The Complete Guide to

Gazebos and Arbors

Philip Schmidt

Creative Publishing international

CHANHASSEN, MINNESOTA
www.creativepub.com

Creative Publishing international

Copyright © 2007
Creative Publishing international, Inc.
18705 Lake Drive East
Chanhassen, Minnesota 55317
1-800-328-3895
www.creativepub.com

Printed in China

10 9 8 7 6 5 4 3
Library of Congress
Cataloging in Publication on file

President/CEO: Ken Fund

Home Improvement Group

Publisher: Bryan Trandem
Managing Editor: Tracy Stanley
Senior Editor: Mark Johanson
Editor: Jennifer Gehlhar

Senior Design Manager: Brad Springer
Design Managers: Jon Simpson, Mary Rohl
Production Artist: Dave Schelitzche

Director of Photography: Tim Himsel
Lead Photographer: Steve Galvin
Photo Coordinators: Julie Caruso, Joanne Wawra
Shop Manager: Randy Austin

Production Managers: Linda Halls, Laura Hokkanen

Author: Philip Schmidt
Project Designer: Brian K. Nelson
Page Layout Artist: Kari Johnston
Photographers: Peter Caley, Joel Schnell, Andrea Rugg

THE COMPLETE GUIDE TO GAZEBOS & ARBORS
Created by: The Editors of Creative Publishing international, Inc., in cooperation with Black & Decker.
Black & Decker® is a trademark of The Black & Decker Corporation and is used under license.

Contents

The Complete Guide to Gazebos & Arbors

Introduction

Garden structures are born of a unique blend of architecture and landscaping. While they define our natural spaces and provide comfortable rooms for outdoor living, they are often just as sculptural and ornamental as they are practical. They are havens for people and plants alike. Vines love to climb the framework, and in doing so they create a cool shady spot for lounging.

Gazebos and arbors—both quintessential garden structures—represent a range of outdoor architecture meant for everything from alfresco dining to afternoon naps; thus the inspiration for this book. All 15 original building projects are variations on the theme of better outdoor living.

Some tend toward the exotic, like the lattice-walled gazebo inspired by Japanese teahouses, while others are playful and lighthearted, like the arbor that mimics a beach umbrella. Of course, there are plenty of traditional favorites, including a stately garden pergola with classical columns and a 6-sided gazebo designed for year-round use.

Each project comes with complete plans and instructions on how to build the structure. Once you've picked a project, have the plans reviewed by the local building and zoning departments to make sure your project conforms to the building codes in your area. Finally, when it comes to decorative details, don't be afraid to embellish. After all, an outdoor room, like a garden, is best when marked by personal touches.

The Inspiration

Time to dream. When you look through the kitchen window and out over the yard, what's missing? What could you place in the garden to make it the perfect outdoor retreat? And what about that spot just beyond the hedge, or on the deck, or by the pool?

In This Section

- Arbors
- Gazebos
- Pergolas
- Pavilions & Summerhouses

A deep arbor with built-in seating is both an inviting destination and a casual outdoor room.

Lightweight, trellis-like arbors often play a supporting role in dramatic garden presentations.

Arbors

Big brother to the trellis, an arbor can be anything from a quaint archway over a garden gate to a heavy timber structure shading an entire patio. A typical design uses post-and-beam construction, with horizontal roof slats providing not only shade but also support for climbing plants and vines.

With its simple form, an arbor conveys a sense of wellbeing, especially when host to a tangle of leafy climbers or bundles of colorful blooms. As an inherently versatile structure, an arbor can arch over a path, become a canopy above a garden bench, or serve as a focal point to break up a large expanse of ground.

Adding simple custom details to a garden structure make it seem right at home.

One traditional use of arbors is to create fragrant, light-dappled tunnels to draw strollers between areas of the grounds.

Decorative arbors (right) make beautiful focal points and are perfect for showcasing special garden accents.

Nestled among trees, an intimate gazebo becomes a special "surprise" destination.

A lean frame makes the most of a gazebo's 360° view, while screening provides a haven from bugs.

Gazebos

Generally defined as a freestanding, roofed structure (often intended for enjoying a nice view), the gazebo has been reinterpreted throughout history. There are classical versions with Greek columns, Oriental styles with pagoda roofs, and rustic American examples made of rough-hewn logs. Today, backyard gazebos can bear the influence of Victorian to Colonial styles and everything in between.

With four, six, or eight symmetrical sides, gazebos have a sculptural beauty that enhances almost any setting. There's just a special feeling you get inside a gazebo, whether it's perched on a hillside commanding a panoramic view or tucked in the corner of a garden beneath overhanging limbs. It is perhaps the best example of the perfect balance of enclosure and openness that only an outdoor room can offer.

The gazebo's unusual form inspires creative designs—for walls, roof, and decoration.

In the off-season, a classic gazebo adds a touch of nostalgia to a winter landscape.

The temple of love (right), an ancient form of gazebo, exemplifies the gazebo's character as both showpiece and sanctuary.

Wrapped in fragrant roses, the formal backdrop
of a pergola makes for a romantic summer setting.

Pergolas

A Greco-Roman invention, the pergola originated as an extension to a building, an awning with structural heft that bridged an interior and the outdoors.

Modern pergolas are more often freestanding and monolithic, but they still echo the majestic column and heavy beam construction of their ancient ancestors.

A pergola with just the right amount of shading members, or accessories, creates the perfect outdoor dining room.

Pergolas are great for defining pathways and for softening the edge between home and garden.

A pavilion with surrounding vegetation adds privacy and convenient shelter for a backyard pool area.

Pavilions & Summerhouses

Pavilions and summerhouses are free-standing, fair-weather structures. They offer a quaint and intimate setting unmatched by their distant cousin, the gazebo.

A pavilion can range from a striped canvas beach hut to an open-air, public arcade. In essence, it is a shelter from the sun, but it also allows cool breezes to waft in and out thanks to the open sides—the perfect companion to a swimming pool or play yard.

Summerhouse is self-explanatory. The word alone evokes the sounds of lapping waves and crickets chirping at nighttime. Is there anything better than an outdoor room with a cot waiting in the corner for a midday nap?

Like a giant umbrella, an open pavilion gives you a break from the sun with almost no feeling of enclosure.

The relaxed and cozy atmosphere of a screened summerhouse makes it a special place at any hour.

The Drawing Board

Big or small, these projects require some planning. Take a little time up front to run through the details, check with the local building departments (and your neighbors), and make sure you're placing the new structure where you'll get the most from it.

In This Section

- Choosing a Site
- Building Codes & Zoning Laws
- Planning for Sun & Shade
- Working with Plans

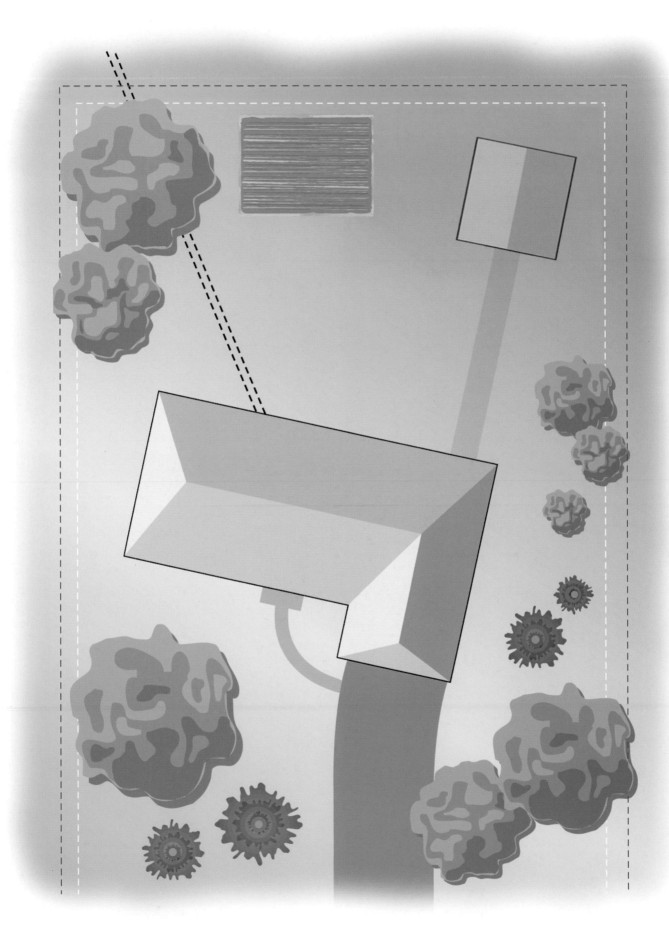

Choosing a Site

Placement and orientation can have a huge impact on how much you enjoy an outdoor structure. The following considerations should help you decide what you really want from the new space and alert you to common pitfalls.

What's the use?

That is, how do you plan to use your new structure? If you want a private getaway for daydreaming or napping, tuck the structure into a corner of the garden or behind a fence or a dense group of plantings. If you plan to dine in your outdoor room you'll probably want it close to the house for convenience. Also consider which seasons you spend the most time outside. This allows you to plan for the right amount of sunlight and shelter from the elements (see page 22).

Your view from the house

Placement affects the privacy in the outdoor space as well as the structure's impact on the look of your yard. A space that's not visible from the house is considerably more private; however, if your kids will use it, you might want it in plain sight. You may want to strategically locate the structure to block your view of the street or a neighbor's ugly storage shed. A more prominent structure can serve as a focal point, drawing your eye to the garden or framing a distant view.

Your view of the house

When you're lounging in your gazebo or entertaining under your pergola, what will you see? Often the best view is that of your own house. Of course, if you haven't painted in a while, you might not want that constant reminder.

Consult thy neighbor

Don't jeopardize that Good Citizen award by being secretive about your project. If your new structure will have any impact on your neighbors' lots or views, discuss your plans with them.

Soil & drainage

For obvious reasons, choose an area with solid soil, and avoid sites where water collects. Be aware of gutter downspouts and the paths water takes in heavy rains. It's much easier to move a structure than to redesign your home's drainage.

When planning a gazebo or arbor project, consider how the finished design will fit in with the natural surroundings and how it will look from your house.

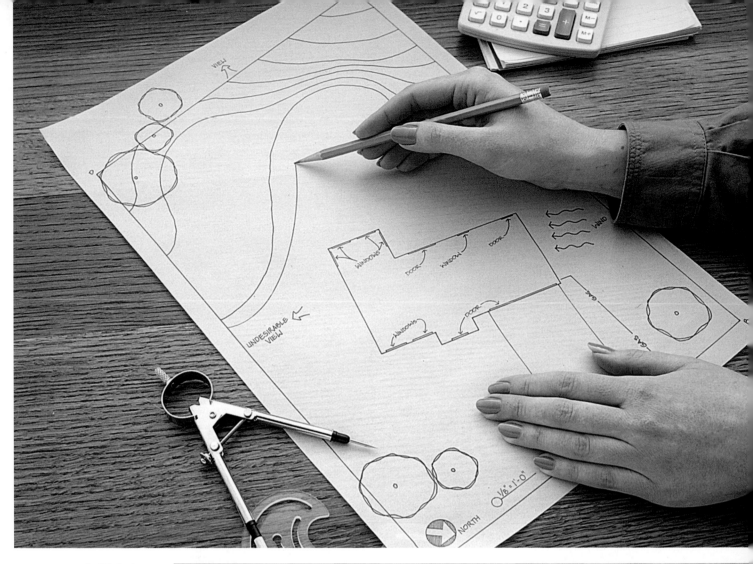

Your initial plans should take into account: structure location, wind, sun, views from the house, and landscaping.

Once you have the architectural renderings, you must have the project approved by the city. Include as many details in your plan proposal as possible— including material you intend to use.

Building Codes & Zoning Laws

As loath as you may be to consult the authorities about your personal project, it's important to get the go-ahead from the building and zoning departments. They can review your plans and note any design modifications necessary to make your project safe and legal for your area. Just give them a call to find out about the process. Usually, it's quite simple. In many municipalities, it's also the law.

Building code

The building code outlines safety and structural standards for all types of buildings in a given municipality. It supercedes all national, regional, and state building codes. Because it's impossible for any single project design—including those in this book—to meet the requirements of all codes, the local code sets the standards for your specific conditions. Depending on the project, the building department might require that you get a permit and pass scheduled inspections. If so, you can be fined for not getting one.

Zoning laws

These govern a number of restrictions that may directly affect your project, including:

- **Setback from property line:** How closely to your property line you can build. This may range from 6" to 3' or more.
- **Building size and height.**
- **Easements:** Restricted zones on your property that must be left open for utilities, emergency access, or other contingencies..
- **Allowable lot coverage:** The total area or percentage of your lot that can be covered with buildings.

Call before you dig

The familiar public service message is aimed directly at you—and anyone else planning to make holes in their yard. Don't forget that lurking beneath your well-tended lawn are gas and power lines, telephone and TV cables, and possibly plumbing drains (that means sewage). They may be closer the surface than you think. Utility companies will come out and mark your lines for free, so there's no excuse for accidentally cutting into a 100-amp electrical line with a steel shovel.

Most states are part of the North American One Call Referral System, which will contact all of the utilities in your area and notify them of your construction plans. Utility companies that have lines in your yard will automatically send out a representative to mark the lines. Call 888-258-0808.

The Right-brained Approach

Feeling creative? You might find it helpful to draw a site plan of your lot and use it to experiment with different ideas. If you have your home's original blueprints, make copies at a copy store, or use tracing paper to create your plan sketches. Otherwise, you can just take rough measurements of your house and yard and scale them down to a workable size, such as 1/8" = 1'0".

Make it easy on yourself by buying a cheap, plastic scale ruler at an art supply store. This automatically sets the scale for you so you don't have to do the math. Trying to make scaled drawings with a standard ruler will quickly become tedious.

Create a complete picture by adding trees, plantings, fences, pathways, and other items in your yard. Mark the locations of your home's windows and doors, as well as gutter downspouts and yard drainages. Finally, include the site's orientation to the sun and prevailing winds.

Planning for Sun & Shade

Sunlight is an integral part of any outdoor space. How you block or filter it sets the tone of a structure's interior and largely dictates how the space is used. Another consideration is how your structure will shade or reflect light onto neighboring areas, such as a garden.

Seasonal sunlight

Each day the sun crosses the sky at a slightly different angle, moving from its high point in summer to its low point in winter. Shadows change accordingly. In the summer, shadows follow the east-west axis and are very short at midday. Winter shadows point to the northeast and northwest and are relatively long at midday.

Generally, the south side of a building is exposed to sunlight throughout the year, while the north side may be shaded in fall, winter, and spring. Geographical location is also a factor: as you move north from the equator, the changes in the sun's path become more extreme.

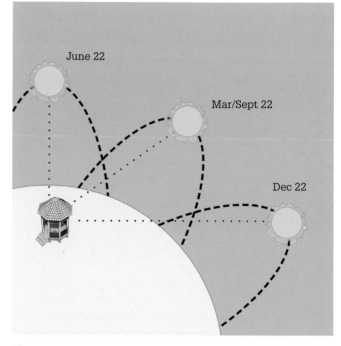

The sun moves from its high point in summer to its low point in winter. Shadows change accordingly.

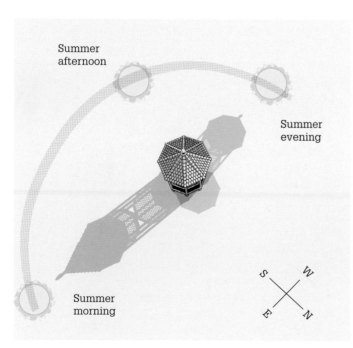

Shadows follow the east-west axis in the summer.

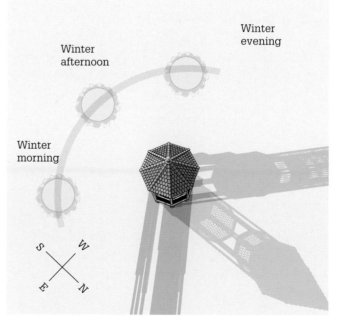

Winter shadows point to the northeast and northwest and are relatively long at midday.

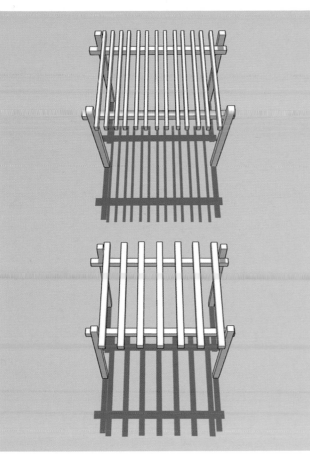

A good amount of detail should be put into slat design for overheads. Changing the size and orientation of slats allows you to customize the amount of shade they provide at different times of the day.

Knowing when and how you most use your patio will allow you to plan for shade at the perfect times.

Designing with Shade

If you're building an arbor or pergola to create an overhead to an outdoor room, you can easily modify the roof slats to meet your needs. The first thing to decide is when you will use the space the most: morning, afternoon, or evening? How much shade or sunlight do you want at your favorite times?

You can modify your project by changing the size, orientation, number, and spacing of the overhead slats or cross pieces. For example, you might decide to slant the slats for a desired effect.

With basic arbor and pergola projects, you can experiment with slat options during the building process. After the primary structure of posts and main beams are in place, lay the slats on top in different configurations. Permanently fasten them after you find the right arrangement.

Note ▸

Just like the old rule of never leaving your tools on top of a ladder, don't leave any unfastened slats on your structure—airborne lumber is never a good thing. Also, however you decide to lay out your slats, have your plans reviewed by the building department, to make sure the structure will hold up under local weather conditions.

Mother Nature's method

Vines on a roof know how to deal with the sun. In summer, when vines are full of leaves, they provide shade when it's needed most. In winter, the sun passes through their bare branches.

Working with Plans

The projects in this book include complete construction drawings in the style of architectural blueprints. If you're not used to reading plans, don't worry; they're easy to use once you know how to look at the different views. Each project also includes a 3-D model of the completed structure. Flipping back and forth between this and the two-dimensional plans allow you to visualize the actual structure.

Shown here are the various plan views used in this book. Occassionally you will see "Typ." This stands for "typical" and means the detail applies to all similar elements.

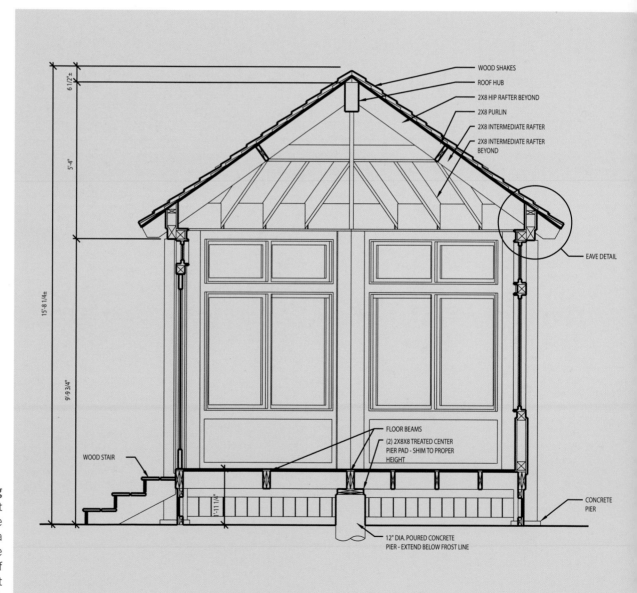

WOOD SHAKES

ROOF HUB

2X8 HIP RAFTER BEYOND

2X8 PURLIN

2X8 INTERMEDIATE RAFTER

2X8 INTERMEDIATE RAFTER BEYOND

EAVE DETAIL

FLOOR BEAMS

(2) 2X8X8 TREATED CENTER PIER PAD - SHIM TO PROPER HEIGHT

WOOD STAIR

CONCRETE PIER

12" DIA. POURED CONCRETE PIER - EXTEND BELOW FROST LINE

6 1/2"±

5'-4"

15'-8 1/4±

9'-9 3/4"

1'-11 1/4"

The building section is the most comprehensive drawing, giving you a side view of the structure sliced in half down the middle. It shows both the framing and finish elements.

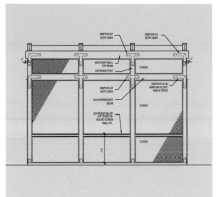

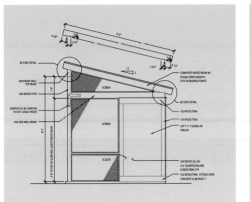

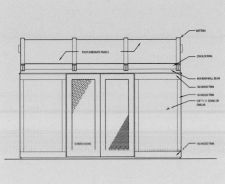

Elevations give you a direct, exterior view of the building from all sides. Plans may include elevations for both the framing and the exterior finishes.

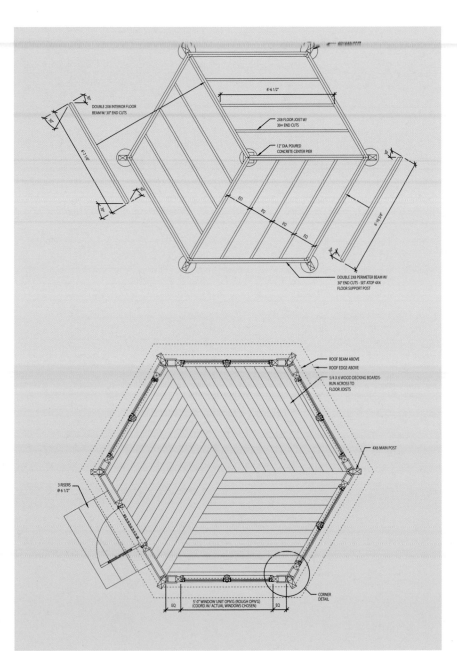

Plan views are overhead perspectives looking straight down from above the structure. Floor plans show the layout of the walls or upright supports, with the top half of the structure sliced off. There are also foundation plans, roof framing plans, and other plan views.

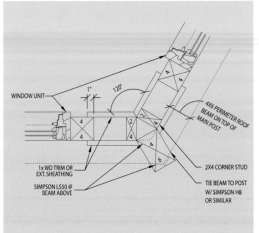

Detail drawings and templates show a close-up of a specific area or part of the structure. They typically show a side or overhead perspective.

Gazebo & Arbor Projects

In This Section

- Arbor Retreat
- Lattice Gazebo
- Classical Pergola
- Wood & Copper Arbor
- 3-Season Gazebo
- Gabled Entry
- Umbrella Arbor
- Pool Pavilion
- Summerhouse
- Corner Lounge
- Classic 8-Sided Gazebo
- Party Shelter
- Wall of Arbors
- Freestanding Arbor
- Trellis Gate

Arbor Retreat

The airy, sun-filtered space under an arbor always makes you want to stay awhile—thus, it's a perfect place for built-in seating. The arbor getaway we've chosen (page 30) has plenty of room for lounging or visiting, but it's designed to do much more: Viewed from the front, the Arbor Retreat becomes an elegant passageway. The bench seating is obscured by latticework, and your eyes are drawn toward the central opening and striking horizontal beams. This makes the structure perfect as a grand garden entrance or a landscape focal point. For added seclusion, tuck this arbor behind some foliage.

Sitting inside the Retreat you can enjoy privacy and shade behind the lattice screens. The side roof sections over the seats are lowered to follow a more human scale and create a cozier sense of enclosure. Each bench comfortably fits three people and the two sides face each other at a range that's ideal for conversation.

We found plenty of ideas for our Arbor Retreat (page 30); several of them are shown in these original structures: extended beams for hanging flowers or training vines (opposite page); comfortable seating for two or more (top); and light screening at the sides to establish a strong sense of space while maintaining an airy feel.

Material List

Description (No. finished pieces)	Quantity/Size	Material
Posts		
Inner posts (4)	4 @ field measure	4 × 4
Outer posts (4)	4 @ field measure	4 × 4
Concrete	Field measure	3,000 PSI concrete
Gravel	Field measure	Compactable gravel
Roof		
Beams (6 main, 4 cross)	8 @ 8'	4 × 4
Roof slats (10 lower, 11 upper)	21 @ 8'	2 × 2
Seats		
Seat supports, spacers, slats (6 horizontal supports, 6 vertical supports, 4 spacers, 16 slats)	16 @ 8'	2 × 6
Aprons (2)	2 @ 6'	1 × 8
Lattice Screens		
Arches (4)	1 @ 8'	2 × 8
Slats—arched sides (20 horizontal, 8 vertical)	12 @ 8'	2 × 2
Slats—back (8)	8 @ 8'	2 × 2
Hardware & Fasteners		
3/8" × 7" galvanized lag screws	12, with washers	
3" deck screws		
3½" deck screws		
2½" deck screws		
¼" × 3" galvanized lag screws	16, with washers	

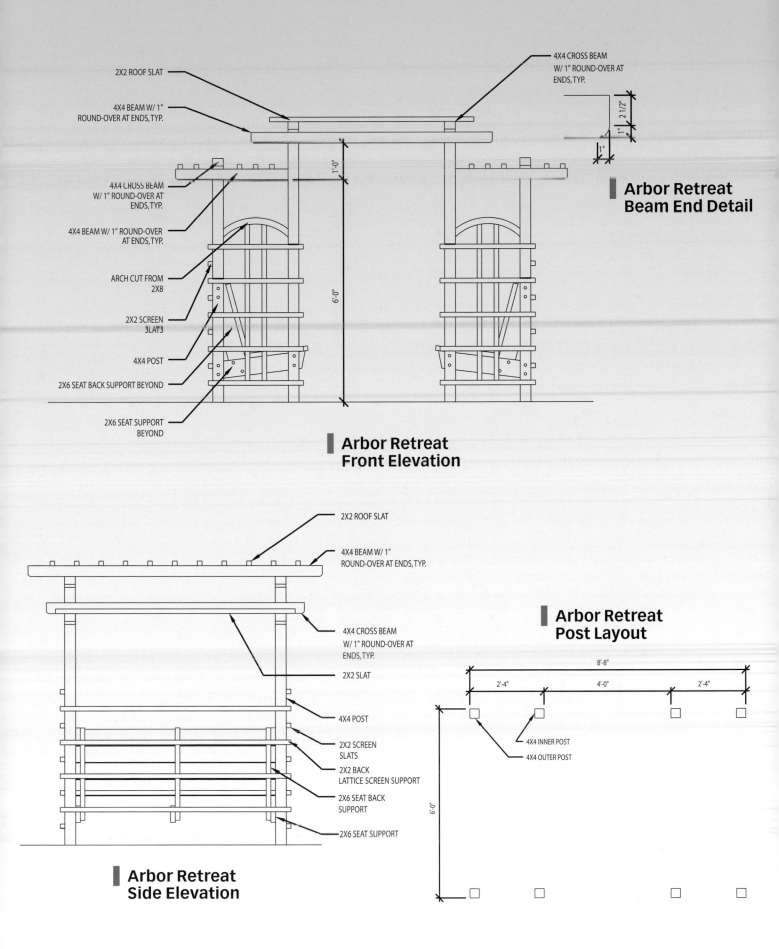

2X2 ROOF SLAT

4X4 CROSS BEAM
W/ 1" ROUND-OVER AT
ENDS, TYP.

2 1/2"

1"

1"

**Arbor Retreat
Beam End Detail**

4X4 BEAM W/ 1"
ROUND-OVER AT ENDS, TYP.

4X4 CROSS BEAM
W/ 1" ROUND-OVER AT
ENDS, TYP.

4X4 BEAM W/ 1" ROUND-OVER
AT ENDS, TYP.

ARCH CUT FROM
2X8

2X2 SCREEN
SLATS

4X4 POST

2X6 SEAT BACK SUPPORT BEYOND

2X6 SEAT SUPPORT
BEYOND

1'-0"

6'-0"

**Arbor Retreat
Front Elevation**

2X2 ROOF SLAT

4X4 BEAM W/ 1"
ROUND-OVER AT ENDS, TYP.

**Arbor Retreat
Post Layout**

4X4 CROSS BEAM
W/ 1" ROUND-OVER AT
ENDS, TYP.

2X2 SLAT

4X4 POST

2X2 SCREEN
SLATS

2X2 BACK
LATTICE SCREEN SUPPORT

2X6 SEAT BACK
SUPPORT

2X6 SEAT SUPPORT

8'-8"

2'-4"   4'-0"   2'-4"

6'-0"

4X4 INNER POST

4X4 OUTER POST

**Arbor Retreat
Side Elevation**

Arbor Retreat
Upper Level Roof Framing Plan

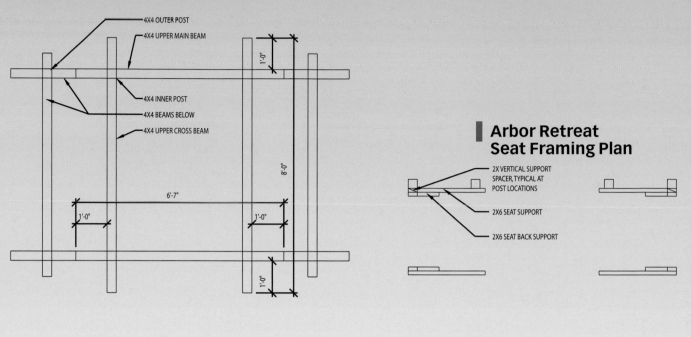

4X4 OUTER POST

4X4 UPPER MAIN BEAM

4X4 INNER POST

4X4 BEAMS BELOW

4X4 UPPER CROSS BEAM

1'-0"

8'-0"

6'-7"

1'-0"

1'-0"

1'-0"

Arbor Retreat
Seat Framing Plan

2X VERTICAL SUPPORT
SPACER, TYPICAL AT
POST LOCATIONS

2X6 SEAT SUPPORT

2X6 SEAT BACK SUPPORT

Arbor Retreat
Roof/Slat Plan

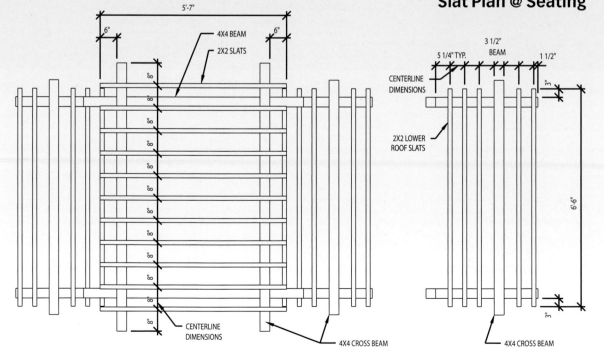

5'-7"

6"

6"

4X4 BEAM

2X2 SLATS

8"
8"
8"
8"
8"
8"
8"
8"
8"
8"
8"
8"

CENTERLINE
DIMENSIONS

4X4 CROSS BEAM

Arbor Retreat
Slat Plan @ Seating

3 1/2"
BEAM

5 1/4" TYP.

1 1/2"

CENTERLINE
DIMENSIONS

3"

2X2 LOWER
ROOF SLATS

6'-6"

3"

4X4 CROSS BEAM

Arbor Retreat
Seat Section

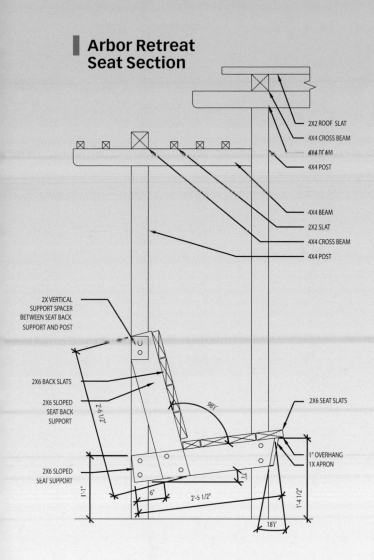

2X2 ROOF SLAT
4X4 CROSS BEAM
4X4 BEAM
4X4 POST

4X4 BEAM
2X2 SLAT
4X4 CROSS BEAM
4X4 POST

2X VERTICAL
SUPPORT SPACER
BETWEEN SEAT BACK
SUPPORT AND POST

2X6 BACK SLATS

2X6 SLOPED
SEAT BACK
SUPPORT

2X6 SLOPED
SEAT SUPPORT

2X6 SEAT SLATS

1" OVERHANG
1X APRON

2'-6 1/2"
98Y
2'-5 1/2"
6"
1'-1"
1'-4 1/2"
18Y

Arbor Retreat
Arch Detail

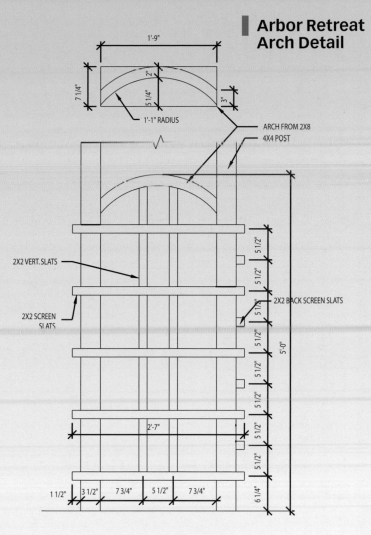

1'-9"
7 1/4"
2"
5 1/4"
3"
1'-1" RADIUS

ARCH FROM 2X8
4X4 POST

2X2 VERT. SLATS

2X2 SCREEN
SLATS

2X2 BACK SCREEN SLATS

5 1/2"
5 1/2"
5 1/2"
5 1/2"
5 1/2"
5 1/2"
5 1/2"
5'-0"

2'-7"

1 1/2" 3 1/2" 7 3/4" 5 1/2" 7 3/4"   6 1/4"

Arbor Retreat
Screen Layout

Arbor Retreat
Seat Level Roof Framing Plan

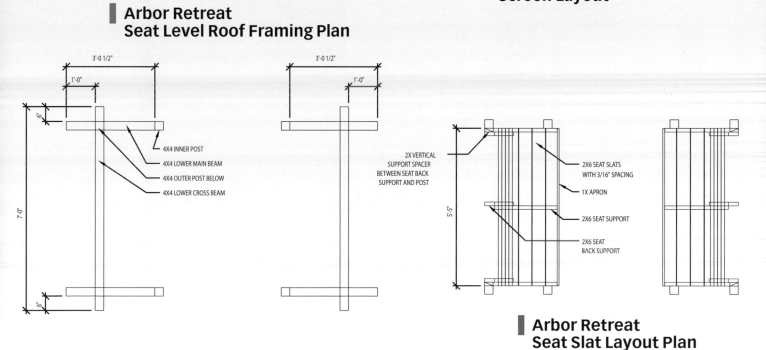

3'-0 1/2"
1'-0"
6"
7'-0"
6"

4X4 INNER POST
4X4 LOWER MAIN BEAM
4X4 OUTER POST BELOW
4X4 LOWER CROSS BEAM

3'-0 1/2"
1'-0"

2X VERTICAL
SUPPORT SPACER
BETWEEN SEAT BACK
SUPPORT AND POST

5'-5"

2X6 SEAT SLATS
WITH 3/16" SPACING

1X APRON

2X6 SEAT SUPPORT

2X6 SEAT
BACK SUPPORT

Arbor Retreat
Seat Slat Layout Plan

How to Build the Arbor Retreat

Step A: Set the Posts

1. Treat the bottoms of the posts for rot-resistance (see page 220).

2. Lay out the eight post locations on the ground, following the POST LAYOUT PLAN on page 32.

3. Follow the basic procedure shown on page 220 to set the posts in concrete. Make sure the size and depth of the post holes conform to the local building code. The post heights don't have to be exact at this stage; however, the four inner posts must stand at least 84" above the ground. The four outer posts must be at least 72" above the ground. Set up mason's lines to make sure the posts are perfectly aligned and the layout is square.

4. Pour the concrete and let it dry completely.

Step B: Cut the Posts to Length

1. You need a long leveling tool to mark the posts for cutting. If you don't own a 6-ft. level, you can make one using a standard 4-ft. level and a straight 2 × 4. Tape the level to a straight edge of a 7-ft.- or 8-ft.-long 2 × 4 so the level is roughly centered along the board's length.

2. Measure up from the ground and mark one of the inner posts at 84". Using the long level, transfer the height mark to the remaining inner posts.

3. Mark one of the outer posts 72" from the ground, and then transfer that mark to the other outer posts.

4. Cut the posts to length (see Cutting Lumber Posts, below). Cut carefully so the post tops are flat and level.

Step C: Cut & Shape the Beams

The Arbor Retreat has two levels of roof beams. The lower seat level has four short main beams running perpendicular to the seats and two cross beams running parallel to the seats (see SEAT LEVEL ROOF FRAMING PLAN, on page 33.) The upper level has

---

DIY Tip ▶ Cutting Lumber Posts

4 × 4 and 6 × 6 posts can be tricky to cut, especially when the post is already standing. Here are some tips for making accurate cuts.

If the combination of power saws and ladders doesn't jive with you, a sharp handsaw can always do the trick, and often with greater accuracy. Start the cut carefully, and watch your lines as you work. Remember: standard handsaws cut only on the push stroke; don't waste energy by applying pressure on the pull stroke.

Extend your cutting line all the way around the post. Use a speed or combination square. This helps you keep your saw on track as you cut from different sides of the post.

Align the posts with mason's lines, and use cross bracing to keep the posts plumb while the concrete sets.

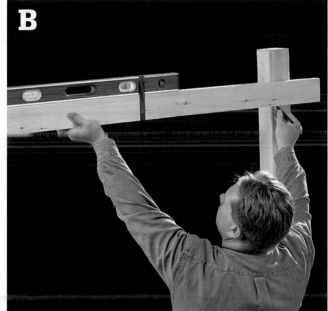

Use a 6-ft. level or a standard level and 2 × 4 to mark each set of posts at a uniform height.

When cutting with a circular saw, set the saw blade to maximum depth. Cut all the way around the post, moving from one side to the next. Be careful to stay on your cutting lines, so the cut surface will be flat. On a 6 × 6, you can cut all four sides, then finish off the center with a handsaw. Because a handsaw blade is thinner than a circular saw blade, keep the handsaw flat against the wood as you cut.

A reciprocating saw with a long, woodcutting blade makes it easy to cut through posts in a single pass. Be careful to keep the saw steady and level to ensure a straight cut.

Power miter saws are the easiest tool for cutting 4 × 4s on a workbench and don't require a continuous cutting line. To cut a 6 × 6—if your saw can accommodate one—set up a stop block. This allows you to evenly rotate the post, cutting from all sides.

Round over the bottom corners of the beams using a router and a roundover bit of desired size.

Test-fit the main beams to the posts, then drill counterbored pilot holes and fasten the beams with lag screws.

two main beams and two cross beams (see UPPER LEVEL ROOF FRAMING PLAN, page 32).

All of the beams are 4 x 4s and have one or two ends rounded over at the bottom corners (see BEAM END DETAIL, on page 31). This is an optional decorative detail that gives the project a finished look.

1. Cut the lower seat level main beams to length at 36½". Cut the lower seat level cross beams at 84".

2. Cut the upper level main beams to length at 79". Cut the upper level cross beams at 96".

3. Shape the beam ends, if desired, using a router with a roundover bit. Or, you can simply make a 45° bevel cut with a saw. The upper level main beams and all four cross beams are shaped at both ends. The short, lower level main beams are shaped only at the outside ends.

Step D: Install the Lower Main Beams

1. For each of the lower level main beams, set the beam on top of an outer post and butt its unshaped end against the corresponding inner post. Hold the beam level, and mark where the top face of the beam meets the inner post. Set the beam aside.

2. On the opposite (inside) face of the inner post, mark a point for drilling a pilot hole so the hole will be centered on the end of the beam.

3. At each pilot hole mark, drill a counterbored hole just deep enough to completely recess the washer and head of a ⅜" × 7" lag screw.

4. Reposition each beam so its top face is on the post reference line. Holding the beam in place, drill a pilot hole for the lag screw through the inner post and into the end of the beam. Fasten each main beam with a ⅜" × 7" lag screw.

5. Drill a counterbored pilot hole down through the top of each lower level main beam and into the end of its outer post. Fasten the beam to the post with a ⅜" × 7" lag screw. Make sure the head of the screw is flush or slightly recessed into the beam (see photo E, page 37).

Step E: Install the Lower Cross Beams & Roof Slats

1. Position the lower (84") cross beams on top of the lower main beams so they are centered over the outer posts and overhang the main beams by 6" at both ends (see SEAT LEVEL ROOF FRAMING PLAN).

2. Drill angled pilot holes through the sides of the cross beams and into the main beams, about ¾" in from the sides of the main beams (to avoid hitting the

lag screws). Drill two holes total on each side of the cross beam at each joint.

3. Fasten the cross beams to the main beams with 3½" deck screws (eight screws total per cross beam).

4. Cut the 10 lower roof slats to length at 78".

5. Mark the roof slat layout onto the tops of the lower main beams, following the SLAT PLAN @ SEATING drawing, on page 32.

6. Position the slats on the layout so they overhang the main beams by 3" at both ends. Drill pilot holes, and fasten the slats to the main beams with 2½" deck screws.

Step F: Install the Upper Main Beams, Cross Beams & Roof Slats

1. Position the upper main beams on top of the inner posts so they overhang the posts by 12" at both ends (see UPPER LEVEL ROOF FRAMING PLAN). Check the fit of the joints, and make adjustments as needed for a good fit.

2. At each post location, drill a counterbored pilot hole and secure the beam to the post with a ⅜" × 7" lag screw with washer, just as you did to fasten the lower main beams to the outer posts.

3. Position the upper cross beams over the upper main beams so they are centered over the inner posts and overhang the main beams by 12" at each end.

4. Drill pilot holes. Fasten the cross beams to the main beams with 3½" deck screws, just as you did with the lower cross beams.

5. Cut the 11 upper roof slats to length at 67".

6. Mark the slat layout onto the upper cross beams, following the ROOF/SLAT PLAN (page 32).

7. Position the slats so they overlap the cross beams by 6" at both ends. Drill pilot holes, and fasten the slats with 2½" deck screws.

Step G: Cut the Seat Supports

Each seat has three horizontal seat supports and three vertical seat back supports, plus two vertical support spacers (see SEAT SECTION, page 33, and SEAT FRAMING PLAN, page 32). The sets of supports and spacers are identical, so once you mark and cut each type, you can use it as a pattern to mark the duplicate pieces.

1. Cut one horizontal seat support and one vertical seat back support, following the SEAT SECTION.

TIP: Cut each of the supports from a different 8-ft. 2 × 6, and save all of the cutoffs for seat slats. Also cut a vertical support spacer from a full 2 × 6.

Fasten the cross beams to the main beams with screws set at an angle. Countersink the screws for best appearance.

Install the upper beams and slats using the same procedure for securing the lower beams and slats.

2. Test-fit the pieces on the arbor posts. Make any necessary adjustments or re-cuts so all of the angles fit properly, as shown in the SEAT SECTION.

3. Use the cut pieces to mark the remaining supports, and then make the cuts. For the two center support assemblies, cut the rear end of the horizontal seat support so it will be flush with the rear edge of the vertical support.

Step H: Install the Outer Seat Supports & Aprons

1. On each side of the structure, measure up from the ground and mark the inner posts at 16½" and the outer posts at 13". These marks represent the top edges of the horizontal seat supports.

2. Position the horizontal seat supports on the marks so their back ends are flush with the outsides of the outer posts. Fasten the supports to the posts with pairs of ¼" × 3" lag screws driven through counterbored pilot holes.

3. Position each vertical seat back support and spacer as shown in the SEAT SECTION, and mark the location of the support spacer onto the post. Fasten the spacer to the post with 3" deck screws driven through pilot holes. Then, fasten the vertical seat back support to the spacer and horizontal seat support with 2½" deck screws; use three or four screws at each end.

4. Measure between the outside faces of the side seat supports, and then cut the 1 × 8 aprons to length at those dimensions.

5. Bevel the top edge of the aprons at 7°. Position them against the seat supports, as shown in the SEAT SECTION. Mark the bottom edges of the aprons for cutting. Bevel the bottom edges at 7°. Fasten the aprons to the ends of the seat supports with 2½" deck screws.

Step I: Install the Seat Slats & Center Supports

1. Measure between the inner posts to determine the length of the seat slats. Using this dimension cut eight slats to length for each side.

2. Position a slat on top of the horizontal seat supports so its front edge overhangs the supports by about 1". Fasten the slat to the supports with pairs of 3" deck screws.

3. Install the next three slats on each side, leaving a ³⁄₁₆" gap between the slats. Rip the final seat slat to fit the remaining space.

4. Install the vertical back seat slats from the top down. Position the top slat so its highest edge is flush with, or just below, the tops of the vertical seat supports. Gap the remaining slats by ³⁄₁₆".

5. Using 2½" deck screws, assemble the two center seat supports so they match the outer supports. Install the center supports at the midpoints of the slats by screwing through the slats and into the supports, using 3" deck screws.

Step J: Build the Arched Lattice Screens

1. Mark the layout of the horizontal lattice pieces onto the posts, following the SCREEN LAYOUT, on page 33; mark along one post, then

Mark the end cuts on the seat supports using a speed square, or you can use a protractor to find the angles (also see page 39).

Fasten the horizontal seat supports to the posts with lag screws. Attach the vertical seat back supports with deck screws.

use a level to transfer the marks to the other post.

2. Cut 20 2 × 2 lattice slats to length at 31". Position the slats on the layout so they overhang the posts by 1½" at both ends. Fasten the slats to the posts with 2½" deck screws driven through pilot holes.

3. To make the arches, make a cardboard template, following the ARCH DETAIL on page 33. Using the template, trace one arch onto a 2 × 8. Cut out the arch with a jigsaw or bandsaw. Test-fit the arch between the post pairs, and make any necessary adjustments for a good fit. Cut the remaining arches. Sand the cut edges smooth.

4. Position each arch on its layout marks so its outside edges are flush with the outside faces of the posts. At each end of the arch, drill an angled pilot hole upward through the bottom of the arch and into the post. Fasten the arch with 2½" deck screws.

5. On the top and bottom horizontal slats, make a mark 7" in from each post. These represent the outside edges of the vertical lattice slats.

6. Cut the eight vertical slats to a rough length of 54". Mark the top ends of the slats to match the arches by holding each slat on its reference marks. Use a compass to transfer the arch curve to the end of the slat. Cut the curved ends and test-fit the slats.

7. Hold each vertical slat in place against the arch and mark the bottom end for length, so it will be flush with the bottom edge of the lowest horizontal slat. Cut the vertical slats to length.

8. Install the vertical slats with 3" deck screws driven down through the arches and 2½" deck screws driven through the lowest horizontal slats.

Step K: Build the Back Lattice Screens

1. Mark the layout for the back lattice slats onto the outer posts, following the SCREEN LAYOUT.

2. Cut the eight 2 × 2 back lattice slats to length at 75". This gives you 1½" overhang at each end.

3. Position the slats on their layout marks so they overhang the posts by 1½" at both ends. Drill pilot holes, and fasten the slats to the posts with 2½" deck screws. See SIDE ELEVATION.

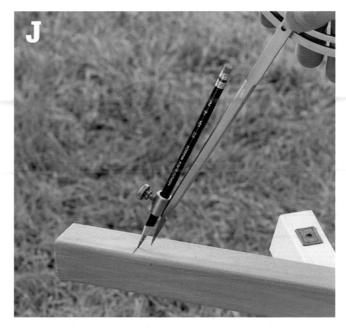

Keeping the compass straight, follow the arch's curve to mark the end of the vertical slat.

Install the center support so it's centered along the length of the seat slats.

Fasten the back slats to the outer posts with 2½" deck screws.

Lattice Gazebo

Agarden retreat surrounded by lattice is a study in dynamic views, both inside and out. The sun's movement fills the interior with ever-changing light patterns made even more compelling by vines twisting along the walls and roof. And with only partial separation from the elements, the sense of enclosure is blended with the sounds and smells of the outdoors.

Borrowing elements from Japanese teahouses and other Asian sources, the Lattice Gazebo featured on page 43 has a gently sloping roofline that brings lightness to its broad, sweeping form. Rounded openings give the walls an uncommon decorative quality and provide visual contrast to the grid pattern of the lattice. In daylight, the shadowed interior offers a pleasant retreat for people as well as sun-shy plants. At night, when lighted from inside, the gazebo glows like a paper lantern.

The simple, symmetrical design of this project makes it easy to alter its size. As shown in the plans, the gazebo is big enough for a patio table and chairs. To create a smaller version, first resize the footprint. Decide how tall you want the structure, being mindful of proper proportions. From there, the pieces can be measured and cut to fit.

Inspired by these and other fanciful garden structures, our Lattice Gazebo (page 43) is as fun to use as it is to look at.

Material List

Description (No. finished pieces)	Quantity/Size	Material
Posts & Foundation		
Posts (4)	4 @ field measure	4 × 4
Concrete	Field measure	3,000 PSI concrete
Compactable gravel	Field measure	
Walls		
Top and bottom rails (14 full-length, 4 door-wall bottom rails)	15 @ 10'	2 × 4
Window headers (6) and sills (6), door headers (2), and jambs (16)	23 @ 10'	2 × 4
Window and door brackets (14)	3 @ 10' 1 @ 6'	1 × 12
Lattice	Field measure	3/4" (total panel thickness) manufactured wood lattice
Roof		
Truss top chord (4)	4 @ 12'	2 × 12
Truss bottom chord (8)	8 @ 8'	2 × 6
Truss strut (4)	1 @ 10'	2 × 4
Hub (1)	1 @ 51"	4 × 4
Support joists (4 outer, 4 inner)	4 @ 14' 4 @ 10'	2 × 4
Slat braces (4)	1 @ 8' 1 @ 3'	2 × 4
Slats	Field measure	2 × 2
Hardware & Fasteners		
3" galvanized wood screws		
1 5/8" galvanized wood screws		
1 1/2" galvanized wood screws		
3/8" × 6" galvanized carriage bolts	16, with washers and nuts	
1/4" × 7" galvanized lag screws	4, with washers	
1/4" × 6" galvanized lag screws	12, with washers	
2 1/2" deck screws		

Note: Truss assembly consists of 2 bottom chords, 1 top chord, and 1 strut.

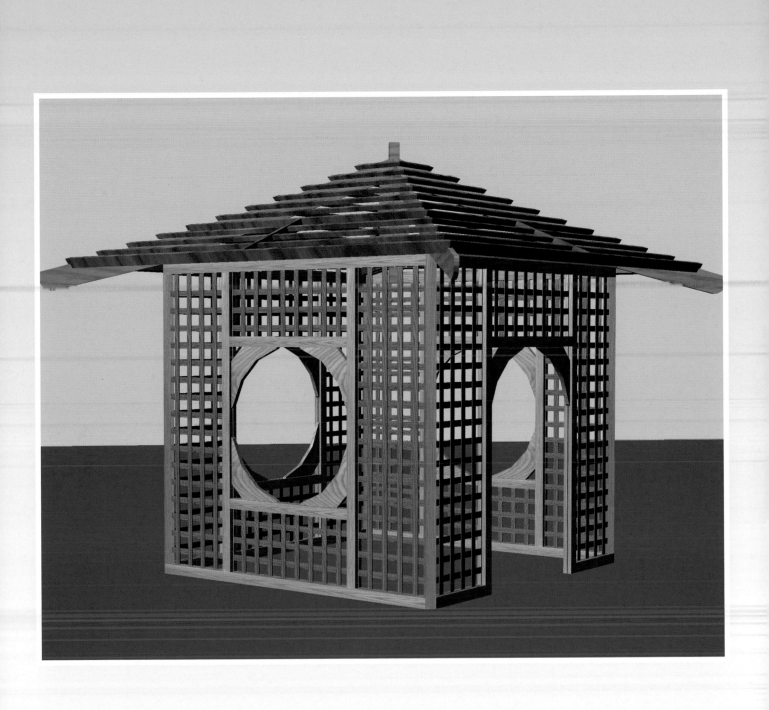

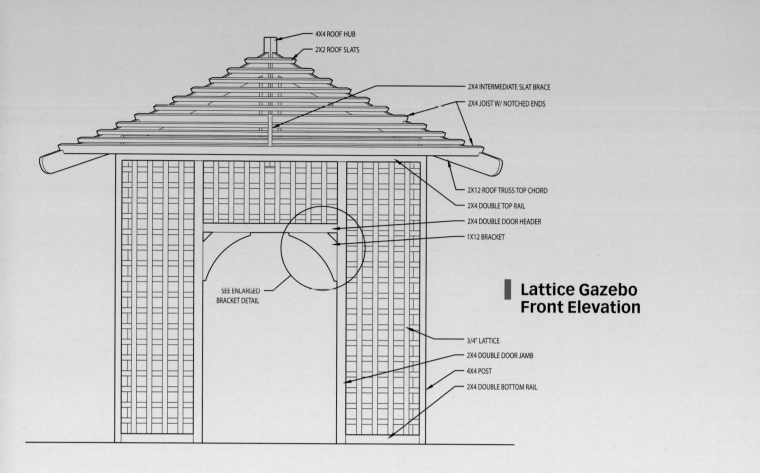

Lattice Gazebo Front Elevation

4X4 ROOF HUB
2X2 ROOF SLATS
2X4 INTERMEDIATE SLAT BRACE
2X4 JOIST W/ NOTCHED ENDS
2X12 ROOF TRUSS TOP CHORD
2X4 DOUBLE TOP RAIL
2X4 DOUBLE DOOR HEADER
1X12 BRACKET
SEE ENLARGED BRACKET DETAIL
3/4" LATTICE
2X4 DOUBLE DOOR JAMB
4X4 POST
2X4 DOUBLE BOTTOM RAIL

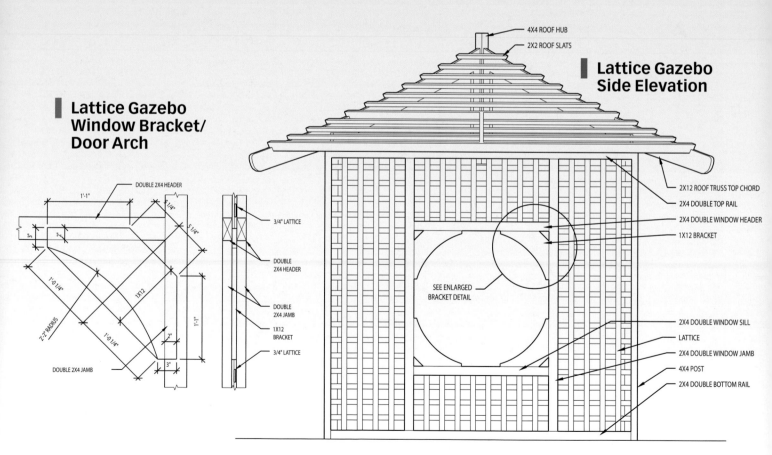

Lattice Gazebo Window Bracket/ Door Arch

DOUBLE 2X4 HEADER
1'-1"
5 1/4"
3"
2"
5 1/4"
1'-0 1/4"
1X12
2'-2" RADIUS
1'-0 1/4"
2"
1'-1"
2"
3"
DOUBLE 2X4 JAMB

3/4" LATTICE
DOUBLE 2X4 HEADER
DOUBLE 2X4 JAMB
1X12 BRACKET
3/4" LATTICE

Lattice Gazebo Side Elevation

4X4 ROOF HUB
2X2 ROOF SLATS
2X12 ROOF TRUSS TOP CHORD
2X4 DOUBLE TOP RAIL
2X4 DOUBLE WINDOW HEADER
1X12 BRACKET
SEE ENLARGED BRACKET DETAIL
2X4 DOUBLE WINDOW SILL
LATTICE
2X4 DOUBLE WINDOW JAMB
4X4 POST
2X4 DOUBLE BOTTOM RAIL

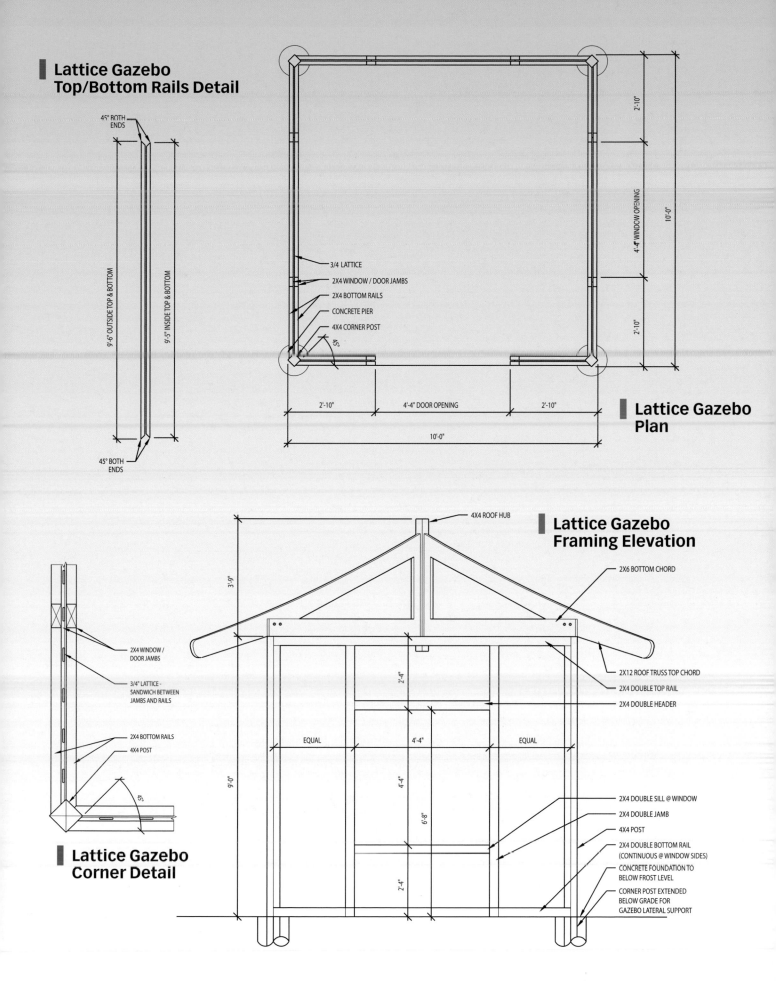

**Lattice Gazebo
Top/Bottom Rails Detail**

45° BOTH ENDS

9'-6" OUTSIDE TOP & BOTTOM

9'-5" INSIDE TOP & BOTTOM

45° BOTH ENDS

**Lattice Gazebo
Plan**

2'-10"

4'-4" WINDOW OPENING

10'-0"

2'-10"

3/4 LATTICE
2X4 WINDOW / DOOR JAMBS
2X4 BOTTOM RAILS
CONCRETE PIER
4X4 CORNER POST

45°

2'-10"   4'-4" DOOR OPENING   2'-10"

10'-0"

**Lattice Gazebo
Framing Elevation**

4X4 ROOF HUB

2X6 BOTTOM CHORD

2X12 ROOF TRUSS TOP CHORD
2X4 DOUBLE TOP RAIL
2X4 DOUBLE HEADER

2X4 DOUBLE SILL @ WINDOW
2X4 DOUBLE JAMB
4X4 POST
2X4 DOUBLE BOTTOM RAIL
(CONTINUOUS @ WINDOW SIDES)
CONCRETE FOUNDATION TO
BELOW FROST LEVEL
CORNER POST EXTENDED
BELOW GRADE FOR
GAZEBO LATERAL SUPPORT

3'-9"

9'-0"

2'-4"

4'-4"

6'-8"

2'-4"

EQUAL   4'-4"   EQUAL

2X4 WINDOW /
DOOR JAMBS

3/4" LATTICE -
SANDWICH BETWEEN
JAMBS AND RAILS

2X4 BOTTOM RAILS
4X4 POST

45°

**Lattice Gazebo
Corner Detail**

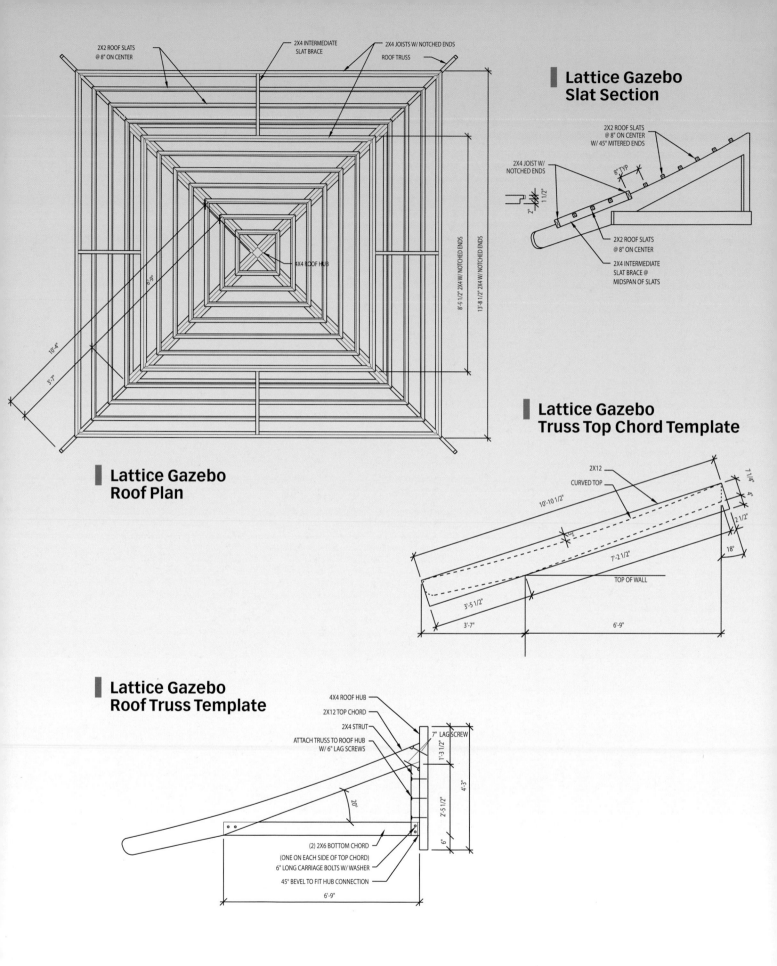

**Lattice Gazebo
Slat Section**

2X2 ROOF SLATS
@ 8" ON CENTER
W/ 45° MITERED ENDS

2X4 JOIST W/
NOTCHED ENDS

8" TYP

1 1/2"

2"

2X2 ROOF SLATS
@ 8" ON CENTER

2X4 INTERMEDIATE
SLAT BRACE @
MIDSPAN OF SLATS

2X2 ROOF SLATS
@ 8" ON CENTER

2X4 INTERMEDIATE
SLAT BRACE

2X4 JOISTS W/ NOTCHED ENDS

ROOF TRUSS

8'-9 1/2" 2X4 W/ NOTCHED ENDS

13'-8 1/2" 2X4 W/ NOTCHED ENDS

4X4 ROOF HUB

5'-9"

10'-4"

3'-7"

**Lattice Gazebo
Roof Plan**

**Lattice Gazebo
Truss Top Chord Template**

2X12

CURVED TOP

10'-10 1/2"

7 1/4"

4"

2 1/2"

18"

7'-2 1/2"

TOP OF WALL

3'-5 1/2"

3'-7"

6'-9"

**Lattice Gazebo
Roof Truss Template**

4X4 ROOF HUB

2X12 TOP CHORD

2X4 STRUT

ATTACH TRUSS TO ROOF HUB
W/ 6" LAG SCREWS

7" LAG SCREW

1'-3 1/2"

4'-3"

2'-5 1/2"

20°

6"

(2) 2X6 BOTTOM CHORD
(ONE ON EACH SIDE OF TOP CHORD)

6" LONG CARRIAGE BOLTS W/ WASHER

45° BEVEL TO FIT HUB CONNECTION

6'-9"

How to Build the Lattice Gazebo

Step A: Install the Posts

The four 4 × 4 posts are buried in concrete; see page 220 for a detailed procedure. The depth and diameter of the post and surrounding concrete pier must meet the requirements of the local building code and extend below the frost line (as a minimum, the posts should be buried 30" deep). Treat the bottom ends of the posts for rot resistance before setting them.

1. Lay out the four post locations onto the ground, following the PLAN drawing, on page 45. Dig the post holes and add a 6" layer of gravel to each for drainage.

2. Set up mason's lines to lay out the precise post locations, following the PLAN drawing. Set the posts in the holes and secure them with cross bracing so they are perfectly plumb and turned at 45° to the square layout. Measure the diagonal between posts to check for squareness: the layout is perfectly square when the diagonal measurements are equal.

3. Pour the concrete and let it dry completely.

4. Measure up from the ground and mark one of the posts at 108". Use a mason's string and a line level to transfer that height mark to the other three posts, then cut the posts to height (see Cutting Lumber Posts, on page 34). Cut carefully so the post tops are flat and level.

Use mason's lines to set up the square post layout and to offset the posts at 45°.

Step B: Build the Outer Wall Frames

In this step, you complete the outer layer of the 2 × 4 wall framing. The main wall structures are made of 2 × 4 frame pieces sandwiched over lattice panels, as shown in the CORNER DETAIL (page 45). Because lattice varies in thickness, test-fit some scrap 2 × 4 frame pieces and lattice to determine how the assembly will fit against the posts.

1. Cut the four 2 × 4 bottom rails to fit between the posts along the sides and rear of the gazebo; cut the ends at 45° to fit flush against the post faces. You will cut and install the front wall, bottom rails in step 6. See TOP/BOTTOM RAILS DETAIL on page 45.

2. Position the bottom rails against the posts at the desired height above the ground, and fasten them to the posts with 3" wood screws.

3. Cut the top rails to fit between the posts on all four sides of the gazebo. Install the rails so their top edges are flush with the tops of the posts.

Install the bottom rail at the desired height. Most likely it will sit close to, if not touching, the ground.

4. Mark the window and door openings onto the rails, following the PLAN drawing. All of the openings are centered on the walls and span 52".

5. Cut the 2 × 4 window jambs to fit snugly between the top and bottom rails. Fasten them to the rails on the layout marks. For each window, cut a 2 × 4 header and a 2 × 4 sill to fit between the jambs. Install them at the desired height to create a square opening.

6. To frame the door opening, cut two jambs to reach from the top rail to the bottom of the bottom rail position. Cut two 2 × 4 bottom rails (left from step #1) to span from the posts to the inside edges of the jambs, as shown in the FRAMING ELEVATION (page 45). Also cut a 2 × 4 door header to length at 52". Assemble the door opening, as shown in the FRAMING ELEVATION, so the top of the opening is 80" from the ground.

Step C: Add the Window & Door Brackets

1. Make a cardboard template for marking the bracket profiles, following the WINDOW BRACK-ET/DOOR ARCH drawing, on page 44.

2. Use the template to mark 14 brackets onto 1 × 12s, then cut the pieces with a jigsaw or bandsaw, and sand the cuts smooth.

3. Draw reference lines 2" in from the angled edges of each bracket; this designates the overlap onto the 2 × 4 wall framing, as shown in the WIN-DOW BRACKET/DOOR ARCH drawings.

4. Position the brackets at the corners of the window and door openings: Each window gets four brackets, while the door gets two at the top of the opening. Fasten the brackets to the frames with 1⅝" wood screws. Drive the screws from inside the gazebo, so the inner wall framing will hide the screw heads.

Step D: Install the Lattice & Inner Wall Frames

You can install the lattice in any configuration you like, using square- or diamond-patterned panels.

1. Working outward from the posts, cut the lattice panel for each framed section (see page 208 for tips on cutting wood lattice). Overlap the 2 × 4 wall framing by at least 3" along the rails and around the window and door openings; overlap about 1½" along the jambs above and below the openings. For best appearance, use a clean factory edge where the lattice meets the posts. You can also bevel those edges so you don't see the end grain of the lattice slats.

2. Fasten the lattice to the framing with 1½" wood screws—drive them through pilot holes to prevent splitting. Use mason's string or layout marks to help keep the lattice panels aligned with one another.

Mark the bracket radius with a 26"-long string or board, pivoting from a centerpoint.

3. Cut and install the inner wall frames, following the same basic procedure used in Step B to install the outer frames. Bevel the ends of the rails where they meet the posts; if necessary, clip the rail ends so they fit together, as shown in the CORNER DETAIL. Fasten the inner framing parts together at the corner joints, as you did with the outer frames, and then fasten the inner and outer framing together with 3" wood screws.

Step E: Build the Roof Trusses

1. Select a straight, 12-ft. 2 × 12 to use as the pattern for the top chords. Check the board for crowning, and mark the top edge (see page 60). Draw the outline of the chord onto the board, following the TRUSS TOP CHORD TEMPLATE (page 46). Make the cuts, and then sand the curved edges smooth.

2. Using the cut board as a pattern, trace the outline onto a second 2 × 12 and make the cuts. For each of the two chords, cut two 2 × 6 bottom chords and one 2 × 4 strut, following the ROOF TRUSS TEMPLATE, on page 46.

3. Assemble the trusses as shown in the TEMPLATE: Sandwich two bottom chords over each top chord and strut and fasten at each end with two ⅜" × 6" carriage bolts. Fasten the strut to the top chord with a ¼" × 7" lag screw driven at an angle through a counterbored pilot hole.

4. Cut the 4 × 4 roof hub to length at 51". If desired, shape the ends to a point with four equal bevel cuts (see page 106). Test-fit the trusses and hub on the gazebo. The outside ends of the bottom chords should be aligned with the outside edges of the posts. Make any adjustments necessary for a good fit.

5. Disassemble one of the trusses and use the parts as patterns to mark the remaining truss pieces. Cut the parts and assemble the remaining trusses.

Step F: Complete the Roof Frame

1. Position two opposing trusses on the posts with their struts centered on the hub. The hub should extend 6" below the bottom chords. Drill pilot holes into the strut. Fasten three ¼" × 6" lag screws through each strut and into the hub (see ROOF TRUSS TEMPLATE). Offset the screws on opposing sides so they don't run into one another. Also fasten through the top chords into the hub with a lag screw driven at an angle through a counterbored pilot hole.

If desired, bevel-cut the edges of lattice that meet the posts, using a circular saw set at 45°.

Bend a long piece of trim or other flexible board against nails to make the top chord arch.

2. Install the two remaining trusses.

3. Mark the top edges of the roof top chords at 8"
and 40" in from their outside ends—these marks represent the outside faces of the 2 × 4 support joists;
see the ROOF PLAN and SLAT SECTION on page
46. If you prefer slat spacing different than 8" on
center, adjust the positions of the joists as desired.

4. Cut the 2 × 4 joists to span between the centers of the chords at the marks. Miter and notch the
ends of the joists, as shown in the SLAT SECTION.

5. Install the joists on the chords with 2½"
deck screws.

6. Cut the four 2 × 4 slat braces to fit between the
joists at their centerpoints. Fasten the braces
between the joists with screws.

Step G: Install the Roof Slats

1. Mark the layout of the roof slats onto the
top edges of the truss chords and slat braces,
using 8" on-center spacing (or different spacing,
as desired); see ROOF PLAN. Also mark the centers of the chords, to facilitate measuring for the
slats.

2. Cut 2 × 2 slats to span from the centers of the
chords to the side faces of the slat braces.

**NOTE: Compound miter the chord ends of the
slats. Fasten the slats with 2½" deck screws
driven through pilot holes. The tops of the slats
should be flush with the tops of the braces.**

3. Continue installing slats up to the roof peak,
mitering the ends so they meet at the centers of the
truss chords.

**If desired, countersink
the lag screws** into the
truss struts to hide
the screw heads.

G

Fasten the slats to the truss, using 2½" deck screws driven through pilot holes.

▶**Tip**

A compound miter saw cuts miters and bevels at the same time, creating slat ends that meet at the centers of the truss chords.

Classical Pergola

Tall and stately, the columned pergola is perhaps the grandest of garden structures. Its minimal design defines an area without enclosing it and makes it easy to place anywhere—from out in the open yard to right up against your house. Vines and flowers clinging to the stout framework create an eye-catching statement of strength and beauty.

In our selected project on page 54, Tuscan-style columns supporting shaped beams mimic the column-and-entablature construction used throughout classical architecture. Painting the columns white or adding faux marbling enhances the classical styling.

The columns used here are made of structural fiberglass designed for outdoor use. They even adhere to the ancient practice of tapering the top ⅔ of the shaft (see The Timeless Column, on page 59).

Structural fiberglass columns, like the ones used in this project, are available from architectural products dealers (see Resources, page 236). You can order them over the phone and have them shipped to your door. This type of column is weather-resistant, but most manufacturers recommend painting them for appearance and longevity. Whatever columns you use, be sure to follow the manufacturer's instructions for all installation and maintenance.

Three variations on the pergola theme present different ideas for using and decorating our Classical Pergola (page 54): built-in seating and a stone floor (opposite page) make this pergola both a place for rest and a beautiful transition between garden areas; an extra layer of overhead slats (top) provides the right amount of shade for this poolside pergola; also poolside (bottom), this pergola clearly separates the bar and entertaining space from the surrounding areas without creating any sense of a barrier.

Material List

Description (No. finished pieces)	Quantity/Size	Material
Columns	6 @ 8"-dia. × 8'	Structural fiberglass column
Concrete Piers		
Concrete tube forms	6—field measure for length	16"-diameter cardboard forms
Gravel	Field measure	Compactable gravel
Concrete	Field measure	3,000 PSI concrete
Beams		
Main beams (4)	4 @ 16'	2 × 8
Cross beams (7)	7 @ 8'	2 × 6
Blocks (6)	1 @ 50"	4 × 4 pressure-treated
Hardware & Fasteners		
½" × 6" J-bolts	6	
Threaded rod for concrete slab foundation only	½"-dia. × 4' corrosion-resistant threaded rod	
Concrete anchoring adhesive— concrete patio installation only		Simpson Acrylic-Tie® adhesive, or similar approved product
Construction adhesive or waterproof wood glue		
16d galvanized common nails		
½"-diameter corrosion-resistant threaded metal rod	6 @ 99"	
½" corrosion-resistant coupler nuts	6	
Corrosion-resistant bearing plates and nuts	6 each	Simpson BP1/2-3 or similar approved bearing plate. Recommended nut for ½" threaded rod
Corrosion-resistant masonry screws		
2½" deck screws		
Paintable caulk		

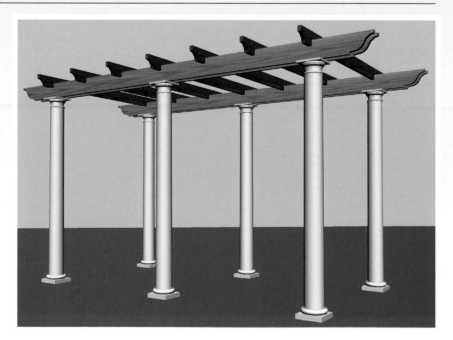

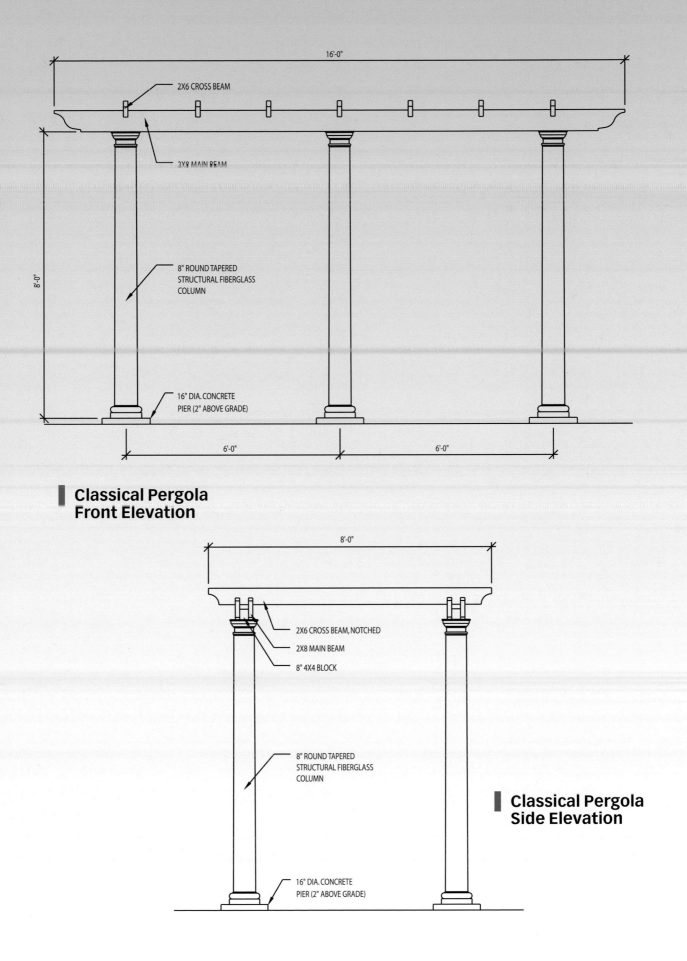

16'-0"

2X6 CROSS BEAM

2X8 MAIN BEAM

8'-0"

8" ROUND TAPERED
STRUCTURAL FIBERGLASS
COLUMN

16" DIA. CONCRETE
PIER (2" ABOVE GRADE)

6'-0"   6'-0"

Classical Pergola
Front Elevation

8'-0"

2X6 CROSS BEAM, NOTCHED

2X8 MAIN BEAM

8" 4X4 BLOCK

8" ROUND TAPERED
STRUCTURAL FIBERGLASS
COLUMN

Classical Pergola
Side Elevation

16" DIA. CONCRETE
PIER (2" ABOVE GRADE)

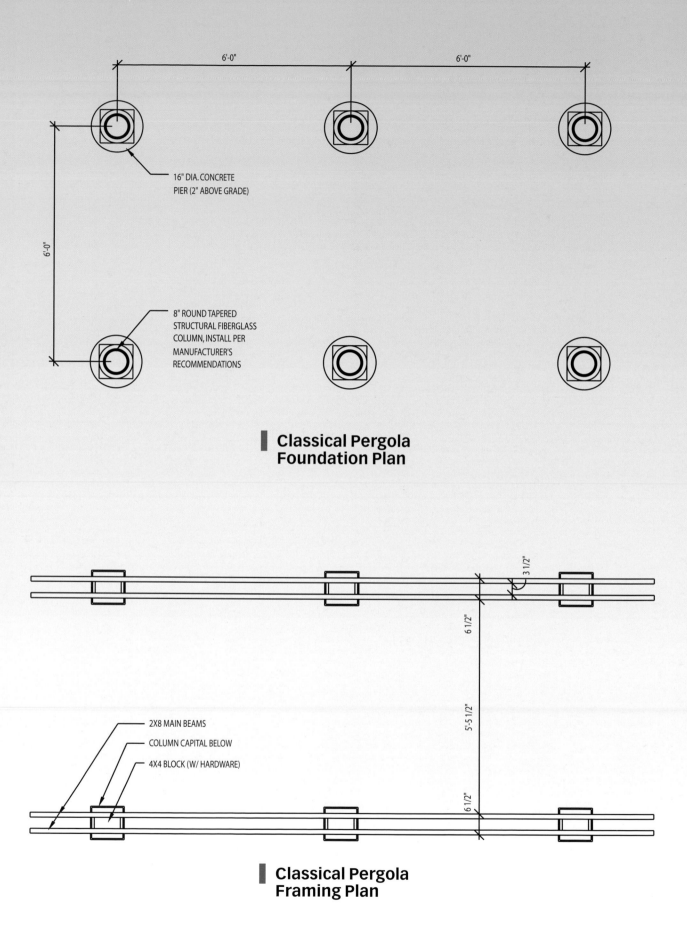

6'-0" **6'-0"**

6'-0"

16" DIA. CONCRETE
PIER (2" ABOVE GRADE)

8" ROUND TAPERED
STRUCTURAL FIBERGLASS
COLUMN, INSTALL PER
MANUFACTURER'S
RECOMMENDATIONS

**Classical Pergola
Foundation Plan**

3 1/2"

6 1/2"

5'-5 1/2"

6 1/2"

2X8 MAIN BEAMS

COLUMN CAPITAL BELOW

4X4 BLOCK (W/ HARDWARE)

**Classical Pergola
Framing Plan**

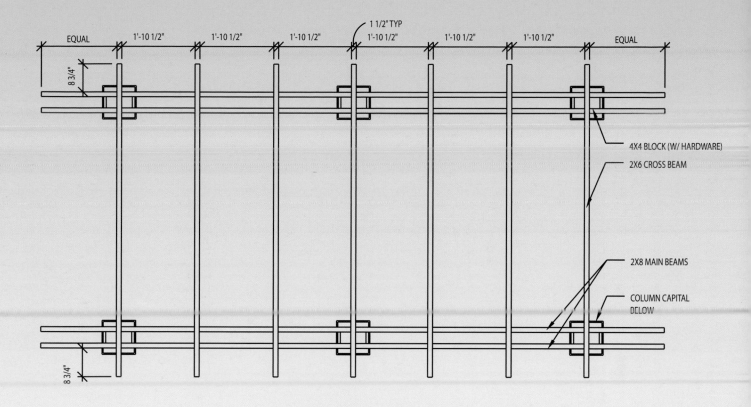

EQUAL   1'-10 1/2"   1'-10 1/2"   1'-10 1/2"   1 1/2" TYP   1'-10 1/2"   1'-10 1/2"   1'-10 1/2"   EQUAL

8 3/4"

8 3/4"

4X4 BLOCK (W/ HARDWARE)

2X6 CROSS BEAM

2X8 MAIN BEAMS

COLUMN CAPITAL BELOW

Classical Pergola
Roof Framing Plan

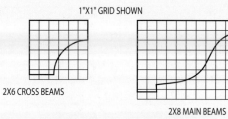

1"X1" GRID SHOWN

2X6 CROSS BEAMS

2X8 MAIN BEAMS

Classical Pergola
Beam End Templates

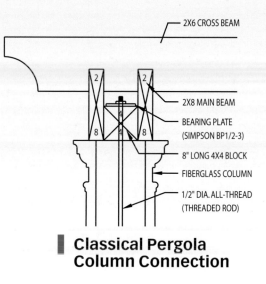

2X6 CROSS BEAM

2X8 MAIN BEAM

BEARING PLATE
(SIMPSON BP1/2-3)

8" LONG 4X4 BLOCK

FIBERGLASS COLUMN

1/2" DIA. ALL-THREAD
(THREADED ROD)

Classical Pergola
Column Connection

How to Build the Classical Pergola

If you're building on poured concrete piers in your yard, complete Step A, below. To build on an existing concrete patio slab, skip ahead to Alternative: Concrete Slab Foundation.

Step A: Pour the Concrete Piers

1. See pages 212 to 215 for detailed instructions on laying out and pouring concrete piers using cardboard forms. Set up batter boards and mason's lines to lay out the pergola columns following the FOUNDATION PLAN on page 56.

2. Dig the six holes for the concrete forms. Add a layer of gravel, then set and brace the forms. Make sure the pier depth and gravel layer meet the requirements of the local building code. For this project, the piers are 16" in diameter and extend at least 2" above the ground. You may have to adjust the height of some piers so that all of them are in the same level plane; measure against your level mason's lines to compensate for any unevenness of the ground.

3. Pour the concrete for each form, and set a 1/2" × 6" J-bolt in the center of the wet concrete. Make sure the bolt is perfectly plumb and extends 1 3/4" to 2" above the surface of the concrete.

4. Following the concrete manufacturer's instructions, finish the tops of the piers to create a smooth, attractive surface. When painted, the piers become part of the finished project.

Alternative: Existing Concrete Slab or Pier Foundation

NOTE: Follow the manufacturer's specifications and instructions for installing the anchor rods in this step.

1. On the patio surface, mark the layout for column centers; follow the FOUNDATION PLAN. The centers must be at least 6" from any edge of the slab. This ensures the column base (plinth) doesn't hang over the edge of the slab and gives you a little bit of wiggle room for adjustments.

2. At each column centerpoint, drill a 5/8"-diameter hole straight down into the concrete, using a hammer drill and 5/8" masonry bit. Make the hole at least 4 1/4" deep.

3. Spray out the holes to remove all dust and debris, using an air compressor with a trigger-type nozzle. Make sure the air is completely oil-free. If necessary, use a clean nylon brush to dislodge any loose material, then spray again with compressed air to completely remove all dust.

4. Cut six pieces of 1/2"-diameter corrosion-resistant threaded rod to length at 8". Make sure the rods are clean and oil-free.

5. Fill each anchor hole 1/2 to 2/3 full with concrete anchor adhesive (see Resources, page 236). Fill the hole starting from the bottom and working up to prevent air pockets. Keep the nozzle of the adhesive dispenser above the adhesive as the hole fills.

6. Insert a rod into each hole, turning the rod slowly until it contacts the bottom of the hole. Position the rod plumb. Leave the rod undisturbed until the adhesive has fully cured.

As the concrete sets, finish the tops of the piers using a concrete float.

For existing foundations, clean the anchor hole thoroughly, and then secure the threaded rod with concrete anchor adhesive.

Drill a 5/8"-diameter hole straight down into the concrete; use a hammer drill and 5/8" masonry bit.

The ancient Greeks and Romans used columns everywhere, and they designed them to exact specifications. A column just wasn't respectable if it didn't have the right shape and proportion. Many of those same rules are still followed today.

According to the ancients, a good column must have a tapered shaft. This is because a perfectly straight shaft appears to be smaller in the center, thus conveying a sense of weakness (not a popular trait among Romans). Some columns are straight along the lowest ⅓ of the shaft and taper inward along the top ⅔; others slightly bulge out in the center (called entasis).

All but the earliest forms of columns had a base and a capital, the style of which largely determined the "order" or type of column it was. Remember art history class? The three Greek orders are Doric, Ionic, and Corinthian. The Roman orders are Tuscan and Composite. Doric and Tuscan have simply ornamented capitals, while Ionic are the ones with the scrolls. Corinthian and Composite follow an anything-goes style and might be decorated with leaves, scrolls, cherubs, goat heads… you name it.

Today, column suppliers offer a variety of capitals and bases. Although it usually costs extra, you can swap out the standard capital or base with one that better suits your style.

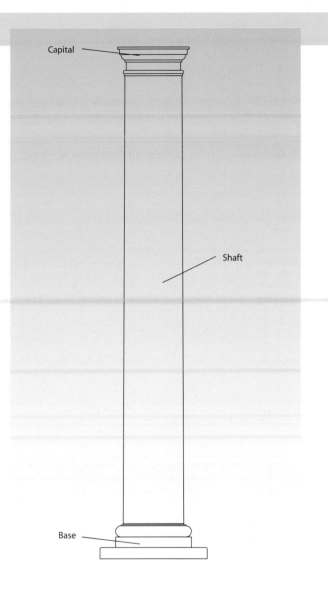

Capital

Shaft

Base

Use a nylon brush to dislodge loose material.

Fill the anchor hole ½ to ⅔ full with concrete anchor adhesive.

Insert a rod into the hole, turning the rod slowly until it contacts the bottom of the hole.

Step B: Cut & Shape the Beams

1. Cut the four main beams to length at 192". Cut the seven cross beams to length at 96".

2. Check all of the beams for crowning—a slight arching shape that's apparent when the board is set on edge. Hold each board flat and sight along its narrow edges. If the board arches, mark the top (convex) side of the arch. This is the crowned edge and should always be installed facing up.

3. Make cardboard patterns for shaping the ends of the main beams and cross beams; follow the BEAM END TEMPLATES on page 57. Use the patterns to mark the shapes onto the beam ends.

4. Shape the beam ends using a jigsaw, coping saw, or bandsaw, and then sand the cuts smooth.

Step C: Construct the Main Beam Assemblies

1. Cut six 4 × 4 blocks at 8".

2. Lay each block flat, and drill a 9/16"-diameter hole through the center of one side.

3. Coat the ends of the blocks and the insides of the holes with wood preservative, following the manufacturer's instructions. The blocks are the main structural connecting points for the pergola, and the preservative helps prevent rot from moisture over the years.

4. Make a mark 20" in from the end of each main beam. These marks represent the outside ends of the blocks.

5. Construct the main beam assemblies by applying construction adhesive or waterproof wood glue to the side faces of the blocks and sandwiching the beams over the blocks. Make sure the blocks are flush with the bottoms of the beams and their ends are on the reference marks. The holes are face up (vertical). Clamp the assembly, and then fasten the beams to the blocks with 16d common nails. Drive four nails on each side, making sure to avoid the center hole in the blocks. Let the glue dry completely.

6. Mark the cross beam layout on to the top edges of main beams, following the ROOF FRAMING PLAN on page 57.

B

Sight along both narrow edges of the beams. If a beam is arched, mark the beam on the convex side of the arch.

Step D: Prepare & Set the Columns

You'll need at least two helpers for this step and the following step. Once you set the columns for one side, continue to the next step to install the main beam. Then, repeat the two steps for the other side of the pergola.

1. Cut the threaded rods to length at 99".

2. Add a corrosion resistant coupler nut to each J-bolt (threaded anchor rod for patio installation).

3. Lay the columns down next to their respective piers. Slip the base and capital over the ends of the column shafts; these will stay loose so you can slide them out of the way until you secure them in Step G.

4. Run the threaded rod through the center of each column.

5. Tip up each column and center it on top of a pier. Check the joint where the column meets the pier; it should make even contact all the way around the column. If necessary, use a rasp to shave the end of the column to ensure even contact.

6. While one person holds the column out of the way, thread the rod into the coupling nut. Adjust the nut so the rod and J-bolt have equal penetration into the nut, and tighten the nut following the manufacturer's instructions. Temporarily brace the column if necessary, or have a helper hold it upright. Repeat steps 4–6 to set the remaining two columns.

Step E: Set the Main Beams

1. Using step ladders set up next to the columns, place one of the main beams onto the columns, inserting the rod ends through the blocks. Check for even contact of the beam on all three columns. If necessary, you can trim a column: Cut from the bottom end only, using a sharp handsaw.

NOTE: If there's a slight gap above the center column due to a crowning beam, it will most likely be gone once the beam is anchored.

2. Add bearing plates and nuts to the end of each threaded rod, loosely threading the nuts.

3. Working on one column at a time, make sure the column shaft is centered on the pier and is centered under the beam block at the top end. Place a 2-ft. level along the bottom, untapered section of the column shaft and check the column for plumb. Hold the column plumb while a helper tightens the nut on the rod. Repeat to adjust and secure the remaining columns.

4. Repeat the procedure to install the columns and beam on the other side of the pergola.

Sandwich the blocks between the main beams, and fasten the assemblies with glue and nails.

Have one person lift up the column while another tightens the coupler nut to the J-bolt and threaded rod.

Step F: Notch & Install the Cross Beams

1. Place each cross beam onto the layout marks on top of the main beams so the cross beam overhangs equally at both ends. Mark each edge where the main beam pieces meet the cross beam. This ensures the notches will be accurate for each cross beam. Number the cross beams so you can install them in the same order. On your workbench, mark the notches for cutting at 2½" deep.

2. To cut the notches, you can save time by clamping two beams together and cutting both at once. Using a circular saw or handsaw, first cut the outside edges of the notches. Next, make a series of interior cuts at ⅛" intervals. Use a chisel to remove the waste and smooth the seats of the notches.

3. Set the cross beams onto the main beams following the marked layout. Drill angled pilot holes through the sides of the cross beams and into the main beams; drill one hole on each side, offsetting the holes so the screws won't hit each other. Fasten the cross beams with 2½" deck screws.

Step G: Finish the Columns

1. Fit each column base against a pier. Secure the base to the pier with corrosion-resistant masonry screws: First, drill pilot holes slightly larger than the screws through the base. Using a masonry bit, drill pilot holes into the pier. Fasten the base with the screws.

2. Fit each capital against the main beam, drill pilot holes, and fasten the capital with deck screws.

3. Caulk the joints around the capital and base with high quality, paintable caulk.

4. Paint the columns—and beams, if desired—using a primer and paint recommended by the column manufacturer.

Center the column at both ends, then tighten the nut over the bearing plate to secure the entire assembly.

Set a circular saw to cut just above the notch seat; clean up the notch with a chisel.

After fastening the base and capital, caulk all of the joints to hide any gaps and create a watertight seal.

Wood & Copper Arbor

As a decorative focal point, this arbor has some unexpected features. With three enclosed sides, its shape is perfect for a corner niche. This arbor is also lovely as a garden centerpiece: it makes for a solid anchor in a garden plan that unfolds to the sides.

Copper accents appear in dramatic sunbursts forming the back panel and in a slatted roof covering that fans out like an art deco awning. Both are made from rigid copper pipe that will develop a beautiful patina over time. Training vines along the slender metal tubing creates a nice contrast of forms while adding shade and privacy.

The interior space of the arbor offers plenty of room for a lawn chair or a small bench. Or, instead of a private sitting area, you might devote the space to displaying a sculpture or a group of special plants.

Material List

Description (No. finished pieces)	Quantity/Size	Material
Posts		
Posts (4)	4 @ field measure	4 × 4
Concrete	Field measure	3,000 PSI concrete
Gravel	Field measure	Compactable gravel
Back Panel		
Horizontal rails (2 top/bottom rails,	1 @ 8'	2 × 4
2 center rails)	1 @ 8'	2 × 2
Copper slats (10)	25 linear feet	½" rigid copper pipe
Side Panels (8 horizontal, 16 vertical)	8 @ 8'	2 × 2
Roof		
Roof beams (4)	2 @ 8'	2 × 6
	1 @ 12'	
Copper slats (10)	51 linear feet	1"-dia. rigid copper pipe
Hardware & Fasteners		
10d galvanized casing nails		
8d galvanized casing nails		
6d galvanized finish nails		
3" deck screws		
6d siding nails		

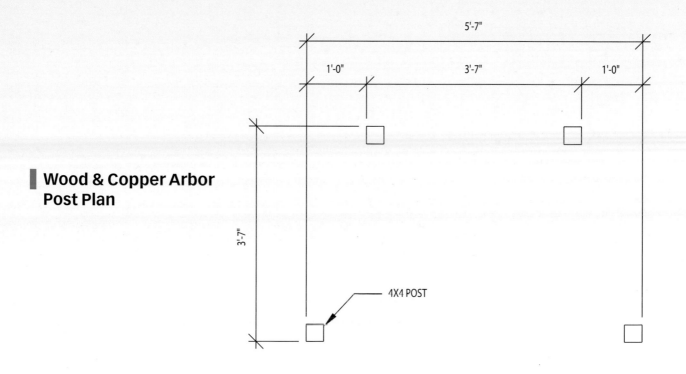

Wood & Copper Arbor
Post Plan

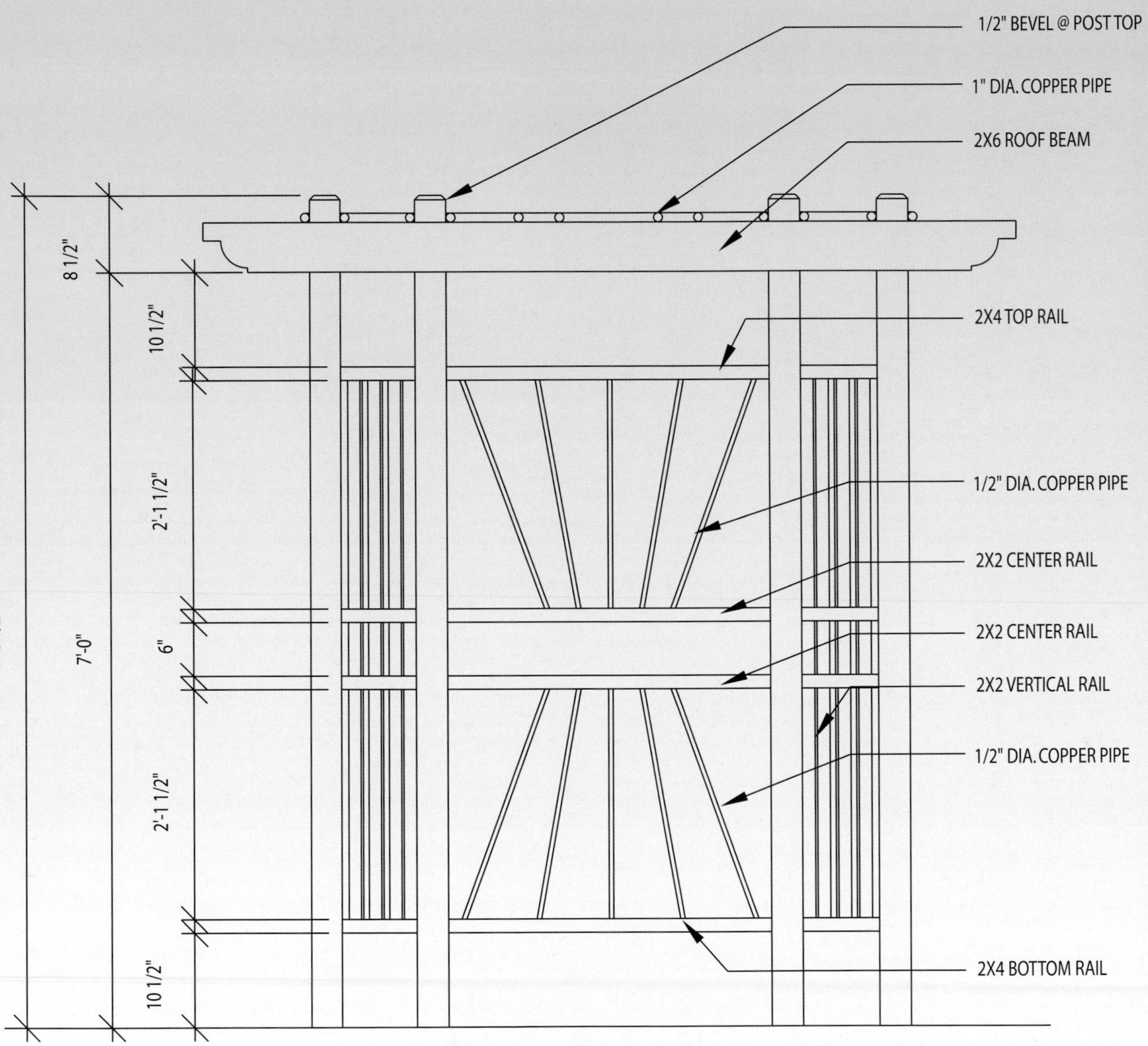
1/2" BEVEL @ POST TOP
1" DIA. COPPER PIPE
2X6 ROOF BEAM
2X4 TOP RAIL
1/2" DIA. COPPER PIPE
2X2 CENTER RAIL
2X2 CENTER RAIL
2X2 VERTICAL RAIL
1/2" DIA. COPPER PIPE
2X4 BOTTOM RAIL
7'-8 1/2"
7'-0"
8 1/2"
10 1/2"
2'-1 1/2"
6"
2'-1 1/2"
10 1/2"

Wood & Copper Arbor
Front Elevation

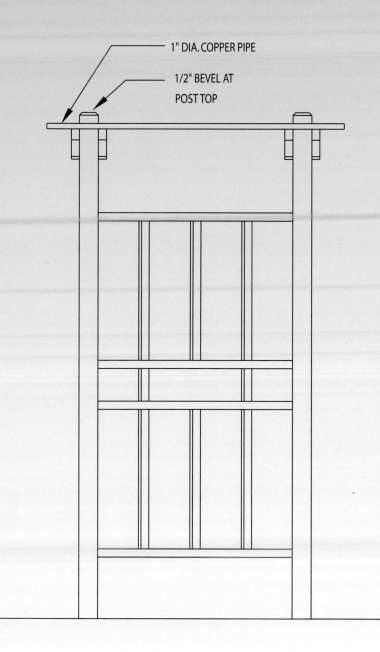

1" DIA. COPPER PIPE

1/2" BEVEL AT
POST TOP

**Wood & Copper Arbor
Side Elevation**

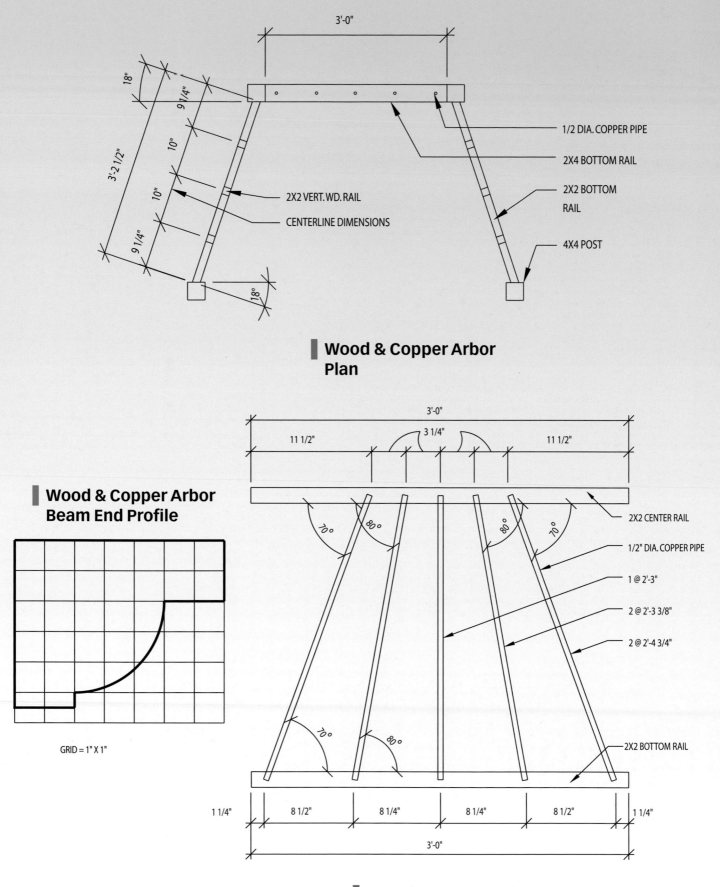

3'-0"

18°

9 1/4"

3'-2 1/2"

10"

10"

9 1/4"

18°

1/2 DIA. COPPER PIPE

2X4 BOTTOM RAIL

2X2 BOTTOM RAIL

4X4 POST

2X2 VERT. WD. RAIL

CENTERLINE DIMENSIONS

Wood & Copper Arbor
Plan

Wood & Copper Arbor
Beam End Profile

GRID = 1" X 1"

3'-0"

11 1/2"   3 1/4"   11 1/2"

70°   80°   80°   70°

2X2 CENTER RAIL

1/2" DIA. COPPER PIPE

1 @ 2'-3"

2 @ 2'-3 3/8"

2 @ 2'-4 3/4"

70°   80°

2X2 BOTTOM RAIL

1 1/4"   8 1/2"   8 1/4"   8 1/4"   8 1/2"   1 1/4"

3'-0"

Wood & Copper Arbor
Back Panel Detail

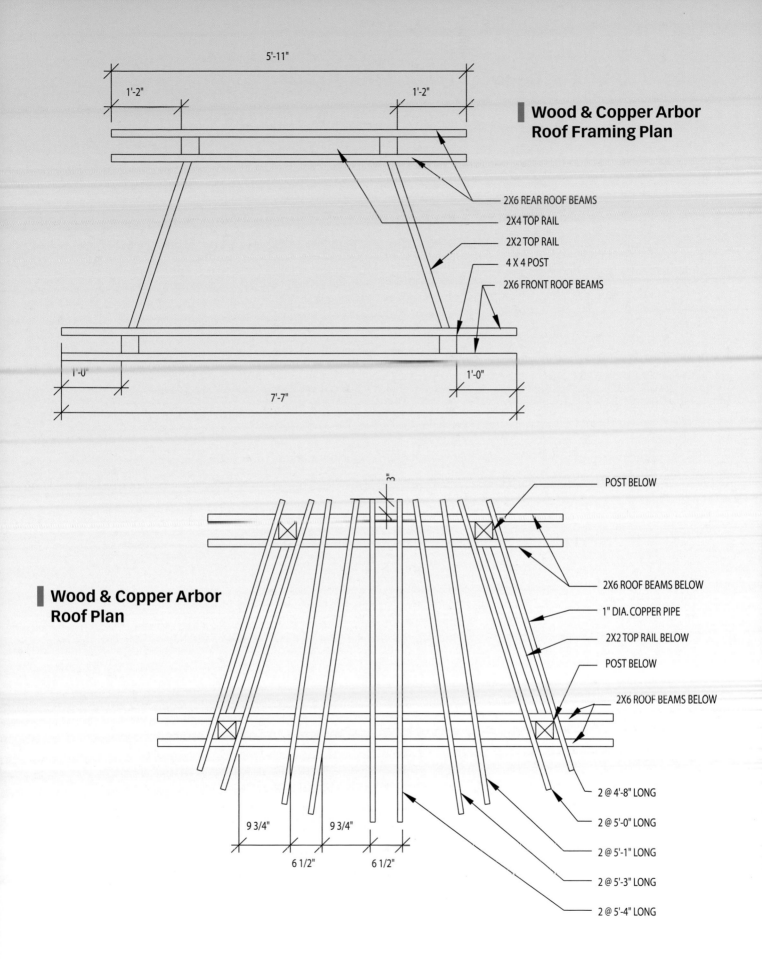

Wood & Copper Arbor
Roof Framing Plan

5'-11"

1'-2"

1'-2"

2X6 REAR ROOF BEAMS

2X4 TOP RAIL

2X2 TOP RAIL

4 X 4 POST

2X6 FRONT ROOF BEAMS

1'-0"

1'-0"

7'-7"

Wood & Copper Arbor
Roof Plan

3"

POST BELOW

2X6 ROOF BEAMS BELOW

1" DIA. COPPER PIPE

2X2 TOP RAIL BELOW

POST BELOW

2X6 ROOF BEAMS BELOW

9 3/4"

9 3/4"

6 1/2"

6 1/2"

2 @ 4'-8" LONG

2 @ 5'-0" LONG

2 @ 5'-1" LONG

2 @ 5'-3" LONG

2 @ 5'-4" LONG

How to Build the Wood & Copper Arbor

Step A: Install the Posts

Set the four posts in the ground with concrete. Treat the bottom ends of the posts for rot resistance before setting them. (See page 220.)

1. Determine the total length of the posts: First find out how deep the posts must be buried in the ground, according to the local building code. To that dimension add 92½" to find the total post length.

2. Cut the posts to length (see Cutting Lumber Posts, page 34). Bevel the top ends of each post at 45°, as shown in the FRONT ELEVATION on page 66.

3. Mark the post layout onto the ground; follow the POST PLAN on page 65. Dig the post holes and add a layer of gravel to each hole. Position and brace one post so its top end is 92½" above the ground.

4. Position and brace the remaining posts, using a level to ensure all of the post tops are at the same height. This compensates for unevenness in the ground and makes sure the structure itself will be level. Add or remove gravel in each post hole as needed to adjust the post height before bracing.

5. Pour the concrete and let it dry completely.

Step B: Prepare the Back Panel Rails

1. Measure up 10½" from the ground and make a mark on one of the posts. Using a level, transfer this height mark to the other posts. You will use this reference line to mark the layouts for the back and side panels.

2. Mark the layout for the four horizontal rails on the inside faces of the rear posts; follow the FRONT ELEVATION. The bottom and top rails are 2 × 4s; the two center rails are 2 × 2s.

3. Measure between the posts to find the exact length of each rail. Cut the rails to length, then test-fit each one to make sure it fits snugly between the posts.

4. Mark the slat hole layouts on the rails; follow the BACK PANEL DETAIL on page 68.

5. Use a drill with a ⁹⁄₁₆" bit and a speed square to make the angled holes for the slats. (If you own an adjustable drill guide, you can use that instead of the square.) Start the hole, using just the tip of the bit.

Then, holding the square in line with the hole's center, position the drill at the prescribed angle to complete the hole. Drill each hole so its shallow edge is about ¾" deep.

TIP: Use masking tape on the bit to gauge the hole depth.

Step C: Install the Back Panels

1. First cut the ½"-diameter copper slats to length, using a tubing cutter or hacksaw: Cut four pieces at 28¾"; cut four pieces at 27⅜"; and cut two pieces at 27" (see page 234 for help with cutting copper pipe).

2. Position the bottom rail on its layout marks, and drill angled pilot holes through the outside edges of the rail and into the posts. Fasten the rail with 10d casing nails. Slightly countersink the nail heads for best appearance. Repeat to install the upper center rail; use 8d casing nails.

3. Set the copper slats into their respective holes on the bottom rail, then fit their top ends into the lower center rail as you position the rail on its layout marks. Drill pilot holes and fasten the lower center rail to the posts with 8d casing nails. Repeat to install the upper slats and top rail.

Step D: Build the Side Panels

1. Mark the layouts for the 2 × 2 horizontal side rails on the insides of the posts, making sure the side rails are aligned with the back panel rails.

2. Measure between the post centers to determine the exact length of each rail; see the PLAN drawing on page 68. Cut the rails to length, beveling the ends at 18°.

3. Position each rail on its layout marks and drill angled pilot holes through the rail and into the posts; drill one hole on each of the accessible sides of the rail. Fasten the rails with 6d finish nails.

4. Mark the layout for the 2 × 2 vertical rails onto the horizontal rails; follow the PLAN drawing. Cut the vertical rails to fit between the horizontal rails. Fasten the rails with two 6d finish nails driven through pilot holes at each joint.

TIP: If the hammering is too jarring on the horizontal rails, drill slightly larger pilot holes.

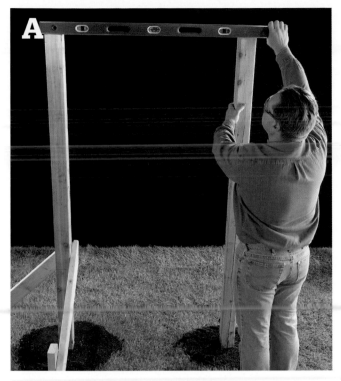

Brace the first post at the proper height, then level over as you set and brace the remaining posts.

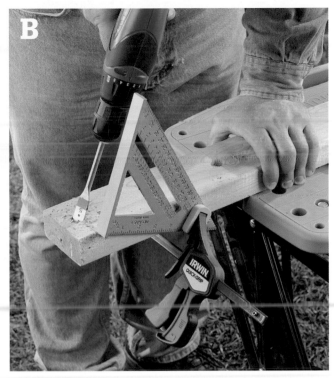

Clamp the square to the workpiece so the 70° mark is aligned with the workpiece. The drill then follows the angle of the square's base.

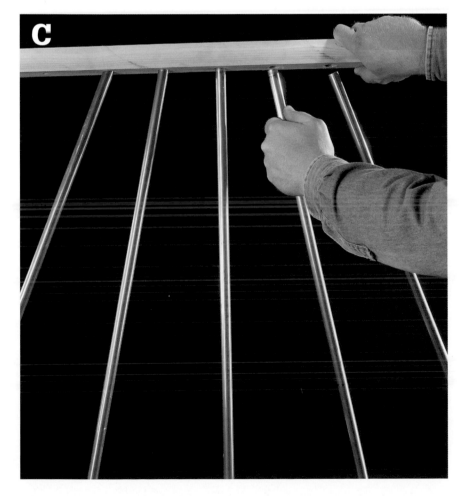

Insert the ends of the copper slats into the holes as you fit the upper rails between the posts.

Drill angled pilot holes to fasten the horizontal side rails, starting about ¾" in from the ends of the rails.

Use a level to make sure the beams are in the same plane so that the roof slats will sit flush across the tops.

Step E: Install the Roof Beams

1. Cut the two front 2 × 6 roof beams to length at 91"; cut the two rear 2 × 6 beams at 71".

2. To shape the beam ends, make a cardboard template following the BEAM END PROFILE drawing on page 68. Trace the pattern onto the beams and make the cuts with a jigsaw or bandsaw. Sand the cuts smooth.

3. Measure down from the tops of each post and make a mark at 3". Position the roof beams so their top edges are on the 3" marks and they overhang the posts equally at both ends. Drill pilot holes and fasten the beams to the posts with 3" deck screws. As you work, set a level across the tops of the beams to make sure they are all level with one another.

Step F: Cut & Install the Roof Slats

1. Mark the roof slat layout onto the top edges of the outer roof beams; follow the ROOF PLAN on page 69.

2. Cut the ten 1"-diameter copper roof slats to length, using the dimensions shown in the ROOF PLAN.

3. Mark pilot holes for fastening the slats: Position the slats on the tops of the roof beams. Measure straight out from the rear-most roof beam to make sure all of the slats overhang 3". Using a permanent marker, draw a dot on top of the slats at the center-points, where the slats cross the inner roof beams.

4. On your workbench, drill a pilot hole at each mark, drilling straight down, completely through the pipe. The holes are slightly larger than the nails you use to fasten the slats.

TIP: It's easier to start the holes if you punch them first with a center punch.

5. Reposition the slats on their layout and fasten them to the roof beams with 6d siding nails.

NOTE: Select a nail that is flat on the underside of the head, so that it sits flush against the slats for minimal visibility.

Nail the roof slats carefully, so the nail head is just snug to the pipe, to avoid any flattening of the pipe.

Like this beautiful octagonal gazebo, our simpler 6-sided version (page 77) offers plenty of opportunity to add personal touches, such as divided-light windows and a custom door.

3-Season Gazebo

A large, windowed gazebo is the ultimate outdoor room. In summer, fully screened openings usher cooling breezes through the shaded interior. During the cooler days of spring and fall, slide-up storm windows provide comfort without limiting the full, 360-degree view. Because the gazebo is enclosed, you can decorate the interior and keep it furnished year-round, or use the space for off-season storage.

The 3-season Gazebo on page 77 has a classic hexagonal floor plan. Five of the walls are framed identically and are designed with standard-sized combination storm windows and standard fixed utility windows. The sixth wall contains a standard pre-hung storm door and a utility window. You can follow the plan's specifications for window and door sizes or choose custom sizes and alter the framing accordingly. Either way, it's a good idea to buy the units and have them on hand for measuring before you frame the walls.

As with the 8-sided Gazebo (page 148), making the many angled cuts on this project is much easier with a power miter saw, preferably a compound saw.

This gazebo (above) is the same design as the one on page 74, but it shows how a change in finish and hardware greatly alters the look. Consider custom details like these while you look over the plans on the following pages to make your gazebo unique.

Inspired partly by screened gazebos such as this one (left), our version (on page 77) has combination windows with screen and glass, but you could fill the wall openings with screen only.

Material List

Description (No. finished pieces)	Quantity/Size	Material
Foundation		
Concrete	Field measure	3,000 PSI concrete
Concrete tube forms	7—field measure for length	12"-diameter cardboard forms
Compactable gravel	2 cubic feet	
Framing		
Main posts (6)	6 @ 10'	4 × 6
Floor support posts (6)	1 @ 8'	4 × 4
Center pier pad (2–3 pieces)	1 @ 3'	
Exterior-grade plywood as needed for shim material		2 × 8
Floor frames:		
Perimeter and Interior Floor Beams (18)	18 @ 8'	2 × 8
Floor Joists (9)	9 @ 8'	2 × 8
Perimeter roof beams (6)	6 @ 8'	4 × 6
Roof hub (1)	1 @ 1'	6 × 6
Hip rafters (6)	6 @ 10'	2 × 8
Purlins (6)	2 @ 10'	2 × 8
Intermediate rafters (18)	9 @ 12'	2 × 8
Trim nailers (24)	3 @ 8', plus cutoffs from intermediate rafters	2 × 4
Widow & door frames	Field measure	4 × 4
Corner studs (12)	12 @ 10'	2 × 4
Roof		
Truss top chord (4)	4 @ 12'	2 × 12
Truss bottom chord (8)	8 @ 8'	2 × 6
Truss strut (4)	1 @ 10'	2 × 4
Hub (1)	1 @ 51"	4 × 4
Support joists (4 outer, 4 inner)	4 @ 14' 4 @ 10'	2 × 4
Slat braces (4)	1 @ 8' 1 @ 3'	2 × 4
Slats	Field measure	2 × 2
Floor Decking	39 @ 8'	5⁄4" × 6" decking boards
Roofing (roof covering)		
Roof sheathing	9 @ 4' × 8'	3⁄4" exterior-grade plywood
Shingles and 15# building paper	Coverage for 220 square feet, plus ridge caps	
Stairs		
Stringers (3) and stair pad (1)	2 @ 8'	pressure-treated 2 × 12
Treads (6)	3 @ 10'	5⁄4" × 8" decking boards
Risers (optional, 3)	1 @ 10' 1 @ 6'	1 × 6

Description (No. finished pieces)	Quantity/Size	Material
Wall Finishes & Trim		
Top-of-wall trim	6 @ 8'	1 × 12
	6 @ 8'	1 × 10
Window/door header trim	Field measure	1×
Exterior sheathing/trim	Field measure	
Interior sheathing/trim	Field measure	
Optional skirt framing	12 @ 8'	2 × 4
Optional skirt sheathing/trim	Field measure	
Framing Connectors		
Post bases, main posts	6, with standoff plates and anchoring hardware	Simpson ABU46, or similar approved connector
Post bases, floor support posts	6, with standoff plates and anchoring hardware	Simpson AB44, or similar approved connector
Beam hangers	3, with recommended fasteners	Simpson LS50Z, or similar approved connector
Hurricane ties	6, with recommended fasteners	Simpson H8, or similar approved connector
Rafter connectors	6, with recommended fasteners	Simpson FB26, or similar approved connector
Stair stringer framing connectors	6, with recommended fasteners	Simpson L30, or similar approved connector
Hardware & Fasteners		
5⁄8" × 12" J-bolts	7, with washers and nuts	
1⁄2" × 12" J-bolts	6, with washers and nuts	
1⁄4" × 10" galvanized carriage bolts	12, with washers and nuts	
3½" x 1⁄4" galvanized lag bolt	6, with washers and nuts	
Construction adhesive		
10d galvanized common nails		
16d galvanized common nails		
2¼" deck screws		
2½" deck screws		
8d galvanized box nails		
Heavy-duty staples		
Roofing nails		
3½" galvanized wood screws		
1⁄4" × 6" galvanized lag screws, with washers		

* Wall Frames are made up of the corner studs and door and window frames.

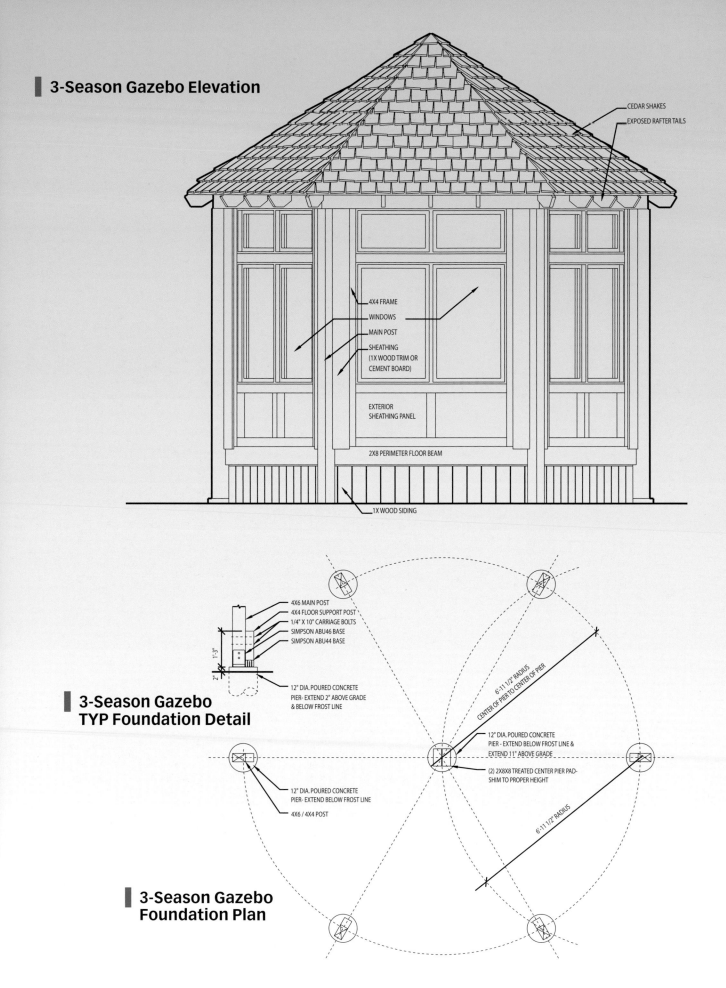

3-Season Gazebo Elevation

CEDAR SHAKES

EXPOSED RAFTER TAILS

4X4 FRAME

WINDOWS

MAIN POST

SHEATHING
(1X WOOD TRIM OR
CEMENT BOARD)

EXTERIOR
SHEATHING PANEL

2X8 PERIMETER FLOOR BEAM

1X WOOD SIDING

4X6 MAIN POST
4X4 FLOOR SUPPORT POST
1/4" X 10" CARRIAGE BOLTS
SIMPSON ABU46 BASE
SIMPSON ABU44 BASE

1'-3"

2"

12" DIA. POURED CONCRETE
PIER- EXTEND 2" ABOVE GRADE
& BELOW FROST LINE

3-Season Gazebo
TYP Foundation Detail

6'-11 1/2" RADIUS
CENTER OF PIER TO CENTER OF PIER

12" DIA. POURED CONCRETE
PIER - EXTEND BELOW FROST LINE &
EXTEND 11" ABOVE GRADE

(2) 2X8X8 TREATED CENTER PIER PAD-
SHIM TO PROPER HEIGHT

12" DIA. POURED CONCRETE
PIER- EXTEND BELOW FROST LINE

4X6 / 4X4 POST

6'-11 1/2" RADIUS

3-Season Gazebo
Foundation Plan

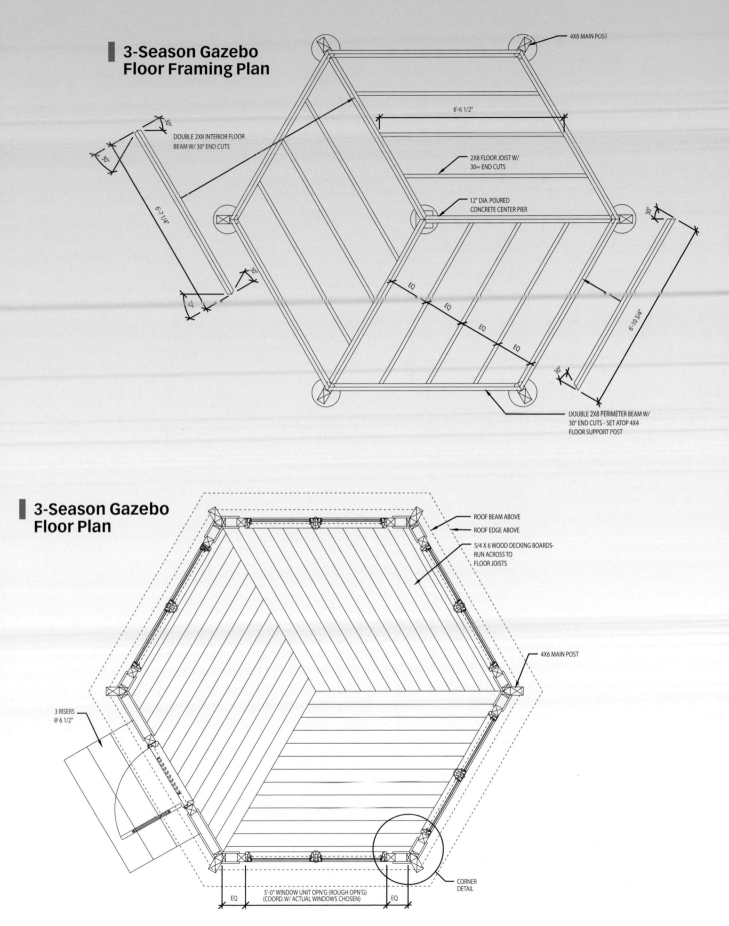

3-Season Gazebo Floor Framing Plan

4X6 MAIN POST

6'-6 1/2"

DOUBLE 2X8 INTERIOR FLOOR BEAM W/ 30° END CUTS

2X8 FLOOR JOIST W/ 30∞ END CUTS

12" DIA. POURED CONCRETE CENTER PIER

30°

30°

6'-7 1/4"

30°

4"

30°

EQ

EQ

EQ

EQ

EQ

30°

6'-10 3/4"

30°

DOUBLE 2X8 PERIMETER BEAM W/ 30° END CUTS - SET ATOP 4X4 FLOOR SUPPORT POST

3-Season Gazebo Floor Plan

ROOF BEAM ABOVE

ROOF EDGE ABOVE

5/4 X 6 WOOD DECKING BOARDS- RUN ACROSS TO FLOOR JOISTS

4X6 MAIN POST

3 RISERS @ 6 1/2"

CORNER DETAIL

EQ

5'-0" WINDOW UNIT OPN'G (ROUGH OPN'G) (COORD. W/ ACTUAL WINDOWS CHOSEN)

EQ

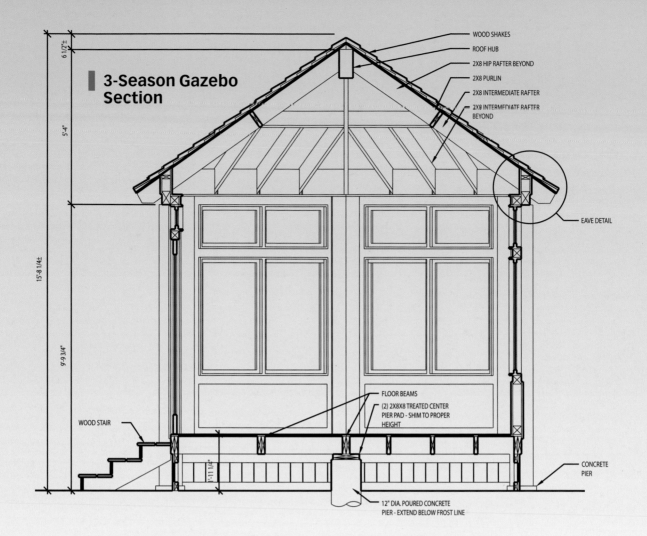

3-Season Gazebo Section

WOOD SHAKES

ROOF HUB

2X8 HIP RAFTER BEYOND

2X8 PURLIN

2X8 INTERMEDIATE RAFTER

2X8 INTERMEDIATE RAFTER BEYOND

EAVE DETAIL

6 1/2"±

5'-4"

15'-8 1/4"±

9'-9 3/4"

WOOD STAIR

1'-11 1/2"

FLOOR BEAMS

(2) 2X8X8 TREATED CENTER PIER PAD - SHIM TO PROPER HEIGHT

CONCRETE PIER

12" DIA. POURED CONCRETE PIER - EXTEND BELOW FROST LINE

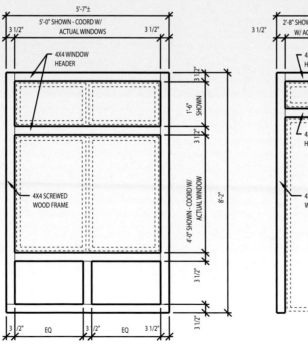

5'-7"±

5'-0" SHOWN - COORD W/ ACTUAL WINDOWS

3 1/2"   3 1/2"

4X4 WINDOW HEADER

3 1/2"

1'-6" SHOWN

3 1/2"

4X4 SCREWED WOOD FRAME

4'-0" SHOWN - COORD W/ ACTUAL WINDOW

8'-2"

3 1/2"

3 1/2"

3 1/2"   EQ   3 1/2"   EQ   3 1/2"

3-Season Gazebo
Window Frame Template

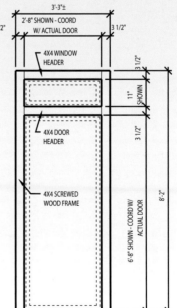

3'-3"±

2'-8" SHOWN - COORD W/ ACTUAL DOOR

3 1/2"   3 1/2"

4X4 WINDOW HEADER

3 1/2"

11" SHOWN

4X4 DOOR HEADER

3 1/2"

4X4 SCREWED WOOD FRAME

6'-8" SHOWN - COORD W/ ACTUAL DOOR

8'-2"

3-Season Gazebo
Door Frame Template

3-Season Gazebo
Roof Framing Plan

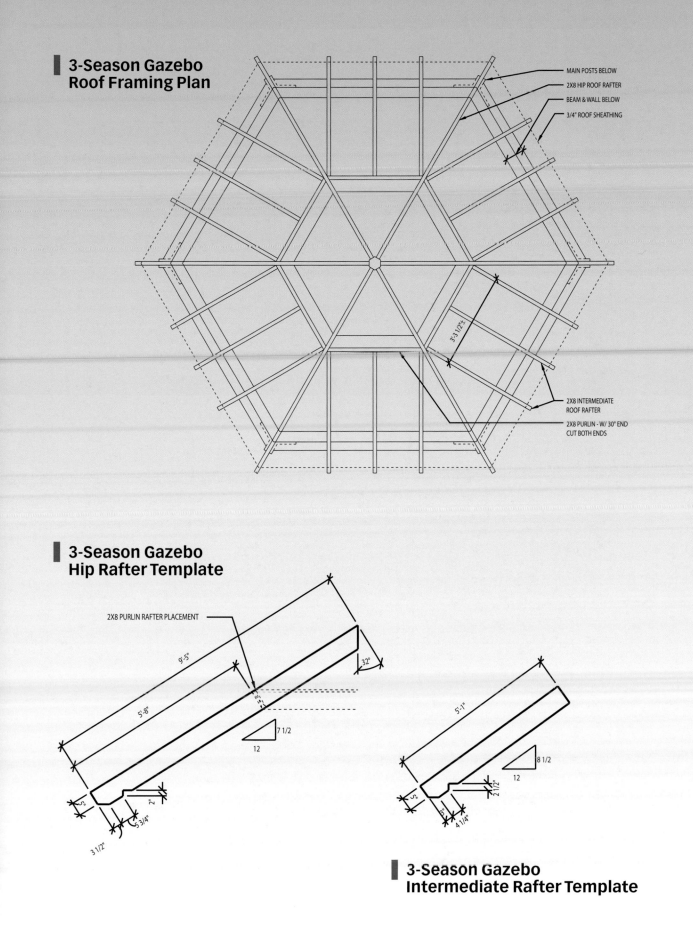

MAIN POSTS BELOW

2X8 HIP ROOF RAFTER

BEAM & WALL BELOW

3/4" ROOF SHEATHING

3'-3 1/2"

2X8 INTERMEDIATE ROOF RAFTER

2X8 PURLIN - W/ 30° END CUT BOTH ENDS

3-Season Gazebo
Hip Rafter Template

2X8 PURLIN RAFTER PLACEMENT

9'-5"

5'-8"

32°

7 1/2
12

5"

2"

5 3/4"

3 1/2"

5'-1"

8 1/2
12

5"

2 1/2"

4 1/4"

3-Season Gazebo
Intermediate Rafter Template

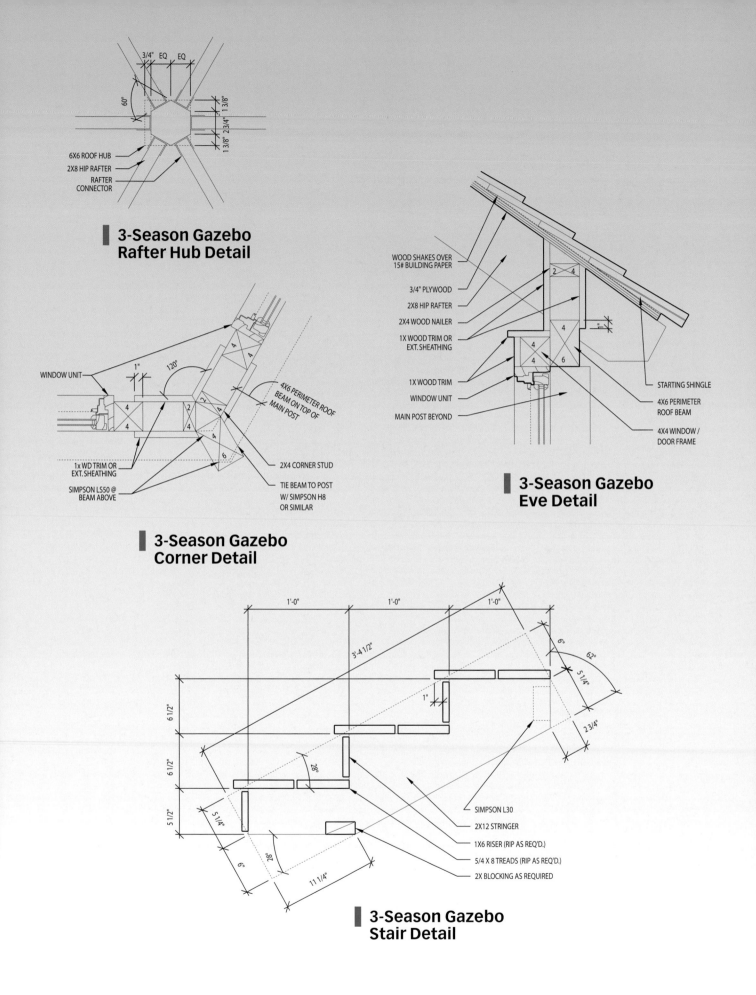

**3-Season Gazebo
Rafter Hub Detail**

3/4" EQ EQ
60°
1 3/8" 1 3/8"
2 3/4"
1 3/8"

6X6 ROOF HUB
2X8 HIP RAFTER
RAFTER CONNECTOR

**3-Season Gazebo
Corner Detail**

WINDOW UNIT
1"
120°
4
4
2
2
4
4
4
6
4X6 PERIMETER ROOF BEAM ON TOP OF MAIN POST
1x WD TRIM OR EXT. SHEATHING
SIMPSON LS50 @ BEAM ABOVE
2X4 CORNER STUD
TIE BEAM TO POST W/ SIMPSON H8 OR SIMILAR

**3-Season Gazebo
Eve Detail**

WOOD SHAKES OVER 15# BUILDING PAPER
3/4" PLYWOOD
2X8 HIP RAFTER
2X4 WOOD NAILER
1X WOOD TRIM OR EXT. SHEATHING
1X WOOD TRIM
WINDOW UNIT
MAIN POST BEYOND
2 4
4
4
4
6
STARTING SHINGLE
4X6 PERIMETER ROOF BEAM
4X4 WINDOW / DOOR FRAME

**3-Season Gazebo
Stair Detail**

1'-0" 1'-0" 1'-0"
3'-4 1/2"
6 1/2"
6 1/2"
5 1/2"
5 1/4"
6"
28°
28°
11 1/4"
1"
6"
62°
5 1/4"
2 3/4"

SIMPSON L30
2X12 STRINGER
1X6 RISER (RIP AS REQ'D.)
5/4 X 8 TREADS (RIP AS REQ'D.)
2X BLOCKING AS REQUIRED

How to Build the 3-Season Gazebo

Step A: Pour the Concrete Piers

See pages 212 to 215 for basic instructions on laying out and pouring concrete pier footings. Detailed steps for laying out a hexagon are given below. Use 12"-diameter concrete tube forms for the six outer piers and the center pier.

TIP: There's a convenient mathematical rule that makes it easy to lay out a hexagon: the centerpoint and all six outer points are equidistant. Therefore, if you measure the same distance from the center and one outer point, the intersection of those measurements is the location of a second outer point, and so on.

1. Drive a stake into the ground at the gazebo's centerpoint, then drive a nail into the center of the stake. Set up batterboards on opposing sides of the gazebo footprint, and run a mason's line that passes directly over the centerpoint.

2. Mark the string at the centerpoint, then measure out in both directions and mark the string at 83 ½". Drive a stake and a nail at outer mark, using a plumb bob to transfer the string markings to the ground. These points represent the centers of two outer piers.

3. With two helpers, pull one tape measure from the centerpoint and one from an outer stake. Cross the tapes so they meet at 83½"—at that intersection, drive a stake and nail to represent a third outer pier. Repeat the process to lay out the three remaining piers. Each time, measure from the centerpoint and one of the original two outer piers to avoid compounding inaccuracy. Untie the mason's string.

4. Dig the holes and set the concrete forms, following the steps on page 214 and the requirements of the local building code. The outer forms should extend 2" above the ground; the center form should extend 11" above the ground.

5. Set up batterboards behind all of the piers. Run three mason's strings over the centers of opposing piers, making sure they all cross over the centerpoint (on the center pier).

NOTE: The strings stay in place for the concrete pour, so make sure they're high enough to allow easy access to the forms. Use the measuring technique from step 3 to mark the centers of the piers onto the strings. Confirm that each concrete form is centered on the layout.

6. Make two more marks on the strings to indicate the J-bolt locations: one at 80¾" from the centerpoint and one at 85¼" from the centerpoint.

7. Pour and screed the concrete. Into each outer pier, set a ½" × 12" J-bolt at the 80¾" string marking. Set a ⅝" × 12" J-bolt at the 85¼" mark. Position the bolts so they are plumb and extend ¾" to 1" above the concrete (follow the post base manufacturer's specifications). Set a ⅝" × 12" J-bolt into the center of the center pier so it extends 5" above the concrete.

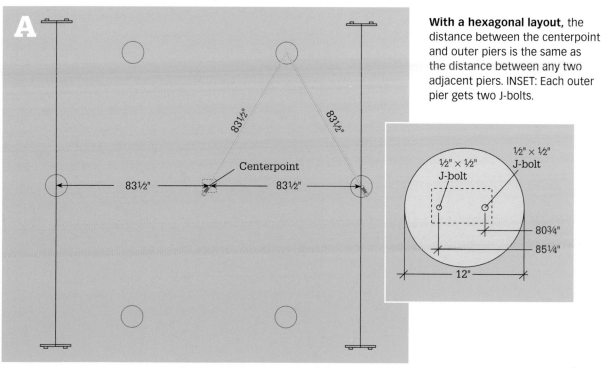

With a hexagonal layout, the distance between the centerpoint and outer piers is the same as the distance between any two adjacent piers. INSET: Each outer pier gets two J-bolts.

Step B: Set the Posts

1. Use a straight board to mark reference lines for squaring the post bases: Set the board flat against the J-bolts on the center pier and each outer pier and mark along the board across the top of the outer pier.

2. Center a 4 × 6 post base over each outer J-bolt and use a framing square to make sure the base is square to the reference line. Secure the bases with washers and nuts; use the hexagon measuring technique to make sure all points are equidistant. Add the provided standoff plate to each base.

3. Leaving the 4 × 6 main posts long, set them into the bases, and position them so their outside edges are 88" from the centerpoint. Tack each post in place with a nail, then install cross bracing so the post is perfectly plumb. Re-check for equidistant placement, then fasten the posts as recommended by the base manufacturer.

4. On the inside face of one of the main posts, make a mark 15" above the top of the pier. Using a mason's string and a line level, transfer this height mark to the other main posts.

5. Install the 4 × 4 post bases (with standoffs) so the floor support posts will be flush against the inside edges of the main posts. Measure from the standoff to the height mark and cut each floor support post to fit.

6. Anchor the support posts to their bases, using the recommended fasteners. Then, anchor each support post to a main post with two ¼" × 10" carriage bolts, as shown in the FOUNDATION DETAIL on page 78.

Step C: Add the Center Pier Pad

1. Run a level line across the tops of two opposing floor support posts. Measure from the top of the center pier to find the thickness of the center pier pad.

2. Create a pad from 2 × 8 lumber, adding exterior-grade plywood as needed for shim material to achieve the proper thickness. Assemble the pad with construction adhesive and nails.

3. Drill a counterbored hole in the pad's center for the J-bolt, and anchor the pad to the center pier. Cut off any excess bolt so it's flush with top of pad.

Mark a line across the tops of the piers; this helps ensure all post bases are facing the gazebo's center.

Countersink the J-bolt nut and washer into the wood pier pad, so the floor beams sit flush on top.

Step D: Frame the Floor

1. Build the six double 2 × 8 perimeter floor beams following the FLOOR FRAMING PLAN, on page 79. Check the boards for crowning (see page 60), making sure the crowned edges are up; then cut the beam ends at 30° so they break on the centers of the floor support posts. Join the two boards for each beam with construction adhesive and 10d common nails.

2. Install the perimeter beams by toenailing into the main posts and floor support posts with 16d common nails. Also nail the beam ends together.

3. Build the three double 2 × 8 interior floor beams like the perimeter beams. Cut the ends at 30°, too (as shown in the INTERIOR BEAM DETAIL).

4. Fasten the interior beams to the center pier pad and to one another with 16d nails. Anchor the outer ends of the beams to the perimeter beams with beam hangers, using the recommended fasteners.

5. Mark the floor joist layout onto the beams following the FLOOR FRAMING PLAN; space the joists equally across each section of the floor frame.

6. Measure and cut each joist to fit, beveling the ends at 30°. Install the joists crown up; driving three 16d common nails into the beams at each end. Make sure the joists are flush with the tops of the floor beams.

Join the interior beams to the perimeter beams with framing connectors, making sure the tops of the beams are flush.

Step E: Install the Floor Decking

As shown in the FLOOR PLAN, the 5⁄4 × 6 decking is laid nearly perpendicular to the floor joists (see photo, right). Each of the three flooring sections starts with a full-width piece aligned with the center of an interior floor beam. Install the decking one section at a time.

1. Starting with any one of the three flooring sections: Cut the outside end of the first decking board at 30° to fit flush with the outside face of the perimeter beam. The pointed end should touch the main post. Let the inside end of the decking board run long over the center of the floor frame.

2. Align the decking board with the center of the interior floor beam (the seam between the two beam boards), and fasten the decking to the beams and joists with two 2¼" deck screws driven through pilot holes.

3. Install the remaining boards in the section, running the ends long over the interior and perimeter beams. Snug the boards tightly together to prevent gaps that could let in insects. Rip the last board to fit flush along the perimeter beam.

4. Trim the decking boards in the first section so the outside ends are flush with outside edge of

Cut along chalk lines to trim the ends of the decking boards along the floor beams.

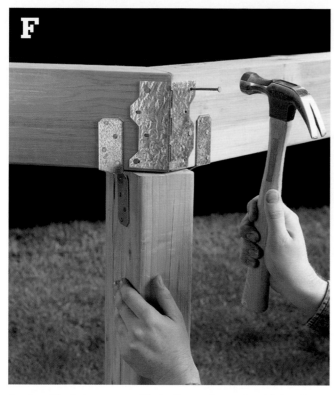

Anchor the beam assembly to the main posts with hurricane ties, and then tie the roof beams together with metal angles.

Install the hip rafters so their top ends are flush with the top of the hub. Inset: Toenail the rafters to the sides of the hub for extra support.

perimeter beam and the inside ends are aligned with the center of the interior beam. Snap a chalk line to ensure a straight cut, and use a circular saw set to cut just through the decking.

5. Complete the remaining sections of flooring using the same procedure. For the final section, pre-cut the inside ends of the boards at 30° to fit against the first board in the first section.

Step F: Install the Roof Beams

1. Measure up from the floor deck and mark one of the main posts at 94¼". Transfer that height mark to the remaining posts using a mason's string and a line level. Cut off the posts at the height marks (see Cutting Lumber Posts, page 34).

2. Cut the 4 × 6 roof beams to span across the tops of the main posts, as shown in the ROOF FRAMING PLAN, on page 81, the EAVE DETAIL and the CORNER DETAIL, on page 82. Miter the ends at 30° so the joints break over the centers of the posts.

3. Toenail the beams to the main posts with 16d common nails, then anchor the beams together with hurricane ties. Reinforce the beam-post connection with adjustable-angle framing connectors.

Step G: Install the Hip Rafters

1. Cut the 6 × 6 roof hub to length at 12".

2. On a table saw, trim off ¾" from one side so the hub measures 4¾" × 5½". Set the saw blade to 30° and make four full-length cuts to create six facets at 2¾", as shown in the RAFTER HUB DETAIL, on page 82.

3. Select two straight 2 × 8s to use for the pattern hip rafters. Check the boards for crowning, then cut them following the HIP RAFTER TEMPLATE, on page 81 (see page 222 for marking and cutting rafters). The slope for the hip rafters is 7½ -in-12.

4. Test-fit the rafters and hub on the gazebo frame. Make any necessary adjustments for a good fit. Use one of the rafters to mark the remaining four hip rafters, and make the cuts.

5. Install the hip rafters so their top ends are flush with the top of the hub and their bottom ends fall over the joints of the roof beams. Fasten the rafters to the framing connectors using 3½" x ¼" lag bolts. Toenail the sides of the hip rafters to the hub with 2½" deck screws.

Step H: Install the Purlins & Intermediate Rafters

1. Measure up from the ends of the hip rafters and mark the side faces at 68". These marks represent the bottom faces of the 2 × 8 purlins.

2. Cut the six 2 × 8 purlins to fit between the rafters, beveling the ends at 30°.

3. Nail the purlins to the rafters with 16d common nails, so their faces are perpendicular to the rafter faces and all edges are flush along the top.

4. Mark the layout for the intermediate rafters onto the purlins and roof beams; follow the ROOF FRAMING PLAN on page 81.

5. Cut a pattern intermediate rafter from a 2 × 8, following the INTERMEDIATE RAFTER TEMPLATE, on page 81. Test-fit the rafter against the purlins and roof beams, and make any adjustments necessary for a good fit.

6. Using the pattern rafter, mark and cut the 17 remaining intermediate rafters.

7. Install the rafters on their layout marks, using 16d common nails.

Step I: Sheath & Shingle the Roof

1. Starting at the eave and working up, cut ¾" plywood to span between the centers of the hip rafters.

NOTE: Starting with a 4 × 8-ft. sheet of plywood means that about 2–3" of the rafter tails will be seen, as shown in the ROOF FRAMING PLAN. If desired, you can slightly adjust the amount of exposure.

2. Fasten the sheathing with 8d box nails driven every 6" along the perimeter and every 12" along intermediate rafters and purlins.

3. Cut and install the remaining sheathing. At the roof peak, cut the pieces to a point so they enclose the hub.

4. Install 15# building paper and cedar shingles, following the steps on pages 226. Install the shingles so their top ends run long over the ridges of the roof, then trim them off with a saw.

5. Cap the ridges with custom-beveled shingle caps or 1× cedar boards. Use a T-bevel to find the angle of the ridge (see Step D, on page 231), then bevel the edges of the cap shingles on a table saw. Alternate the overlap with each cap.

Endnail or toenail the intermediate rafters to the purlins. Toenail the rafters to the roof beams.

Bevel the edges of both shingles for each cap, and alternate the overlap between courses.

Step J: Frame the Walls

The wall frames consist of 2 × 4 corner studs at the ends of each wall section and 4 × 4 frames for the window and door openings. You can build the window and door frames on the ground, then tip them up and secure them to the gazebo framework.

Follow the WINDOW FRAME TEMPLATE and DOOR FRAME TEMPLATE, page 80, for the basic layout of the frames. Modify any dimensions as needed to fit your window and door units.

1. At each corner inside the gazebo, measure up from the bottom edges of the roof beams and make a mark at 3½". Cut the 12 2 × 4 corner studs to fit between the floor and the marks on the roof beams.

2. Position the studs, as shown in the FLOOR PLAN on page 79, making sure they are flush to the outside edges of the floor decking. Fasten the studs to the floor and roof beams with 16d common nails.

3. Cut the 4 × 4 members for each window and door frame, using the rough opening dimensions specified by the window/door manufacturer. When the frames are installed, the bottom faces of the top horizontal pieces should be flush with the bottom faces of the roof beams, as shown in the EAVE DETAIL.

4. Assemble the frames with 3½" wood screws driven at an angle through pilot holes. Drive four screws at each joint, locating the screws on the faces that will be least visible after the windows and door are installed. For example, on the horizontal header and sill pieces, drive two screws through the top and bottom faces and into the vertical jambs.

5. Center each window and door frame within its wall section. Measure the diagonals to make sure the frame is square, then fasten the frame to the roof beam and floor with ¼" × 6" lag screws. Countersink the screws below the surface of the frame pieces.

Step K: Build the Stairs

1. Use a framing square to lay out the first 2 × 12 stair stringer; follow the STAIR DETAIL on page 82. Starting at one end of the board, position the framing square along the board's top edge. Align the 12" mark on the square's blade (long part) and the 6½" mark on the tongue (short part) with the edge of the board. Trace along the outer edges of the blade and tongue, then use the square to extend the blade, marking across the width of the board. The tongue mark represents the first riser.

2. Measure down 1" from the blade mark and make another line parallel to it—this is the cutting line for the bottom of the stringer (the 1" offset compensates for the thickness of the treads on the first step).

3. Continue the step layout, starting at the point where the first riser mark meets the top edge of the board. Mark the top cutting line by extending the third tread mark across the board's width. Mark the top end cut 12" from the top riser.

4. Cut the stringer and test-fit it against the gazebo. Make any adjustments necessary for a good fit, then use the stringer as a pattern to mark the remaining two stringers, and make the cuts.

5. Anchor the top ends of the stringers to the floor beam, using framing connectors. Secure the bottom ends as required for your specific application, such as with 2× blocking nailed between the stringers and anchored to a concrete pad or spiked into the ground. You can cut the blockin from leftover 2 × 12 stringer material.

6. Cut the stair treads to fit the stringer assembly, overhanging the risers as desired. Start with a full-width ⁵⁄₄ × 8 tread at the front of each step, then rip the next piece to fit. Fasten the treads with 2¼" deck screws. If desired, add 1× riser boards to enclose the back of each step.

When installed, the tops of the window and door frames are level with the tops of the corner studs.

Step L: Add the Wall Finishes

How you sheath and trim the walls of your gazebo is up to you and will likely be determined by the style of the windows and door. The trim details shown in the plans are merely suggestions for enclosing the walls and covering some of the framing for a more finished appearance.

The openings in the wall frames can be covered with exterior-grade plywood, T1-11 siding, or another type of siding. The spaces above the roof beams should be covered with 1× trim or exterior sheathing and secured at the top to 2 × 4 nailers installed between the rafters; see EAVE DETAIL. Also, see CORNER DETAIL for interior/exterior corner trim ideas.

You also have the option of adding a skirt below the floor frame between the main posts. To do this, install 2 × 4 nailers between the posts, then add exterior sheathing, as shown in the SECTION drawing, on page 80.

Position the square on the board, using the tread and riser dimensions, then trace along the square to mark the cutting lines.

Overlap the framing with trim or sheathing by at least 1" to make room for nailing and to help weather-proof the structure. Consider filling in the cavities below windows with siding installed with molding, as shown here.

This dramatic structure is sparer in design than our Gabled Entry (page 93) but features similar construction and styling. Open sides and a lighter roof covering, as shown here, might be preferred if the structure is away from the house.

Gabled Entry

An attractive, shaded entryway can do a great deal for a home's exterior. It can dress up a bare front entrance while adding both shelter and a welcoming feature to the façade. At a rear entrance, it can serve as a bridge between the indoor and outdoor spaces, helping to draw the house and garden closer together. Often gabled entries are self-supporting and do not need to be tied into the house, thus you can also place them out in the yard or garden, or use them as portals to enclosures.

The timber frame construction and custom wood details of the Gabled Entry on page 93 create a natural beauty. That beauty is enhanced when the post-and-beam framework and lattice roof are covered with climbing vines, transforming the structure into a lush garden enchantment.

Attached to the house at one end, this rear-entry structure also serves as an overhead for a deck.

Flowering vines fill an entryway with dappled light and fragrant air to be enjoyed with each pass through.

Material List

Description (No. finished pieces)	Quantity/Size	Material
Posts & Foundation		
Posts (4)	4 @ field measure	6 × 6
Concrete	Field measure	3,000 PSI concrete
Gravel	Field measure	Compactable gravel
Post trim (16)	1 @ 10'	1 × 6
	1 @ 10'	¾" × ¾" cove molding
Roof		
Roof beams (2)	2 @ 8'	6 × 6
Top chords (12)	6 @ 12'	2 × 6
Bottom chords (3)	3 @ 8'	2 × 6
Struts (3)	1 @ 10'	2 × 4
Ridge boards (2)	1 @ 6'	2 × 6
Lattice (4)	4 panels @ 4 × 8'	Cedar or redwood manufactured lattice with ½" or thicker slats
Brackets (4 front/rear, 4 side)	1 @ 10' 2 @ 8'	2 × 8
Railing		
Rails (6)	6 @ 8'	2 × 4
Pickets (22 lower, 10 upper)	5 @ 8' 1 @ 4'	2 × 2
Hardware & Fasteners		
Post-to-beam ties	8, with recommended fasteners	Simpson 1212HLPC, or similar approved connector
¼" × 5" galvanized carriage bolts	30, with washers and nuts	
16d galvanized common nails		
10d galvanized common nails		
8d siding nails		
¼" × 4" galvanized lag screws	16, with washers	
6d galvanized finish nails		
4d galvanized finish nails		
3" deck screws		

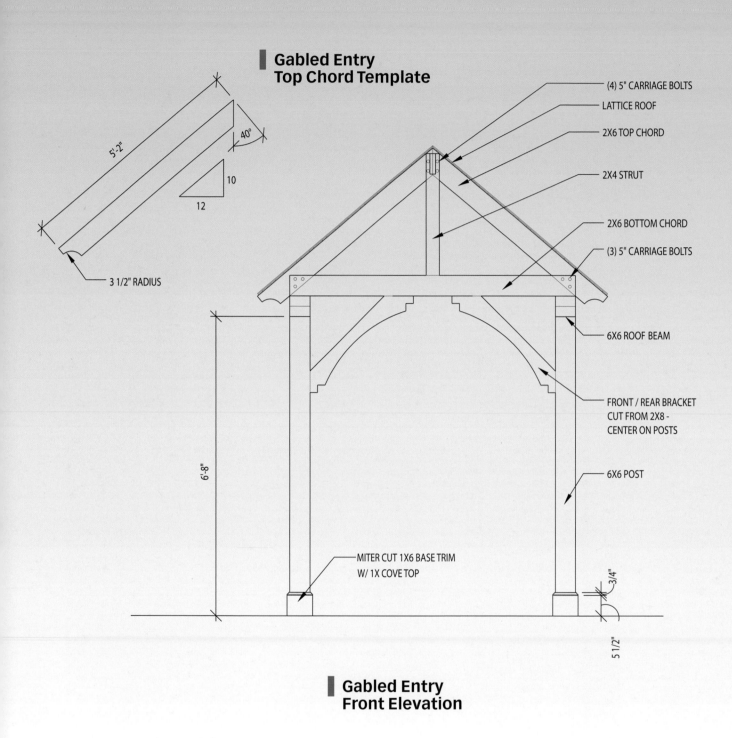

Gabled Entry
Top Chord Template

5'-2"

40°

10

12

3 1/2" RADIUS

(4) 5" CARRIAGE BOLTS

LATTICE ROOF

2X6 TOP CHORD

2X4 STRUT

2X6 BOTTOM CHORD

(3) 5" CARRIAGE BOLTS

6X6 ROOF BEAM

FRONT / REAR BRACKET
CUT FROM 2X8 -
CENTER ON POSTS

6X6 POST

6'-8"

MITER CUT 1X6 BASE TRIM
W/ 1X COVE TOP

3/4"

5 1/2"

Gabled Entry
Front Elevation

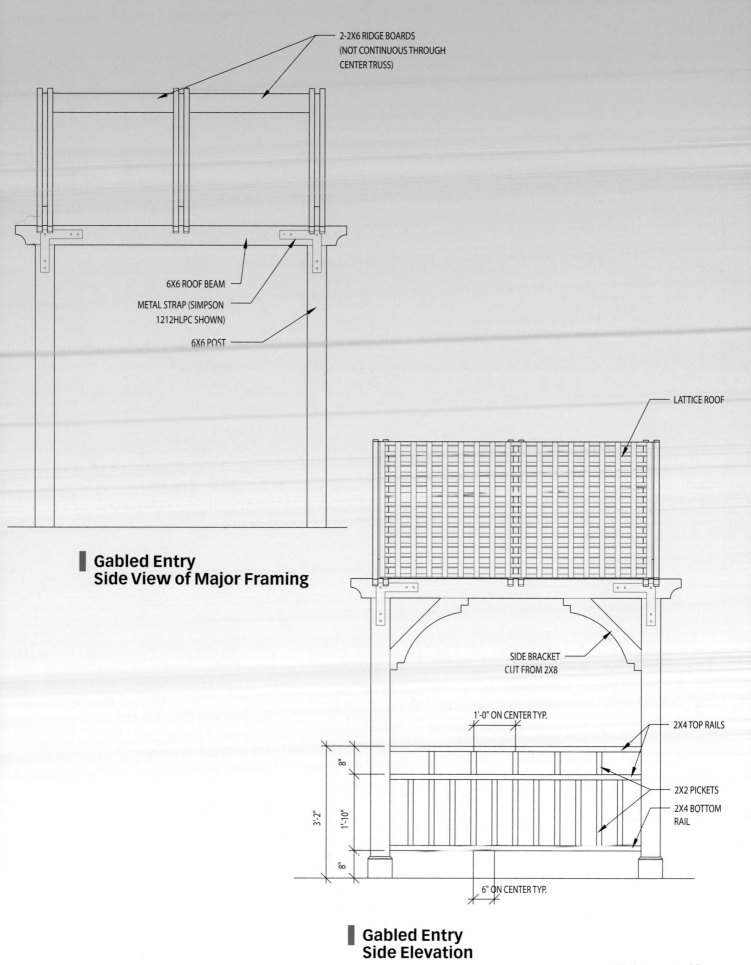

2-2X6 RIDGE BOARDS
(NOT CONTINUOUS THROUGH
CENTER TRUSS)

6X6 ROOF BEAM

METAL STRAP (SIMPSON
1212HLPC SHOWN)

6X6 POST

**Gabled Entry
Side View of Major Framing**

LATTICE ROOF

SIDE BRACKET
CUT FROM 2X8

1'-0" ON CENTER TYP.

2X4 TOP RAILS

8"

2X2 PICKETS

3'-2"

1'-10"

2X4 BOTTOM
RAIL

8"

6" ON CENTER TYP.

**Gabled Entry
Side Elevation**

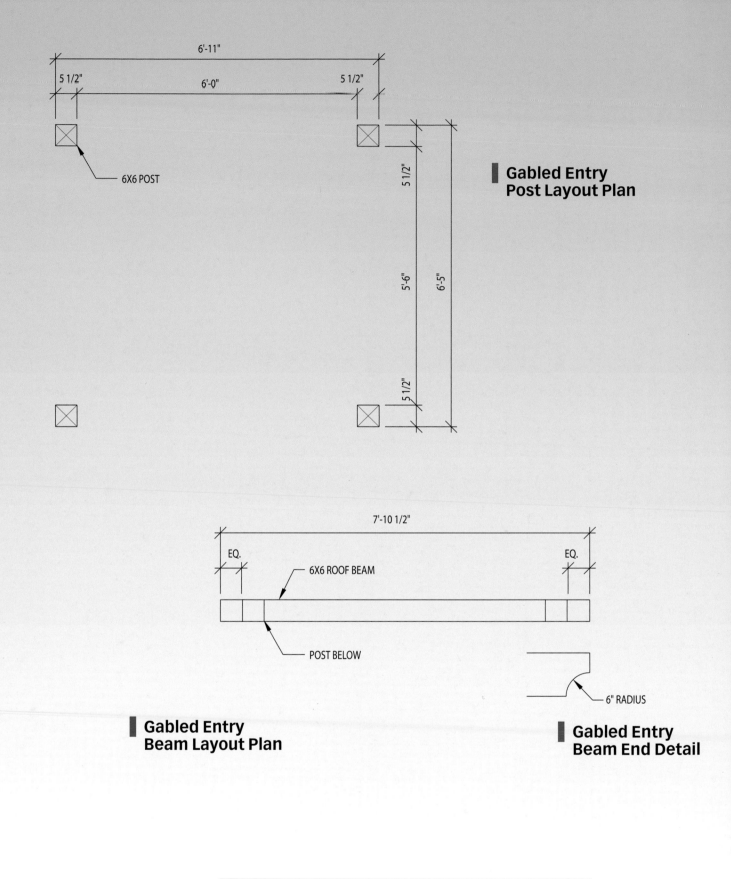

6'-11"

5 1/2"   6'-0"   5 1/2"

6X6 POST

**Gabled Entry
Post Layout Plan**

5 1/2"

5'-6"   6'-5"

5 1/2"

7'-10 1/2"

EQ.   EQ.

6X6 ROOF BEAM

POST BELOW

6" RADIUS

**Gabled Entry
Beam Layout Plan**

**Gabled Entry
Beam End Detail**

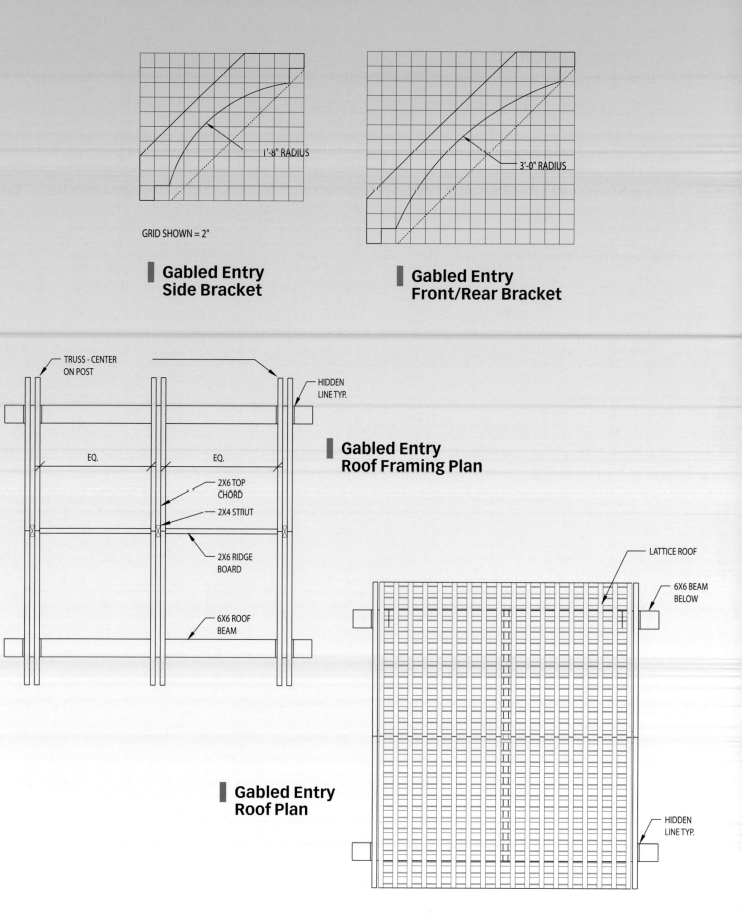

GRID SHOWN = 2"

1'-8" RADIUS

3'-0" RADIUS

Gabled Entry
Side Bracket

Gabled Entry
Front/Rear Bracket

TRUSS - CENTER
ON POST

HIDDEN
LINE TYP.

EQ.

EQ.

Gabled Entry
Roof Framing Plan

2X6 TOP
CHORD

2X4 STRUT

2X6 RIDGE
BOARD

6X6 ROOF
BEAM

LATTICE ROOF

6X6 BEAM
BELOW

Gabled Entry
Roof Plan

HIDDEN
LINE TYP.

How to Build the Gabled Entry

Step A: Set the Posts

The four 6 × 6 posts are set in the ground with concrete. See page 220 for detailed steps on digging the post holes and setting the posts. The post depth must extend below the frost line and meet the requirements of the local building code. Treat the bottom ends of the posts for rot resistance before setting them.

1. Mark the post layout onto the ground; follow the POST LAYOUT PLAN on page 96. Dig the post holes and add a layer of gravel to each hole. Position and brace each post so its top end is at least 84" above the ground. Diagonally measure between the posts to check for squareness: the layout is square when the two diagonal measurements are equal.

2. Pour the concrete and let it dry completely.

3. If you don't own a 6-ft. level, create a long leveling tool to mark the posts for cutting: Tape a standard 4-ft. level to the narrow edge of a straight, 7-ft.- or 8-ft.-long 2 × 4 so the level is roughly centered along the board's length (see Photo B on page 35). Another option is to use a mason's string and a line level.

4. Measure up from the ground and mark one of the posts at 80". Using your extended level, transfer the height mark to the other three posts. Cut the posts to length (see Cutting Lumber Posts, on page 34).

Step B: Cut & Install the Roof Beams

1. Cut the 6 × 6 roof beams to length at 94½".

2. Make a cardboard template for shaping the beam ends; follow the BEAM END DETAIL on page 96. Trace the profile onto the beams and make the cuts with a reciprocating saw or bandsaw. Sand the cuts smooth.

3. Position the beams on top of the posts so they overhang the posts equally at both ends. At each joint, hold a beam tie in position according to the tie manufacturer's specifications, and mark the anchor holes. Use two ties for each joint.

4. Drill through pilot holes for the anchor bolts. Secure the ties using the manufacturer-recommended bolts.

Step C: Build the Roof Trusses

All three trusses have identical parts. You can save time and ensure accuracy by building one truss completely and test-fitting it on the structure. Assemble the truss with a few screws; when you know everything fits, disassemble it and use its parts as patterns to make the other trusses.

1. Each truss has four identical 2 × 6 top chords, with a plumb cut on the top end and a profiled cut on the bottom end. Cut two top chords; follow the TOP CHORD TEMPLATE on page 94 (see pages 222 to

Measure the diagonals as you position the posts to ensure a square layout. Measure again after the posts are braced.

223 for marking plumb cuts). The slope of the roof is 10-in-12. Use a cardboard template to mark the profile for the bottom-end cuts.

2. Cut one 2 × 6 bottom chord to length at 77". Cut one 2 × 4 strut at 32".

3. To assemble the truss, sandwich the strut and bottom chord between the two sets of top chords; follow the layout shown in the FRONT ELEVATION on page 94. Align the bottom corners of the bottom chord with the bottom edges of the top chords. The strut sits on top of the bottom chord and is centered side-to-side on the truss. Tack the parts together with a minimal number of screws.

4. Test-fit the truss on the beams: The bottom chord should sit flush on both beams, with the top chords touching the outside corner edges of the beams. Test-fit the truss at both ends of the beams and at the center. Make any necessary adjustments to the truss for a good fit.

5. Using the cut truss parts as patterns, mark and cut the remaining parts so you have a total of 12 top chords, three bottom chords, and three struts.

6. Assemble the trusses with ¼" × 5" carriage bolts, as shown in the FRONT ELEVATION. To fasten the strut to the bottom chord, toenail a 16d common nail into each narrow edge of the strut and into the bottom chord.

Anchor the beams to the posts with pairs of beam ties, one tie on each side of the joint.

Build the trusses by laying out all the parts on the ground. Fasten them together with carriage bolts and nails.

Step D: Install the Trusses & Ridge Boards

1. Measure in from the ends of the beams and mark the middle truss position so it will be centered on the roof beams; see the ROOF FRAMING PLAN on page 97.

2. Position the center truss on the layout marks. Fasten it to the beams with two 16d common nails driven through each side of the bottom chord (eight nails total for each truss). Use a level to make sure the truss stays plumb as you fasten it.

3. Install the end trusses so they are centered over the tops of the posts.

4. Cut two 2 × 6 ridge boards to fit between the trusses; see the ROOF FRAMING PLAN.

5. Position the ridge boards between the trusses so their top edges are flush with the tops of the top chords (not the truss peaks, where the pointed ends of the chords meet), and toenail them to the chords with 10d common nails.

Step E: Install the Roof Lattice

In addition to providing a partial-shade covering, the lattice panels tie together the trusses and are an important part of the roof structure. Therefore, be sure to use quality manufactured lattice made with ½" or thicker slats (1" panel thickness). Stronger panels hold up better over time.

1. Cut each lattice panel to size: The width should span from the center of the end truss to the center of the middle truss; the length should span from the peak to the bottom ends of the trusses.

TIP: Whenever possible, make the cut edges fall at the center truss and along the roof peak, for best appearance.

2. Fasten the roof panels to the truss chords and ridge boards with 8d siding nails driven through pilot holes to prevent splitting.

Step F: Cut & Install the Brackets

1. Make cardboard templates for marking the bracket shapes; follow the BRACKET DETAILS on page 97.

2. Trace the side bracket profiles onto a 10-ft. 2 × 8, alternating their orientation so you can cut four brackets from one board. Trace the front and rear brackets onto two 8-ft. 2 × 8s.

3. Cut out the brackets with jigsaw or bandsaw. Sand the cuts smooth.

4. Make a mark 2" in from the outside faces of the beams and posts. Position each bracket on the insides of these lines. Align the top ends of the front and rear

Install the trusses by toenailing through the truss bottom chords and into the beams.

Install the roof panels so the seams fall over the center truss and the ridge boards.

Install the corner brackets so they are centered on the posts and beams.

brackets with the bottom chords of the end trusses. Drill counterbored pilot holes through the flat part of the notched ends of the bracket, and fasten the bracket with one ¼" × 4" lag screw at each end. The top ends of the side brackets should be on the 2" marks on the roof beams. These are centered on the beams, while the end brackets are flush side by side under the chords.

Step G: Add the Post Trim

1. Miter-cut four 1 × 6 trim boards to wrap around each post, as shown in the FRONT ELEVATION. Test-fit the pieces as you work, and don't nail them until you know all of the joints fit well. Fasten the trim with 6d finish nails driven through pilot holes.

TIP: To make accurate cuts without measuring, hold the trim boards against the post and mark them for length.

2. Miter-cut ¾" × ¾" cove molding to fit along the top of the trim boards. Nail the trim to the posts with 4d finish nails driven through pilot holes.

Step H: Build the Railings

1. On the inside faces of the posts, mark the layout for the 2 × 4 top rails; follow the SIDE ELEVATION on page 95. Also make vertical marks 1" in from one of the side edges on each post.

2. Cut the three rails (of the first side) to length, so they fit snugly between the posts.

3. Position the rails flat on their layout marks—they should be centered side-to-side on the posts. Drill angled pilot holes through the narrow edges of the rails and into the posts. Fasten the rails with 3" deck screws, countersinking the screw heads.

4. Mark the layouts for the 2 × 2 pickets onto the rails, as shown in the SIDE ELEVATION. Space the upper, short pickets 12" on center; space the lower, long pickets 6" on center. Center all of the pickets from side to side on the rails.

5. Cut the 16 pickets (of the first side) to length, so they fit snugly between the rails.

6. Position the pickets on their layout marks and fasten them with 6d finish nails driven through angled pilot holes. Use at least two nails at each end of the pickets.

7. Repeat for other side.

Hold together the mitered ends of two trim boards and mark the uncut ends along the post.

Nail the finish nails into the pickets. To further hide the nail heads, countersink the nails with a nail set.

Umbrella Arbor

The general definition of an arbor leaves plenty of room for interpretation. This project is a case in point. Taking obvious inspiration from the familiar pop-up shelter, the Umbrella Arbor is a permanent garden structure that becomes a year-round symbol of the bright, breezy days of summer.

This clever project is easier to build than it may appear. It starts with a 6 × 6 post buried in the ground. To the post you attach eight identical rib assemblies, which can be built on a workbench. Lastly, you add the final touch of 1 × 3 lattice roof slats. You might want to use fewer slats for just the suggestion of a canopy or substitute manufactured lattice panels for the slats.

The umbrella spans about 10½ feet, so there's plenty of shelter for a small center table and chairs, or two loungers positioned to give you a view through the slatted canopy covered with vines.

Material List

Description (No. finished pieces)	Quantity/Size	Material
Post (1)	1 @ field measure	6 × 6
Concrete	Field measure	3,000 PSI concrete
Gravel	Field measure	Compactable gravel
Rib Assemblies*		
Ribs & Brackets (8 ea.)	8 @ 10'	2 × 4
Connectors (8)	4 @ 8'	2 × 2
Roof slats	Field measure	1 × 3
Hardware & Fasteners		
#10 × 3" galvanized wood screws		
¼" × 4" galvanized lag screws,	40, with washers	
6d siding nails		

* Each rib assembly has 1 rib, 1 brace, and 1 connector.

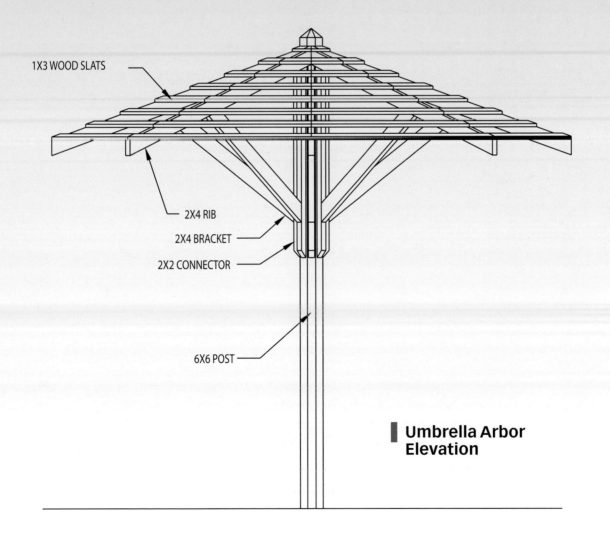

1X3 WOOD SLATS

2X4 RIB

2X4 BRACKET

2X2 CONNECTOR

6X6 POST

**Umbrella Arbor
Elevation**

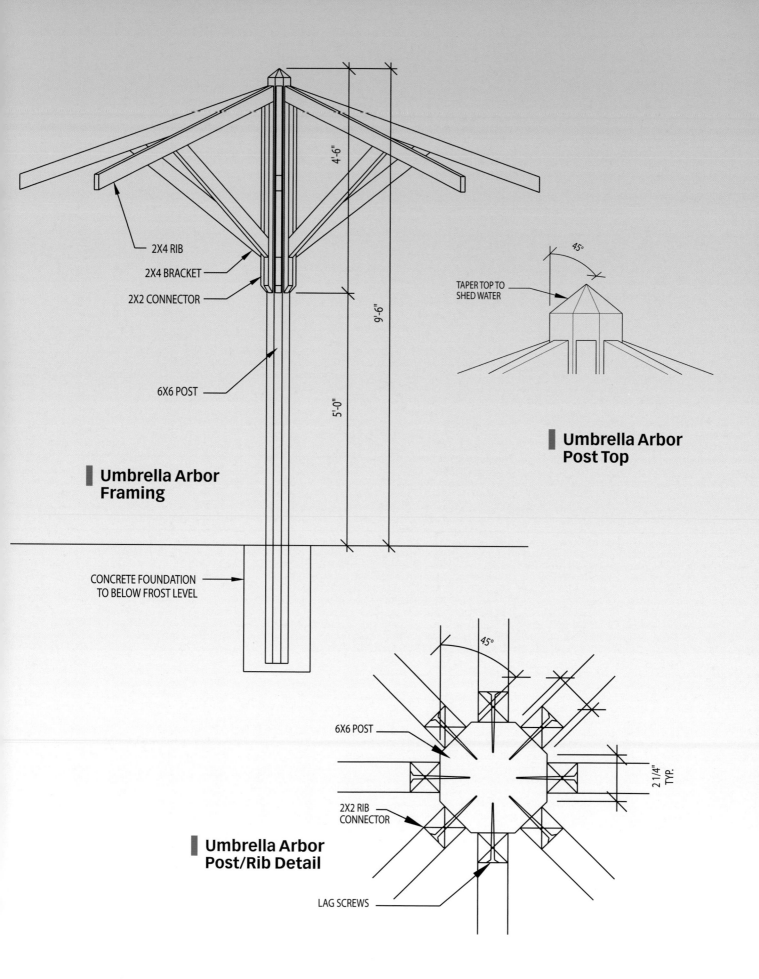

2X4 RIB

2X4 BRACKET

2X2 CONNECTOR

4'-6"

9'-6"

5'-0"

6X6 POST

Umbrella Arbor
Framing

CONCRETE FOUNDATION
TO BELOW FROST LEVEL

45°

TAPER TOP TO
SHED WATER

Umbrella Arbor
Post Top

45°

6X6 POST

2 1/4"
TYP.

2X2 RIB
CONNECTOR

Umbrella Arbor
Post/Rib Detail

LAG SCREWS

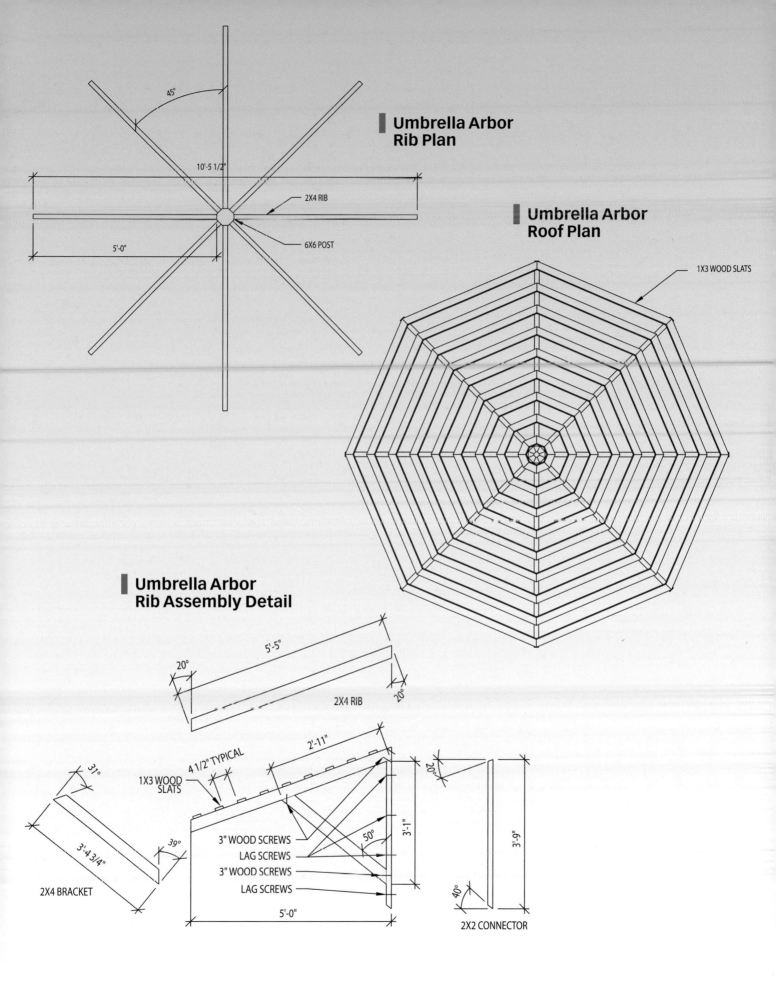

Umbrella Arbor Rib Plan

45°

10'-5 1/2"

5'-0"

2X4 RIB

6X6 POST

Umbrella Arbor Roof Plan

1X3 WOOD SLATS

Umbrella Arbor Rib Assembly Detail

20°

5'-5"

20°

2X4 RIB

31°

3'-4 3/4"

39°

2X4 BRACKET

1X3 WOOD SLATS

4 1/2" TYPICAL

2'-11"

3" WOOD SCREWS

LAG SCREWS

3" WOOD SCREWS

LAG SCREWS

50°

3'-1"

5'-0"

20°

3'-9"

40°

2X2 CONNECTOR

How to Build the Umbrella Arbor

Step A: Cut & Shape the Post

The umbrella's post is made from a single 6 × 6 timber, which you cut into an octagon by making four full-length 45° bevel cuts, using a table saw or circular saw. Beveling the top of the post to a point is an optional step. You might choose to leave the top flat and add a finial or garden ornament.

1. Determine the total length of the post: First find out how deep the post must be buried in the ground, according to the local building code (as a minimum, the post should be buried 30" deep and below the frost line). To that dimension add 114" to find the total post length. Cut the post to length (see Cutting Lumber Posts on page 34).

To make the bevel cuts with a table saw:

1. Set the blade of your table saw to cut at 45°. If your blade tilts to the right, move the saw fence to the left side of the blade; if your blade tilts to the left, move the fence to the right side. Position the fence about 3⅞" from the blade.

2. Make a couple of test cuts on adjacent sides of a scrap piece of 6 × 6 post. Measure the facets and readjust the fence as needed so all eight facets will be the same width (approx. 2¼"). Complete the four cuts to create eight equal sides.

3. To bevel the top of the post, position the saw fence on the other side of the blade and use a stop block and miter gauge to make the cuts at the desired depth. To prevent dangerous kickback, make sure the post is not contacting the stop block when it reaches the blade.

Cut off each corner of the post to make eight equal sides. INSET: To shape the post end, use a circular saw.

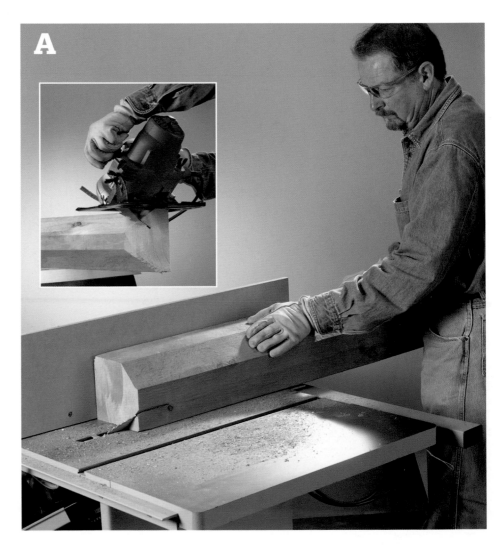

To make the cuts with a circular saw:

1. On the bottom end of the post, mark cutting lines 1⅝" from two adjacent edges.

2. Set the saw blade to cut at 45°. Make two short test cuts on a scrap piece of 6 × 6 post, then measure the facets and adjust the cutting lines as needed so all eight facets will be equal (approx. 2¼").

3. Mark four cutting lines along the full length of the post, then make the cuts.

4. To bevel the top of the post, mark a cutting line on all eight sides at the desired distance from the end. Make the cuts with the blade set at 45°.

Step B: Set the Post in Concrete

See page 220 for detailed steps on digging the post hole and setting the post in concrete.

1. Treat the bottom of the post for rot resistance (see page 220). Dig the post hole and add a layer of gravel to the hole. Position and brace the post so its top end is 114" above the ground and the post stands perfectly plumb.

2. Pour the concrete and let it dry completely. Remove the braces.

Set the post in concrete, following the requirements of the local building code.

C

Build the rib assemblies, making sure all of the pieces are flush and the joints are tight.

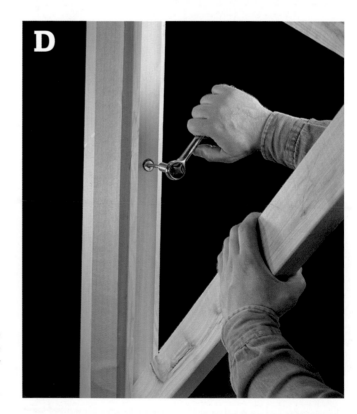

D

Fasten the rib assemblies to the post with evenly spaced ¼" × 4" lag screws.

Step C: Build the Rib Assemblies

1. Cut the eight 2 × 4 ribs, 2 × 4 brackets, and 2 × 2 connectors following the RIB ASSEMBLY DETAIL, on page 104.

TIP: Cut one of each piece, then use it as a template for marking the remaining pieces.

2. Build the assemblies with 3" wood screws, following the layout shown in the RIB ASSEMBLY DETAIL. The bracket and connector should form a 50° angle.

Step D: Install the Rib Assemblies

1. Measure up from the ground and mark all facets of the post at 60". Predrill holes through the backside of the connectors.

2. Position each rib assembly so it's centered on a post facet and its bottom edge is on the layout mark. Fasten the 2 × 2 connector to the post with four ¼" × 4" lag screws with washers. Drive a lag screw at an angle through the top of the 2 × 4 rib and into the post, as shown in the RIB DETAIL.

Step E: Install the Roof Slats

1. Mark a centerline down the length of each rib, along its top edge.

2. Starting at the post, measure between adjacent ribs and cut 1 × 3 slats to fit between the centerlines. Miter the ends of the slats at 22½°.

3. Fasten the slats to the ribs with 6d siding nails driven through pilot holes to prevent splitting. Gap the slats about 5" apart. As you work toward the ends of the ribs, measure the remaining distance and adjust the gaps as needed so the last slat will be flush with the ends of the ribs.

Use temporary spacers set between the slats to maintain consistent gaps while you fasten the slats.

While more enclosed than our Pool Pavilion design (page 113), this playfully detailed structure demonstrates the essence of a casual poolside retreat.

Pool Pavilion

A pavilion creates an outdoor room with a uniquely casual grandeur. Defined by a stately roof, the Pool Pavilion on page 113 has four open sides that invite entry from all directions and offer open views from the shaded interior. Adding curtains that flow with the breezes provides an elegant and relaxing getaway complete with shade and privacy.

Of course, a backyard pool is not required. The Pavilion's simple design makes it suitable for a variety of uses. As shown in the plans, its four support posts are buried in the ground with concrete, but you can adapt the project for an existing patio by using post bases and adding structural supports to the post-and-beam frame for lateral strength (consult a professional for design modifications).

In addition to hanging curtains or shades from the beams, you might consider installing a set of weather-resistant cabinets and a stone or metal countertop to create an outdoor kitchen or bar.

Where shade is desired over a large area, a grouping of pavilions can be far more interesting than a monolithic roof structure.

A pavilion is all about summertime leisure. This ornate structure is also a full-time patio shelter.

Material List

Description (No. finished pieces)	Quantity/Size	Material
Posts (4)	4 @ field measure (114" minimum)	4 × 8 Walls
Post Piers		
Concrete tube forms	4—field measure for length	12"-diameter cardboard forms
Gravel	Field measure	Compactable gravel
Concrete	Field measure	3,000 PSI concrete
Beams		
Main beams (2)	2 @ 12'	4 × 12
Notched brackets (4)	1 @ 10'	4 × 4
Inner brackets (4)	1 @ 8'	2 × 4
Roof Frame		
Rim beams—2 × 6 (2)	2 @ 10'	2 × 6
Rim beams—2 × 8 (2)	2 @ 10'	2 × 8
Roof hub (1)	1 @ 2'	4 × 4
Hip rafters (4)	4 @ 8'	2 × 6
Intermediate rafters (4)	2 @ 12'	2 × 6
Roofing		
Sheathing	4 @ 4 × 8'	¾" exterior-grade plywood
Shingles and 15# building paper	150 square feet, plus ridge caps	
Hardware & Fasteners		
½" × 7" galvanized carriage bolts	16, with washers and nuts	
16d galvanized common nails		
3½" galvanized wood screws		
8d galvanized box nails		
Heavy-duty staples		
Roofing nails		
Metal roof flashing		
Roofing cement		

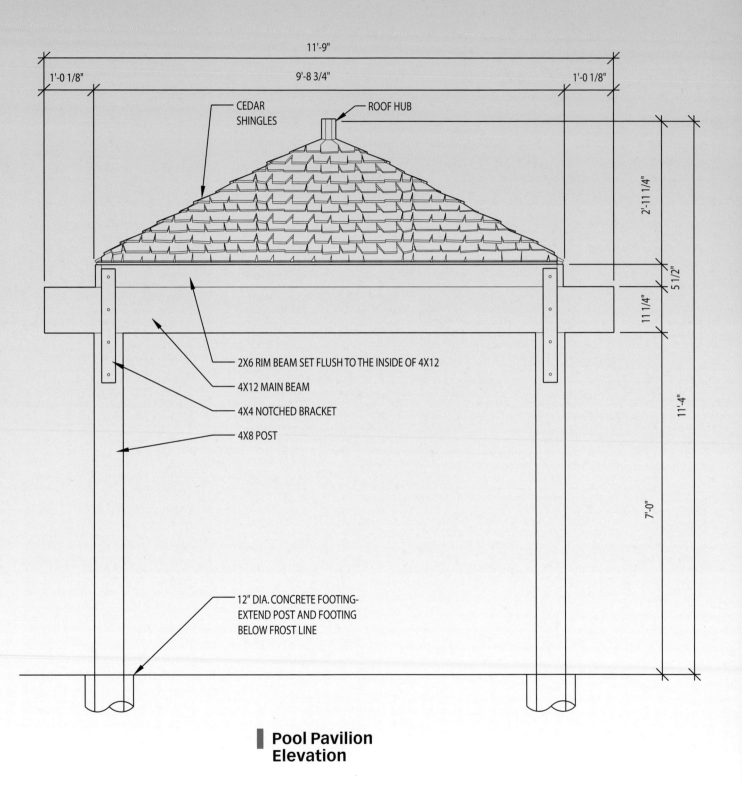

11'-9"

9'-8 3/4"

1'-0 1/8"

1'-0 1/8"

CEDAR
SHINGLES

ROOF HUB

2'-11 1/4"

5 1/2"

11 1/4"

2X6 RIM BEAM SET FLUSH TO THE INSIDE OF 4X12

4X12 MAIN BEAM

4X4 NOTCHED BRACKET

4X8 POST

11'-4"

7'-0"

12" DIA. CONCRETE FOOTING-
EXTEND POST AND FOOTING
BELOW FROST LINE

**Pool Pavilion
Elevation**

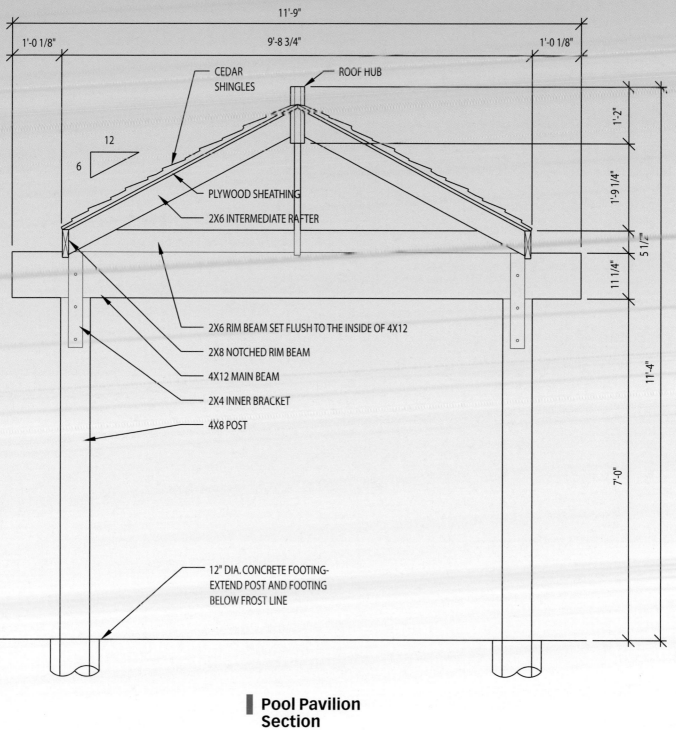

11'-9"

1'-0 1/8"   9'-8 3/4"   1'-0 1/8"

CEDAR SHINGLES

ROOF HUB

12

6

PLYWOOD SHEATHING

2X6 INTERMEDIATE RAFTER

1'-2"

1'-9 1/4"

5 1/2"

11 1/4"

2X6 RIM BEAM SET FLUSH TO THE INSIDE OF 4X12

2X8 NOTCHED RIM BEAM

4X12 MAIN BEAM

2X4 INNER BRACKET

4X8 POST

11'-4"

7'-0"

12" DIA. CONCRETE FOOTING-
EXTEND POST AND FOOTING
BELOW FROST LINE

**Pool Pavilion
Section**

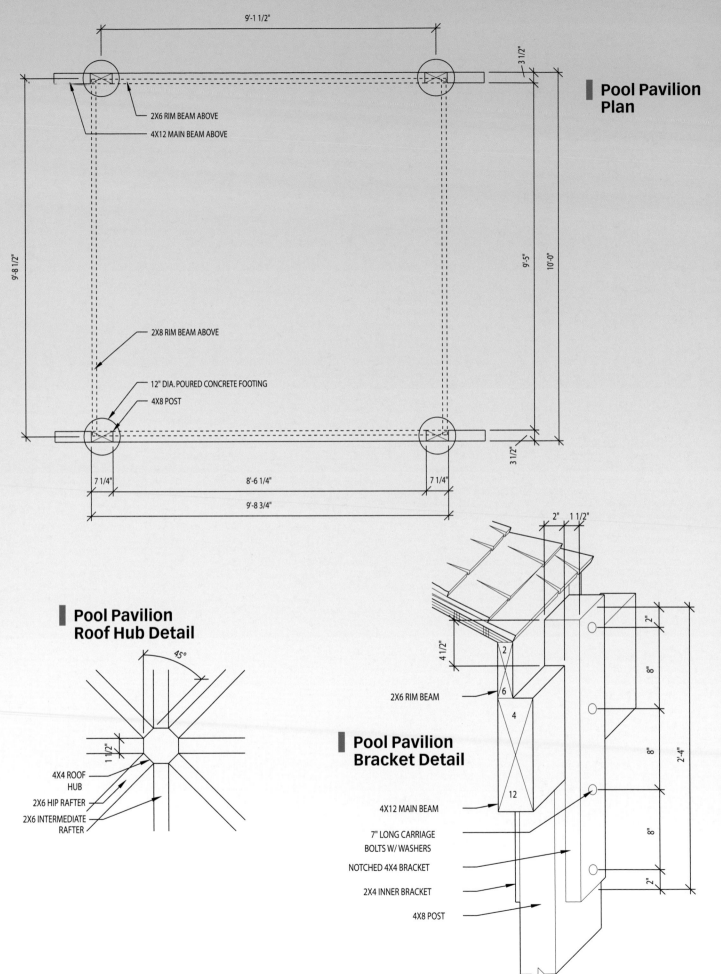

9'-1 1/2"

3 1/2"

Pool Pavilion Plan

2X6 RIM BEAM ABOVE

4X12 MAIN BEAM ABOVE

9'-8 1/2"

9'-5"

10'-0"

2X8 RIM BEAM ABOVE

12" DIA. POURED CONCRETE FOOTING

4X8 POST

3 1/2"

7 1/4"

8'-6 1/4"

7 1/4"

9'-8 3/4"

Pool Pavilion Roof Hub Detail

45°

1 1/2"

4X4 ROOF HUB

2X6 HIP RAFTER

2X6 INTERMEDIATE RAFTER

2" 1 1/2"

4 1/2"

2"

2

2X6 RIM BEAM

6

4

8"

8"

2-4"

Pool Pavilion Bracket Detail

12

8"

4X12 MAIN BEAM

7" LONG CARRIAGE BOLTS W/ WASHERS

NOTCHED 4X4 BRACKET

2X4 INNER BRACKET

4X8 POST

2"

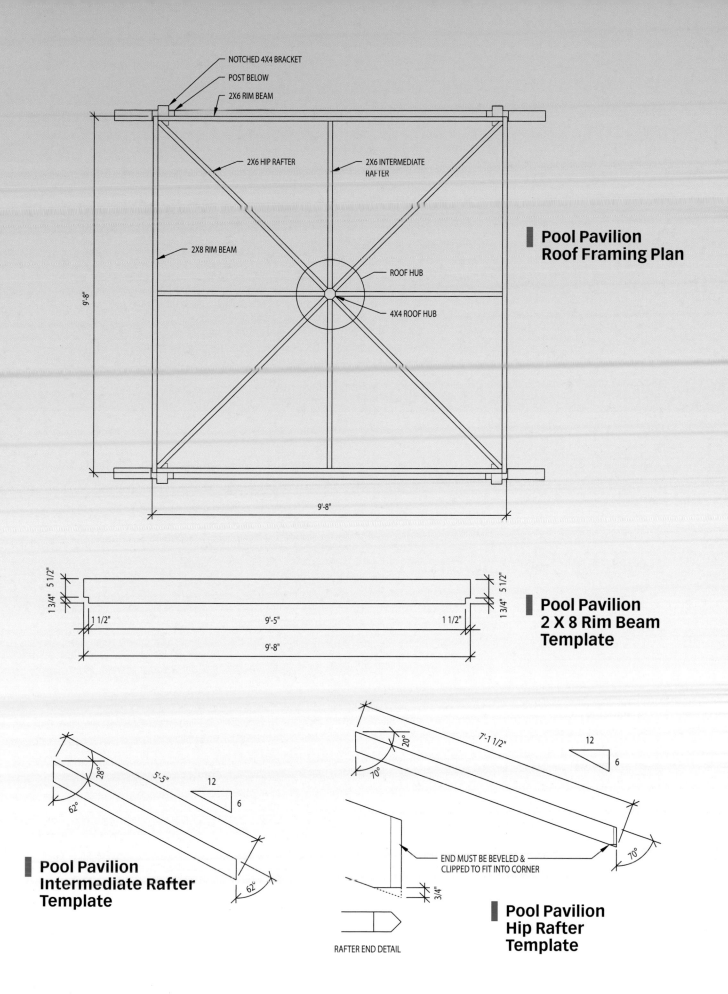

NOTCHED 4X4 BRACKET

POST BELOW

2X6 RIM BEAM

2X6 HIP RAFTER

2X6 INTERMEDIATE RAFTER

2X8 RIM BEAM

ROOF HUB

4X4 ROOF HUB

9'-8"

9'-8"

Pool Pavilion Roof Framing Plan

5 1/2"   5 1/2"

1 3/4"   1 3/4"

1 1/2"   9'-5"   1 1/2"

9'-8"

Pool Pavilion 2 X 8 Rim Beam Template

28°

5'-5"

62°

62°

12

6

Pool Pavilion Intermediate Rafter Template

20°

7'-1 1/2"

70°

70°

12

6

END MUST BE BEVELED & CLIPPED TO FIT INTO CORNER

3/4"

RAFTER END DETAIL

Pool Pavilion Hip Rafter Template

How to Build the Pool Pavilion

Step A: Set the Posts

The four 4 × 8 posts are buried in concrete piers made with 12"-diameter cardboard tube forms. The post depth must extend below the frost line and meet the requirements of the local building code. Treat the bottom ends of the posts for rot resistance (see page 220) before setting them.

1. Lay out the centers of the four post locations onto the ground; follow the PLAN drawing on page 116. Diagonally measure between the posts to check for squareness: the layout is perfectly square when the diagonal measurements are equal.

2. Dig 15"-diameter holes for the post piers at the pier depth required for your area, plus 4". Fill the holes with a 4" layer of compactable gravel.

3. Cut the tube forms to length so they will slightly extend above the ground level. Set the tubes in the holes, hold them plumb, and then tightly pack around the outside with soil.

4. Place a post into each form and brace it in position with 2 × 4 cross bracing. Make sure the posts are perfectly plumb and the layout is square.

5. Fill the forms with concrete, smooth the tops of the piers, and let the concrete dry.

Step B: Set the Main Beams

1. Mark one of the posts 84" above the ground. Using mason's string and a line level, transfer this height mark to the remaining posts. Cut the posts at the height mark (see Cutting Lumber Posts on page 34).

2. Cut four 4 × 4 notched bracket pieces to length at 28". Notch the brackets as shown in the BRACKET DETAIL on page 116.

3. Cut four 2 × 4 inner brackets to length at 23½".

4. Cut the two 4 × 12 main beams to length at 141". Set each beam on a pair of posts so it overhangs the posts equally at both ends.

5. Position a notched bracket on the outer surface over the beam and post so it's centered on the post. Position an inner bracket on the opposite side, centered on the post with its top end flush with the top of the beam. Clamp the pieces together and drill pilot holes for ½" × 7" carriage bolts; follow the layout shown in the BRACKET DETAIL. Anchor the parts with carriage bolts in the three lower positions only.

Step C: Install the Rim Beams

1. Cut the two 2 × 6 rim beams to length at 113".

2. Cut the two 2 × 8 rim beams to length at 116". Check all of the beams for crowning (see page 60). Notch the bottom corners of the 2 × 8 beams; follow the 2 × 8 RIM BEAM TEMPLATE on page 117.

3. Fit the 2 × 8 rim beams over the main beams so their inside faces are flush with the brackets.

4. Set the 2 × 6 rim beams—crown up—between the 2 × 8s, flush with the inside edges of the main beams. Make sure the rim beams are flush at the tops and fasten them together with 16d common nails driven through the 2 × 8s and into the ends of the 2 × 6s.

5. Anchor the 2 × 6 beams to the notched brackets, using the top carriage bolt pilot hole. Countersink the washer and nut on the inside face of the 2 × 6, then cut off the bolt flush with the beam so it won't interfere with the hip rafters.

Set the posts in concrete, then cut off the exposed portion of the cardboard tube form.

B

Anchor the main beams to the posts with two brackets secured with carriage bolts.

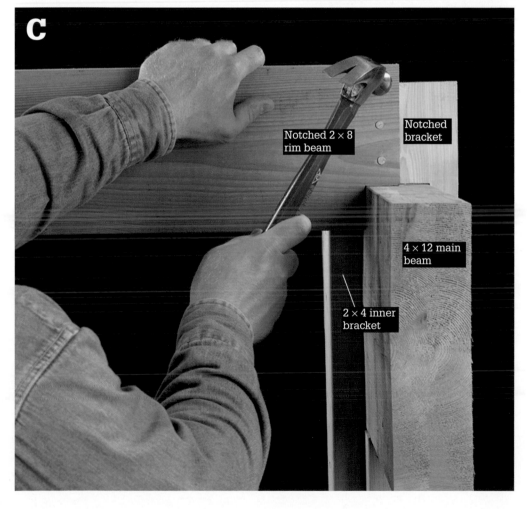

C

Notched 2 × 8 rim beam

Notched bracket

4 × 12 main beam

2 × 4 inner bracket

Endnail through the notched beam into the 2 × 6 rim beams, (not seen), and then anchor the 2 × 6s with carriage bolts.

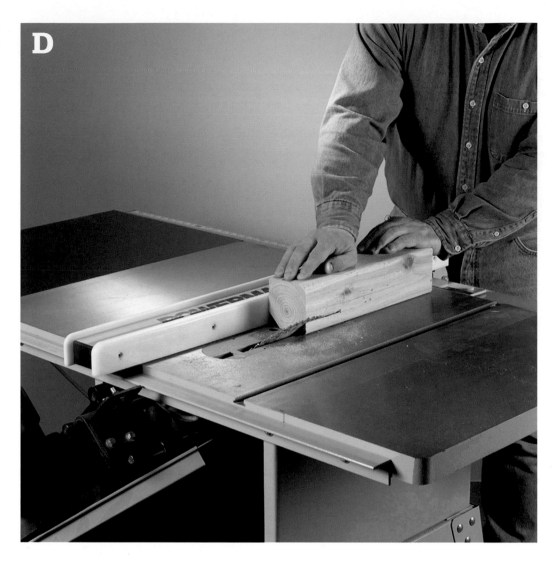

Step D: Cut the Roof Hub

With the blade of a table saw or circular saw set at a 45° angle, four cuts turns a 4 × 4 into an octagon.

TIP: Use a scrap piece of 4 × 4 to set up the cuts, or use one end of the workpiece that you can cut off to create the finished hub.

1. If you're using a table saw, set the saw fence about 2½" from the blade—you'll probably have to position the fence on the left side of the blade. If you're using a circular saw, draw cutting lines down two adjacent sides, about 1" from the corner edges.

2. Make a couple of test cuts, then measure the facets. Adjust the fence or cutting lines as needed so that all eight facets will be equal.

3. Make the final cuts down the full length of the hub. Cut the hub to length at 14".

NOTE: If the facets are slightly smaller than the thickness of the rafters, plane the rafter ends or taper them with a chisel to match.

Step E: Frame the Roof

1. Select two straight 2 × 6s for the pattern hip rafters, and check the boards for crowning (see page 60).

2. Cut the rafters following the HIP RAFTER TEMPLATE on page 117 (see page 222 for cutting rafters). The roof slope is 6-in-12. In addition to having a plumb cut on its bottom end, the hip rafter gets 45° bevel cuts so the end fits into the corner of the beams, as shown in the ROOF FRAMING PLAN on page 117. The bottom end also gets clipped to clear the 2 × 4 inner bracket.

3. Use the roof hub to test-fit the hip rafters against the rim beams. The tops of the rafters should be flush with the inside top edges of the rim beams. Make any necessary adjustments for a good fit.

4. Use one of the pattern rafters to mark the remaining two hip rafters, then make the cuts.

5. Install the hip rafters by screwing through the top and sides of each rafter into the roof hub, using 3½" wood screws. The hub should extend about 6½" above the tops of the rafters. Fasten the bottom ends of the rafters to the beams with 16d common nails. Alternate between opposing sides as you work to ensure the hub remains centered.

6. Repeat the cutting and test-fitting process to cut four 2 × 6 intermediate rafters; follow the INTERMEDIATE RAFTER TEMPLATE on page 117. Install the intermediate rafters so they're flush with the hip rafters at the hub and flush with the tops of the rim beams at the bottom ends. Also make sure the bottom ends are centered along the lengths of the rim beams.

Step F: Sheath & Shingle the Roof

As shown in the plans, the pavilion roof is sheathed with ¾" exterior-grade plywood. For a more attractive ceiling surface—and one that is less likely to show nails coming through—you can use ⁵⁄₄ cedar decking instead of plywood.

1. Install plywood sheathing from the bottom up. To lay out the plywood cuts, measure from the intermediate rafter center to the hip rafter center at the bottom ends. Mark the intermediate rafter 4 feet from the rim beam, and measure straight across to the center of the hip rafter. Transfer the two dimensions to a sheet of plywood, measuring from the square factory edge.

2. Snap a chalk line between the marks. Cut the plywood along the line.

3. Position the plywood so its bottom edge is butted against the rim beam and its side edges break on the centers of the rafters. Fasten the sheathing to the rafters with 8d box nails spaced every 6".

4. Use the angled edge of the leftover plywood and make a square cut for the next piece of sheathing. When the bottom row of sheathing is finished, use the cutoffs to fill in the top row up to the hub.

5. Install 15# building paper and cedar shingles, following the steps on page 226. Install the shingles so their top ends run long over the ridges of the roof, then trim them off with a saw. Cap the ridges with pre-made shingle caps or with 1× cedar boards. Use metal flashing and roofing cement to seal around the roof hub.

Drive angled screws to fasten the rafters to the roof hub.

Align pre-made shingle caps over ridges, working from the bottom up.

Some summerhouses are attached to the main house via a breezeway; these must be built on frost footings or other deep foundation.

Summerhouse

An ideal summerhouse combines the open-air shelter of a screened porch with the remote seclusion of an outbuilding. Add a beautiful view and you have the very essence of leisure. The Summerhouse on page 125 provides everything but the view.

Built on a concrete slab foundation, the Summerhouse is designed for years of outdoor exposure. The fully screened front wall stands about nine feet high and offers a sweeping view of your favorite site. The lower, entry side has solid corner walls for structural support and added privacy. Dual screened doors ensure plenty of airflow for the hottest summer days.

As shown in the plans, the Summerhouse's roof is covered with translucent polycarbonate panels that let in plenty of light while sheltering the interior from showers. However, other roof coverings might better suit your climate and use of the house. For example, you might choose a more opaque material, or hang fabric beneath the panels to help keep the interior cool. Whatever type of roofing you use, make sure it complies with the local building code standards for year-round exposure (e.g., snow loads).

Starting with post-and-beam construction, similar to our Summerhouse design, this custom house gains personality from a unique roof shape, arched openings, and period railing details.

This lightweight variation on the summerhouse features a cupola for decoration, while the continuous half-wall gives it the feel of a screened porch.

Material List

Description (No. finished pieces)	Quantity/Size	Material
Foundation		
Concrete	1.63 cubic yards	3,000 PSI concrete
Gravel	1.25 cubic yards	Compactable gravel
Mesh	100 square feet	6" × 6": W1.4 × W1.4 welded wire mesh
Form materials	See page 212	
Wall Framing		
Corner wall framing (22 studs, 4 bottom plates, 4 top plates)	26 @ 8'	2 x 4 (pressure-treated lumber for plates)
Front wall posts (4)	4 @ 9'	4 × 4
Front wall top beam (1)	1 @ 13'	4 × 8
Front wall intermediate beams (3)	1 @ 8' 1 @ 4'	4 × 6
Side wall beams (2)	2 @ 8'	4 × 6
Rear wall beam (1)	1 @ 13'	4 × 6
Corner Wall Finish		
Corner wall siding (and interior finish)	8 sheets @ 4 × 8'	⅝" T1-11 plywood siding
Horizontal trim (8, exterior only)	4 @ 8'	1 × 6
Vertical trim (12, including interior)	12 @ 8'	1 × 4
End of wall trim (4)	4 @ 8'	1 × 6
Top cap trim	Field measure	1× lumber
Roof Framing		
Roof beam members (8)	8 @ 9'	2 × 6
Roof beam spacers (4)	4 @ 9'	1 × 6
Battens (4)	4 @ 9'	1 × 4 composite decking material
Blocking (6)	3 @ 8'	2 × 6
Cross beams (9)	3 @ 12'	2 × 6
Screens		
Sills (5)	2 @ 8' 1 @ 4'	2 × 4
Screen molding (58, cut to fit)	58 @ 8'	¾" quarter-round
Screen (15, cut to fit)	4'-wide roll × 55' long	
Adhesive rubber weatherstripping	225 linear feet	
Roof Panels (3)	3 @ 4 × 8'	Multi-wall polycarbonate panel
Screen Doors	2 doors, or pre-hung unit; field measure	

Description
(No. finished pieces)

Description (No. finished pieces)	Quantity/Size	Material
Hardware & Fasteners		
⅝" × 8" J-bolts	8, with washers & nuts	
16d galvanized common nails		
8d galvanized finish nails		
8d galvanized box nails		
6d galvanized box nails		
6d galvanized finish nails		
16d galvanized finish nails or 3½" deck screws		
Heavy-duty staples		
2" deck screws		
Post bases	4, with recommended anchoring hardware	Simpson CPS4 or similar approved base with standoff
Post-to-beam T connectors	8, with recommended anchoring hardware	Simpson OT or similar approved connector
Beam-to-beam angles	4, with recommended anchoring hardware	Simpson HL35PC or similar approved connector
Post-to-beam L connectors	6, with recommended anchoring hardware	Simpson OL or similar approved connector
Roof beam to wall beam connectors	8, with recommended fasteners	Simpson H2.5 or similar approved connector
Aluminum tape		
Glazing tape or adhesive sealant		

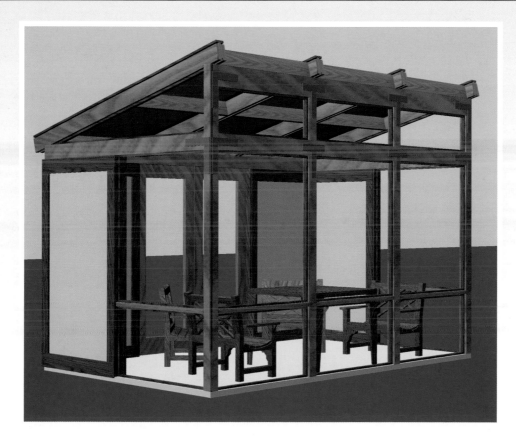

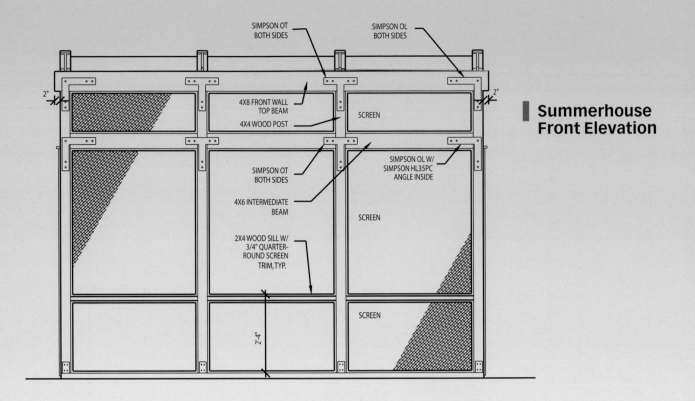

SIMPSON OT
BOTH SIDES

SIMPSON OL
BOTH SIDES

**Summerhouse
Front Elevation**

2"

4X8 FRONT WALL
TOP BEAM

4X4 WOOD POST

SCREEN

SIMPSON OL W/
SIMPSON HL35PC
ANGLE INSIDE

SIMPSON OT
BOTH SIDES

4X6 INTERMEDIATE
BEAM

SCREEN

2X4 WOOD SILL W/
3/4" QUARTER-
ROUND SCREEN
TRIM, TYP.

SCREEN

2"

2'-4"

**Summerhouse
Rear Elevation**

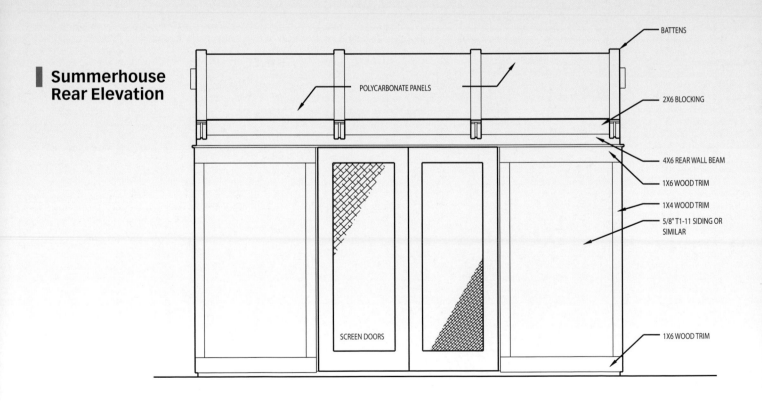

BATTENS

POLYCARBONATE PANELS

2X6 BLOCKING

4X6 REAR WALL BEAM

1X6 WOOD TRIM

1X4 WOOD TRIM

5/8" T1-11 SIDING OR
SIMILAR

SCREEN DOORS

1X6 WOOD TRIM

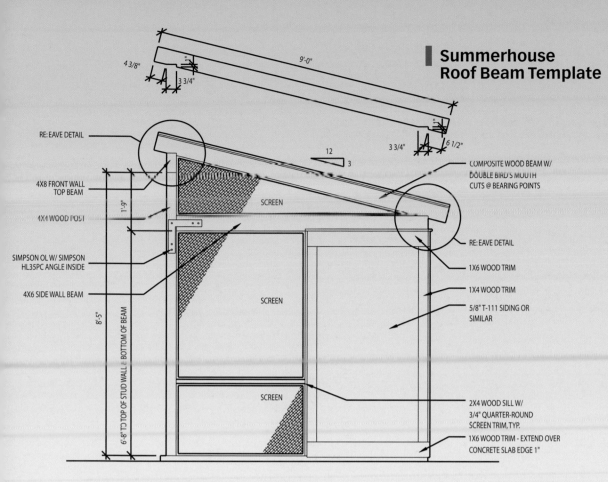

▮ Summerhouse
Roof Beam Template

4 3/8"
9'-0"
1"
3 3/4"
3 3/4"
6 1/2"
12
3

RE: EAVE DETAIL

4X8 FRONT WALL
TOP BEAM

4X4 WOOD POST

SCREEN

COMPOSITE WOOD BEAM W/
DOUBLE BIRD'S MOUTH
CUTS @ BEARING POINTS

SIMPSON OL W/ SIMPSON
HL35PC ANGLE INSIDE

4X6 SIDE WALL BEAM

SCREEN

RE: EAVE DETAIL

1X6 WOOD TRIM

1X4 WOOD TRIM

5/8" T-111 SIDING OR
SIMILAR

SCREEN

1'-9"

8'-5"

6'-8" TO TOP OF STUD WALL / BOTTOM OF BEAM

2X4 WOOD SILL W/
3/4" QUARTER-ROUND
SCREEN TRIM, TYP.

1X6 WOOD TRIM - EXTEND OVER
CONCRETE SLAB EDGE 1"

▮ Summerhouse
Side Elevation

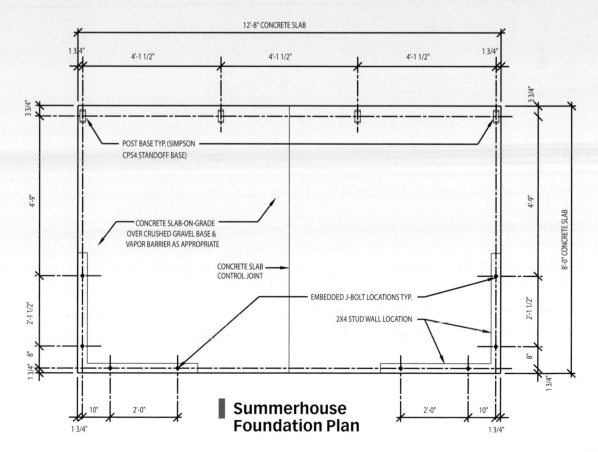

12'-8" CONCRETE SLAB

1 3/4"
4'-1 1/2"
4'-1 1/2"
4'-1 1/2"
1 3/4"

3 3/4"

3 3/4"

POST BASE TYP. (SIMPSON
CPS4 STANDOFF BASE)

4'-9"

CONCRETE SLAB-ON-GRADE
OVER CRUSHED GRAVEL BASE &
VAPOR BARRIER AS APPROPRIATE

CONCRETE SLAB
CONTROL JOINT

4'-9"

8'-0" CONCRETE SLAB

EMBEDDED J-BOLT LOCATIONS TYP.

2'-1 1/2"

2X4 STUD WALL LOCATION

2'-1 1/2"

8"

1 3/4"

8"

10"
2'-0"

2'-0"
10"

1 3/4"

1 3/4"

1 3/4"

▮ Summerhouse
Foundation Plan

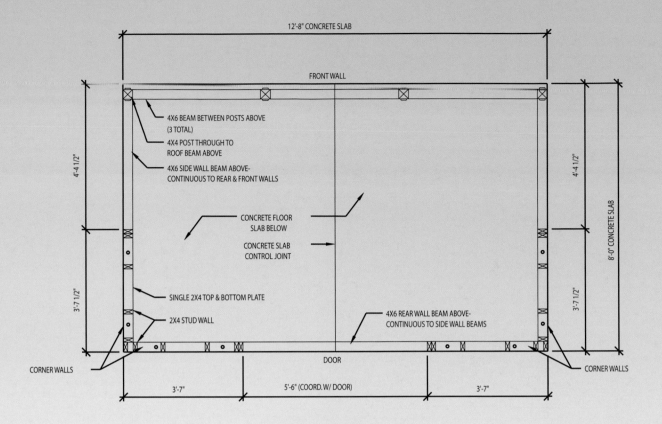

12'-8" CONCRETE SLAB

FRONT WALL

4X6 BEAM BETWEEN POSTS ABOVE
(3 TOTAL)

4X4 POST THROUGH TO
ROOF BEAM ABOVE

4X6 SIDE WALL BEAM ABOVE-
CONTINUOUS TO REAR & FRONT WALLS

CONCRETE FLOOR
SLAB BELOW

CONCRETE SLAB
CONTROL JOINT

4'-4 1/2"

8'-0" CONCRETE SLAB

4'-4 1/2"

3'-7 1/2"

3'-7 1/2"

SINGLE 2X4 TOP & BOTTOM PLATE

2X4 STUD WALL

4X6 REAR WALL BEAM ABOVE-
CONTINUOUS TO SIDE WALL BEAMS

CORNER WALLS

CORNER WALLS

DOOR

3'-7"

5'-6" (COORD. W/ DOOR)

3'-7"

▌Summerhouse Wall Framing Plan

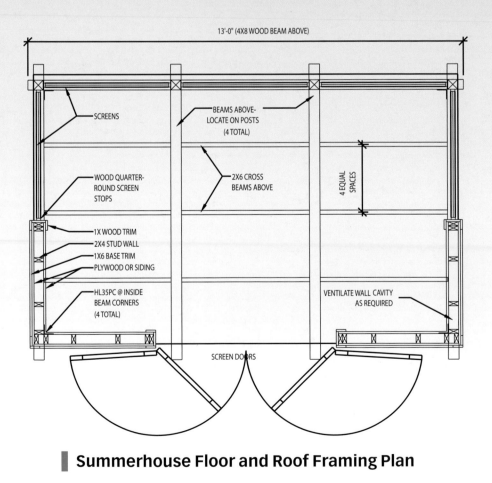

13'-0" (4X8 WOOD BEAM ABOVE)

SCREENS

BEAMS ABOVE-
LOCATE ON POSTS
(4 TOTAL)

WOOD QUARTER-
ROUND SCREEN
STOPS

2X6 CROSS
BEAMS ABOVE

4 EQUAL
SPACES

1X WOOD TRIM
2X4 STUD WALL
1X6 BASE TRIM
PLYWOOD OR SIDING

HL35PC @ INSIDE
BEAM CORNERS
(4 TOTAL)

VENTILATE WALL CAVITY
AS REQUIRED

SCREEN DOORS

▌Summerhouse Floor and Roof Framing Plan

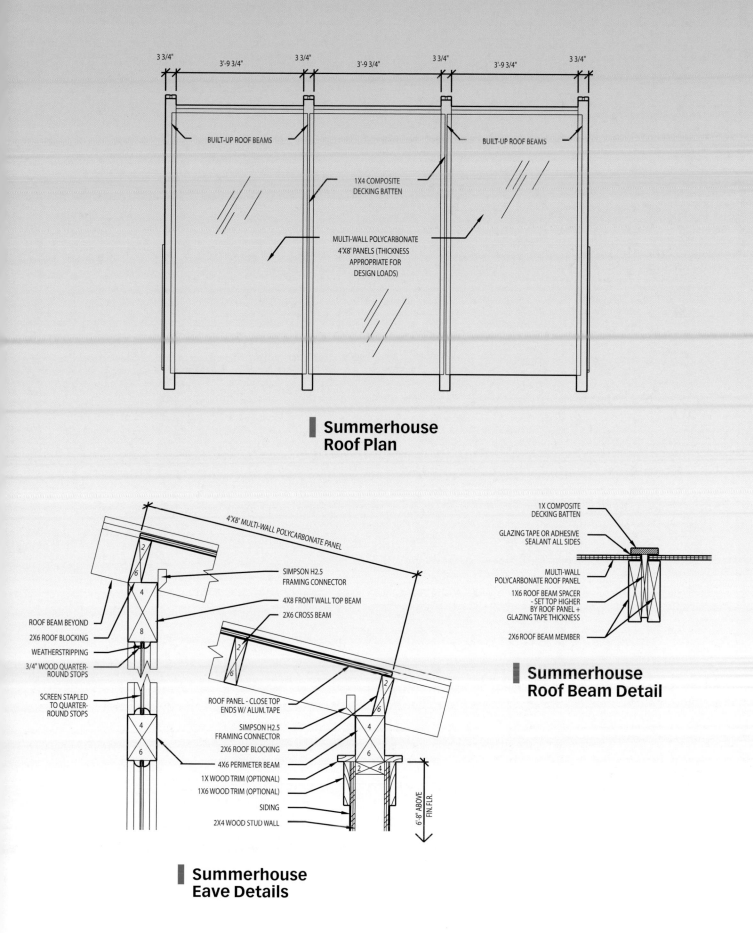

3 3/4"   3'-9 3/4"   3 3/4"   3'-9 3/4"   3 3/4"   3'-9 3/4"   3 3/4"

BUILT-UP ROOF BEAMS

BUILT-UP ROOF BEAMS

1X4 COMPOSITE
DECKING BATTEN

MULTI-WALL POLYCARBONATE
4'X8' PANELS (THICKNESS
APPROPRIATE FOR
DESIGN LOADS)

**Summerhouse
Roof Plan**

4'X8' MULTI-WALL POLYCARBONATE PANEL

1X COMPOSITE
DECKING BATTEN

GLAZING TAPE OR ADHESIVE
SEALANT ALL SIDES

MULTI-WALL
POLYCARBONATE ROOF PANEL

1X6 ROOF BEAM SPACER
- SET TOP HIGHER
BY ROOF PANEL +
GLAZING TAPE THICKNESS

2X6 ROOF BEAM MEMBER

**Summerhouse
Roof Beam Detail**

SIMPSON H2.5
FRAMING CONNECTOR

4X8 FRONT WALL TOP BEAM

2X6 CROSS BEAM

ROOF BEAM BEYOND
2X6 ROOF BLOCKING
WEATHERSTRIPPING
3/4" WOOD QUARTER-
ROUND STOPS

SCREEN STAPLED
TO QUARTER-
ROUND STOPS

ROOF PANEL - CLOSE TOP
ENDS W/ ALUM. TAPE

SIMPSON H2.5
FRAMING CONNECTOR

2X6 ROOF BLOCKING

4X6 PERIMETER BEAM

1X WOOD TRIM (OPTIONAL)

1X6 WOOD TRIM (OPTIONAL)

SIDING

2X4 WOOD STUD WALL

6'-8" ABOVE
FIN. FLR.

**Summerhouse
Eave Details**

How to Build the Summerhouse

Step A: Build the Foundation

See page 216 for step-by-step instructions on pouring and finishing a concrete slab foundation. The finished slab should measure 96" × 152", as shown in the FOUNDATION PLAN on page 127.

Set eight ⅝" × 8" J-bolts in the concrete, following the layout shown in the FOUNDATION PLAN; these are for anchoring the bottom plates of the corner walls. The bolts should extend 2½" from the slab. Also create a control joint down the center of the slab, as shown in the WALL FRAMING PLAN, on page 128.

NOTE: If you live in an area that gets heavy rainfall, you might want to slightly slope the slab toward one side for drainage.

Step B: Frame the Corner Walls

Unless you plan to build custom screen doors, it's best to buy the doors (or a pre-hung door unit) and have them on hand before framing the walls—it's the only way to ensure your door opening will be the right size.

You can frame the four corner walls on the ground, then raise them onto the foundation, using standard wall framing techniques.

1. Mark the rough opening for the screen doors so it is centered along the rear edge of the foundation; see WALL FRAMING PLAN. Size the opening according to the door manufacturer's instructions, but be sure to account for 1× lumber trim at each side; see FLOOR & ROOF FRAMING PLAN on page 128.

2. Measure from your layout marks to determine the lengths of the bottom and top plates of the rear wall frames. Cut two 2 × 4 bottom plates and two top plates using this dimension.

3. For the side walls, cut two bottom plates and two top plates at 40".

4. Cut 22 studs at 77".

5. Mark the stud layouts onto the plates following the WALL FRAMING PLAN. Mark the J-bolt locations onto the bottom plates, then drill holes for the bolts.

6. Assemble the walls with 16d galvanized common nails. Raise each rear wall, setting the bottom plate over the J-bolts. Position the wall so it's flush with the foundation, and secure the plates to the J-bolts with washers and nuts.

7. Raise the side walls and anchor them to the J-bolts. Make sure all of the walls are plumb. Fasten the side walls to the rear walls, driving 16d nails through the end studs.

Step C: Set the Posts

1. Cut four pieces of ⅝"-diameter threaded rod, following the specifications of the post base manufacturer.

2. At the bottom end of each post, drill a ¾"-diameter × 10" hole in the center of the post. Clean dust and debris out of the holes, then fill each hole halfway with the base manufacturer's recommended epoxy. Insert a piece of threaded rod into each hole, and let the epoxy cure.

3. Attach a post base standoff to each post, using the recommended fasteners.

4. Mark the centers of the four front wall posts, following the FOUNDATION PLAN. At each point, drill a ¾"-diameter hole into the slab, following the manufacturer's specifications for anchor depth.

5. Clean the anchor holes and fill them halfway with epoxy. Set the posts by inserting the threaded rods into the foundation holes. Temporarily brace the posts so they are perfectly plumb, then let the epoxy cure.

6. Mark one of the posts at 101" above the slab. Use a level or mason's line to transfer the height mark to the remaining posts, then cut the posts (see page 34).

Step D: Sheath the Corner Walls

You can cover the outsides of the corner walls with any outdoor siding material. However, if you use traditional siding, you must first sheath the walls with ½" or thicker plywood to give the wall frames rigidity. The project as shown here calls for ⅝" T1-11 plywood siding, which takes care of the structural support and siding at once.

1. For each wall, cut the siding to width so it's flush to the framing; cut it to length so it's flush with the top of the top plate and extends 1" below the top of the foundation slab. Overlap the siding where it meets at the outside corners.

2. Fasten the siding to the wall studs and plates with 8d galvanized finish nails; nail every 6" along the

Build the concrete slab foundation following the requirements of the local building code.

Secure the wall frames to the foundation J-bolts, then tack the walls together along the full lengths of the end studs.

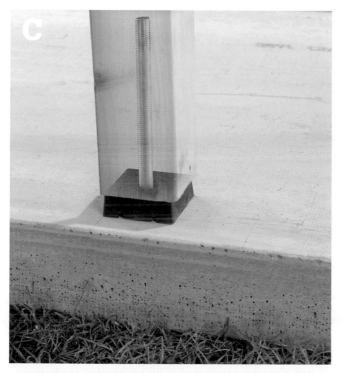

Set the posts into the slab with anchoring rods—brace them so they are perfectly plumb.

Install the plywood siding so it's flush to the framing and overhangs the foundation by 1".

perimeter and every 12" in the field of the sheet.

3. Sheath the insides of the walls with the same plywood siding or another exterior-grade wall finish.

Step E: Install the Wall Beams

NOTE: You will need at least one helper for this step.

1. Cut the 4 × 6 side wall beams to length at 90½".

2. Making sure the crowned edge is up, set each beam on top of the side corner wall so its front end is butted against the corner post and its back end is flush with the rear wall; see SIDE ELEVATION, on page 127. Fasten the beam to the wall's top plate with 16d nails.

3. Anchor the beam to the corner using a post-beam connector on the outside only—you will install a connector on the inside after the front wall beams are in place. Position and fasten the connector following the manufacturer's specifications.

4. Cut the rear wall 4 × 6 beam to length at 145". Position the beam—crown-up—between the ends of the side wall beams so all beams are flush at the top. Anchor the beams together using beam angles and the manufacturer's recommended hardware, then nail the rear beam to the rear walls.

5. Cut the 4 × 8 front wall top beam to length at 156". Set the beam on top of the posts so it overhangs the end posts by 2" and is flush to the faces of all of the posts; see FRONT ELEVATION, on page 126. Anchor the beam with pairs of post-beam connectors at each post.

6. Cut the three 4 × 6 front wall intermediate beams to fit snugly between the posts. Position the beams so they are aligned with the side wall beams and anchor them to the posts with pairs of post-beam

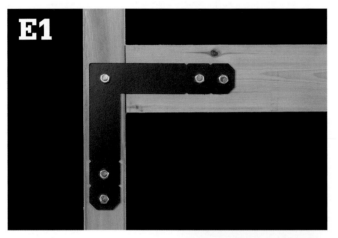

Side wall beam to corner post connection.

Side wall beams to rear wall beam connection.

Front wall beam to post connections.

connectors. On the inside of the Summerhouse, use angle connectors to anchor the two outer intermediate wall beams to the side wall beams.

Step F: Build & Install the Roof Beams

The roof beams are built-up beams made with two 2 × 6s sandwiched over a 1 × 6 spacer, which protrudes above the tops of the 2 × 6s to accommodate the roof panels; see ROOF BEAM DETAIL, on page 129.

1. Cut eight 2 × 6s and four 1 × 6s to length at 108".

2. Select a straight 2 × 6 to use for the pattern beam member. Make the bird's mouth cuts following the ROOF BEAM TEMPLATE, on page 127 (see pages 222 to 223 for help with marking and cutting bird's mouths).

3. Set the pattern on the front and rear wall beams to test-fit the cuts. Make any necessary adjustments so the bird's mouths fit flush against the beams.

4. Use the pattern to mark the bird's mouths on the remaining beam members and the 1 × 6s, then make the cuts. Using construction adhesive and nails, construct the beam so the 1 × 6 extends far enough to accommodate the roof panels, plus a little extra space for glazing tape or adhesive sealant (see Step J, on page 135). Nail the pieces together from both sides using pairs of 16d galvanized common nails driven every 12". Drive the nails at a slight angle so they won't protrude through the opposite side.

5. Mark the layout of the roof beams onto the front and rear wall beams, following the FLOOR AND ROOF FRAMING PLAN.

6. Set the roof beams on their layout marks and fasten them to the wall beams with two 16d nails on each side. Then reinforce each joint with a framing connector.

Step G: Trim the Corner Walls

The four corner walls have 1 × 6 trim along the top and bottom and 1 × 4 trim at the sides. The wall ends are capped with custom-cut 1 × 6 trim. Finally, a 1× cap is added to finish off the walls along the beams. See SIDE ELEVATION, REAR ELEVATION, and EAVE DETAILS. Installing trim on the interior wall as shown is optional.

1. Cap the ends of the walls by ripping 1 × 6 trim to width so it covers the edges of the siding. Install the trim flush to the top and bottom edges of the siding, using 8d galvanized box nails.

2. On the side walls, cut 1 × 6 trim boards to span from the outside corners of the rear walls and overlap

Construct built-up beams with adhesive and nails (INSET). Secure the roof beams to the wall beams with framing connectors fastened with nails.

With the exception of the top cap trim, install the trim so all of the joints are flush.

the end-wall trim. Install the trim flush with the top and bottom edges of the siding.

3. On the rear walls, cut and install 1 × 6 trim boards starting at the door opening and overlapping the side-wall trim.

4. Cut and install 1 × 4 trim to fit vertically between the 1 × 6s. Overlap the 1 × 4s at the outside corners, as shown in the FLOOR AND ROOF FRAMING PLAN.

5. Rip 1× boards to cap the tops of the walls; see EAVE DETAILS. Size the cap trim to overhang the 1 × 6s as much as you like. Install the cap trim with 6d box nails.

Step H: Build the Screens

1. Cut 2 × 4 sills to fit snugly between pairs of posts along the front and side walls (on the side walls, the sills span between the corner post and framed corner wall).

2. Install the sills so their top faces are 28" above the slab. Fasten the sills to the posts and side walls with 16d finish nails or 3" deck screws.

NOTE: All of the screens are built on-site, with each custom-fit to its opening. The simple procedure is the same for every screen.

3. On the inside perimeter of each screened opening, draw a reference line 1⅝" from the outside of the wall. Miter-cut ¾" quarter-round molding to fit around the opening, fitting the pieces into the opening as you work. Cut two frames of molding for each opening; see EAVE DETAILS.

4. Install the outside frame of molding so its flat edge is on the reference lines, using 6d finish nails driven through pilot holes.

5. Using a flexible screen material of your choice, staple the screen to the flat side of the molding, keeping the screen taught and smooth. Trim excess screen after completing the stapling.

6. Cover the edge of the screen with adhesive rubber weatherstripping, positioned so it will be hidden behind the molding. Install the second frame of molding so it's tight against the weatherstripping, further securing the edges of the screen.

Secure the screen with staples and weatherstripping, sandwiched between quarter-round molding.

Nail trim molding

Staple the screen to the inside of the trim

Step I: Install the Roof Blocking & Cross Beams

1. Cut 2 × 6 blocking to fit snugly between the roof beams at the outer edges of the wall beams (six pieces total); see EAVE DETAILS.

2. Rip the bottom edge of each piece of blocking at 14° so the top edge is flush with the tops of the roof beam 2 × 6s, as shown in the EAVE DETAILS. Install the blocking between the roof beams with 16d common nails.

3. Cut nine 2 × 6 cross beams to fit between the roof beams, as shown in the FLOOR AND ROOF FRAMING PLAN. Mark the cross beam layout onto the roof beams, following the PLAN.

4. Position the cross beams at an angle so they are perpendicular to the roof beams and their top edges are flush with the roof beam 2 × 6s. Fasten the cross beams with 16d nails.

Step J: Install the Roof Panels & Doors

The roof framing is sized to accept uncut 4 × 8-ft. sheets of multi-wall polycarbonate panels. Make sure the panels you use are rated for the spans as shown, or install additional blocking or cross beams as needed. The battens that hold down the roof panels are made of composite decking material to prevent rot.

1. Cut four 1 × 4 battens to length at 108".

2. Apply aluminum tape to enclose the ends of the roof panel cells, following the manufacturer's directions.

3. Apply glazing tape or adhesive sealant to the edges of each roof panel or the roof framing, according to the manufacturer's directions. Also add tape or sealant along the top edges of the cross beams and roof blocking.

4. Set each panel on the roof beams so its front edge is flush with the front of the blocking, as shown in the EAVE DETAILS.

5. With the panels in place, center the battens over the beams, drill pilot holes, and fasten them to the beams with 2" deck screws. Make sure the panels are held firmly by the battens.

6. Install the screen doors following the manufacturer's instructions.

Fasten the blocking and cross beams to the roof beams with angled nails or screws.

Center the battens over the roof beams to provide equal overlap on adjacent roof panels.

Corner Lounge

Inspired by custom deck structures like this one, our Corner Lounge (page 138) helps define an outdoor activity space while complementing a natural setting.

Decks and patios are the most-used outdoor rooms. Extending your home into the open air, they're the best places for all kinds of activities—parties, evening meals, afternoon naps, and sunbathing. The Corner Lounge on page 138 is designed to make the most of all the ways you use your deck or patio.

The Corner Lounge combines the sheltering and light-filtering qualities of an arbor roof with the convenience of built-in bench seating. And it fits into the corner, so it won't take up a lot of floor space on your deck. You can add as much or as little lattice screening as you like for just the right amount of shade or privacy. An optional roof design lets you extend the roof over an 11 × 11-ft. area—perfect for adding a table that takes advantage of the bench seating.

You can build this project on most traditional decks and concrete patios. The location will dictate how you install the posts; steps are given here for elevated wood decks, as well as ground-level decks and concrete patios. You can also locate this structure anywhere in your garden by setting the posts in concrete (see page 220).

An arbor-style roof may be just the beginning, providing the framework for a burst of seasonal color and shade for those seated below.

Material List

Description (No. finished pieces)	Quantity/Size	Material
Posts		
Full-height posts* (7)	7 @ field measure	
Add 1 post for optional full roof	4 × 4	
Seat support post (1)	1 @ field measure	4 × 4
Post blocking	2 blocks for each post; field measure	2 × pressure-treated lumber; size to match existing deck joists
Roof Frame		
Beams (8)	8 @ 12'	2 × 8
Roof slats (20)	10 @ 8'	2 × 2
Optional Full Roof		
Beams (6)	6 @ 12'	2 × 8
Roof slats (12 long, 12 short)	18 @ 8'	2 × 2
Seats		
Seat supports (6 sides, 6 ends)	5 @ 8'	2 × 6
Seat slats (27)	9 @ 8'	2 × 6
Lattice Screens		
Lattice slats	Field measure	1 × 1 (¾" × ¾" actual dimensions)
Hardware & Fasteners		
16d galvanized common nails or 3½" deck screws		
Post bases (for concrete patios or ground-level decks only)	8, with recommended anchors and fasteners	Simpson AB44 or similar approved base
⅜" × 7" galvanized carriage bolts	16, with washers and nuts	
¼" × 6¼" galvanized carriage bolts	20, with washers and nuts	
2½" deck screws		
3½" deck screws		
3½" galvanized lag screws	22, with washers	
Galvanized metal angle	1	
4d galvanized finish nails		
Waterproof glue		
6d galvanized finish nails		

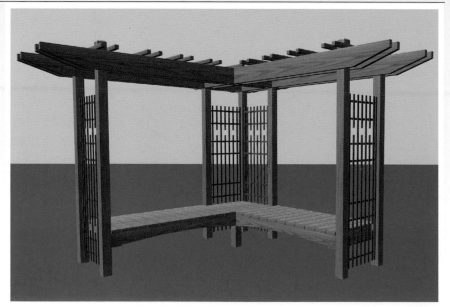

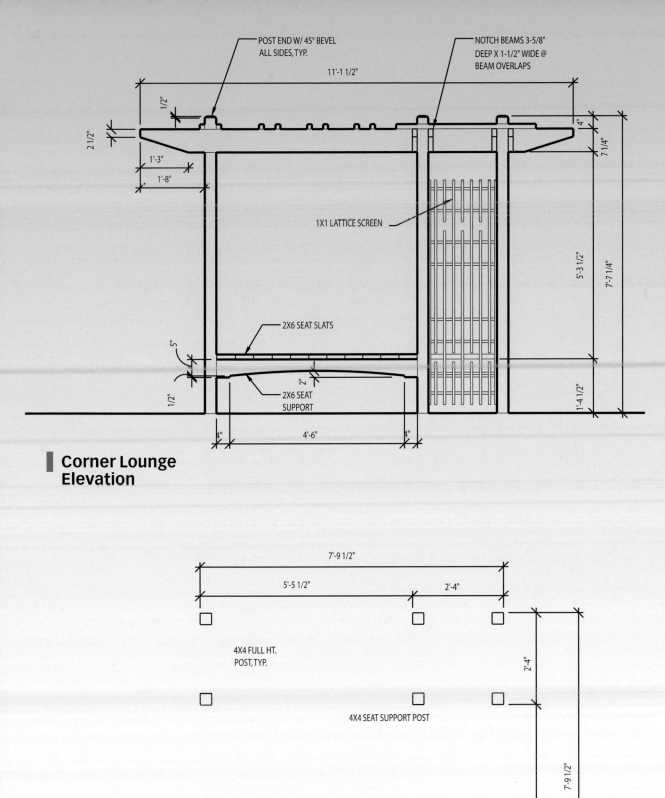

POST END W/ 45° BEVEL ALL SIDES, TYP.

NOTCH BEAMS 3-5/8" DEEP X 1-1/2" WIDE @ BEAM OVERLAPS

11'-1 1/2"

1/2"

2 1/2"

1'-3"

1'-8"

4"

7 1/4"

1X1 LATTICE SCREEN

5'-3 1/2"

7'-7 1/4"

5"

2X6 SEAT SLATS

2"

2X6 SEAT SUPPORT

1/2"

1'-4 1/2"

4"

4'-6"

4"

Corner Lounge Elevation

7'-9 1/2"

5'-5 1/2"

2'-4"

4X4 FULL HT. POST, TYP.

2'-4"

4X4 SEAT SUPPORT POST

7'-9 1/2"

5'-5 1/2"

Corner Lounge Post Layout Plan

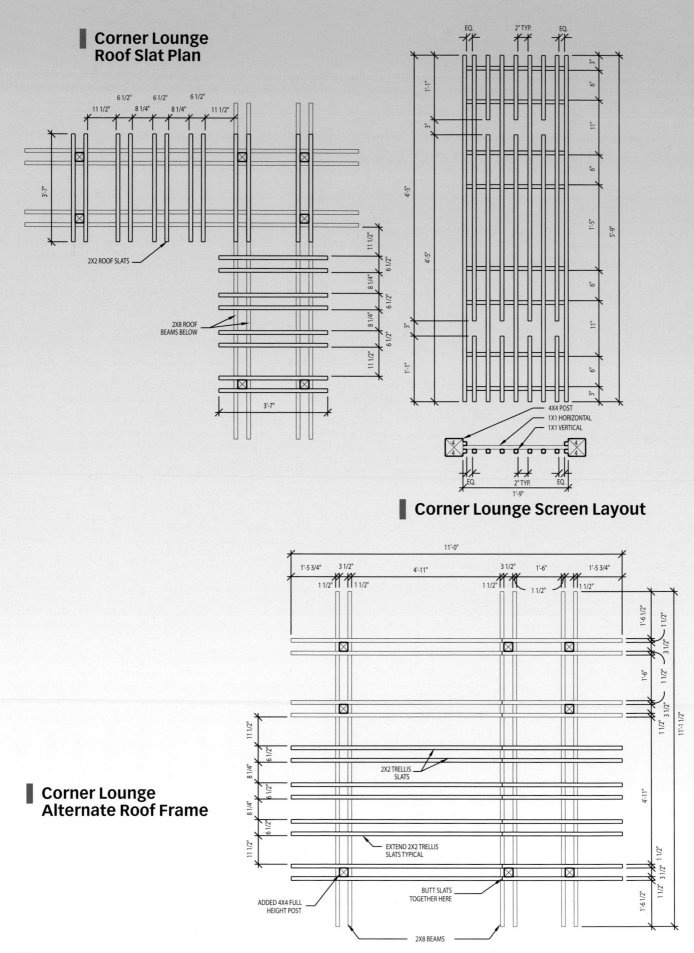

Corner Lounge Roof Slat Plan

6 1/2" 6 1/2" 6 1/2"
11 1/2" 8 1/4" 8 1/4" 11 1/2"

3'-7"

2X2 ROOF SLATS

2X8 ROOF BEAMS BELOW

11 1/2"
6 1/2"
8 1/4"
6 1/2"
8 1/4"
6 1/2"
11 1/2"

3'-7"

Corner Lounge Screen Layout

EQ. 2" TYP. EQ.

1'-1"
3"
3"
6"
11"
6"
1'-5"
5'-9"
4'-5"
6"
3"
11"
4'-5"
6"
3"
1'-1"
6"
3"

4X4 POST
1X1 HORIZONTAL
1X1 VERTICAL

4 4   4 4

EQ. 2" TYP. EQ.
1'-9"

Corner Lounge Alternate Roof Frame

11'-0"

1'-5 3/4" 3 1/2" 4'-11" 3 1/2" 1'-6" 1'-5 3/4"
1 1/2" 1 1/2" 1 1/2" 1 1/2" 1 1/2"

1'-6 1/2" 1 1/2"
1'-6 3 1/2"
1'-6 1 1/2"
1 1/2" 3 1/2"
11'-1 1/2"

2X2 TRELLIS SLATS

11 1/2"
6 1/2"
8 1/4"
6 1/2"
8 1/4"
6 1/2"
11 1/2"

4'-11"

EXTEND 2X2 TRELLIS SLATS TYPICAL

BUTT SLATS TOGETHER HERE

1 1/2"
3 1/2"
1'-6 1/2"

ADDED 4X4 FULL HEIGHT POST

2X8 BEAMS

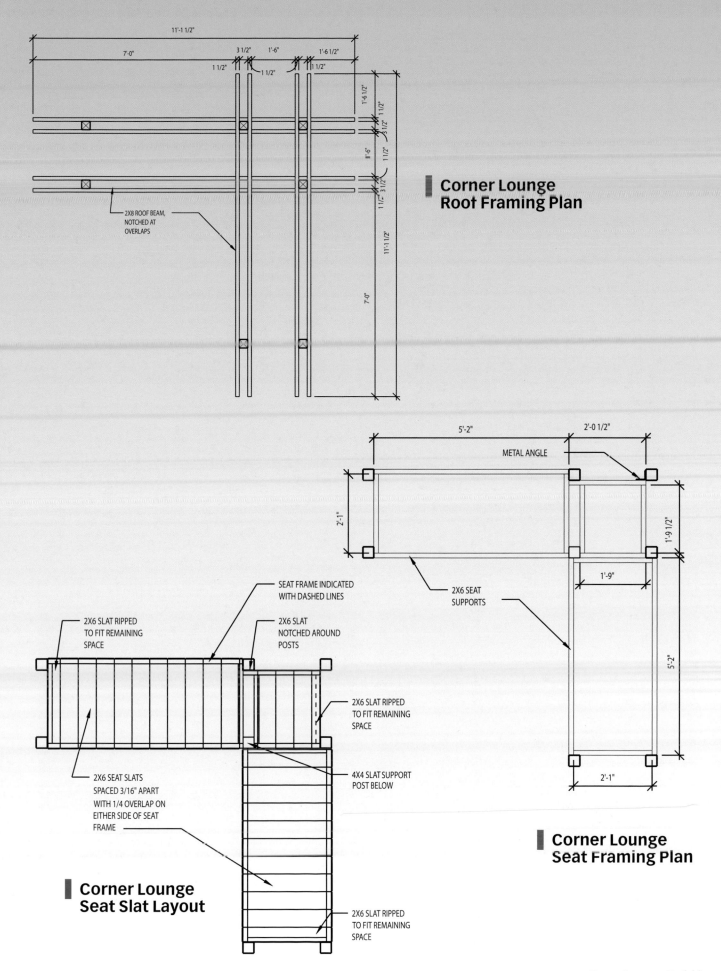

**Corner Lounge
Roof Framing Plan**

2X8 ROOF BEAM, NOTCHED AT OVERLAPS

**Corner Lounge
Seat Framing Plan**

METAL ANGLE

2X6 SEAT SUPPORTS

SEAT FRAME INDICATED WITH DASHED LINES

2X6 SLAT NOTCHED AROUND POSTS

2X6 SLAT RIPPED TO FIT REMAINING SPACE

2X6 SLAT RIPPED TO FIT REMAINING SPACE

4X4 SLAT SUPPORT POST BELOW

2X6 SEAT SLATS SPACED 3/16" APART WITH 1/4 OVERLAP ON EITHER SIDE OF SEAT FRAME

**Corner Lounge
Seat Slat Layout**

2X6 SLAT RIPPED TO FIT REMAINING SPACE

How to Build the Corner Lounge

The proper method for installing the posts depends on your situation:

Elevated wood deck: complete the following steps, but skip the Alternative Post Installation.

Concrete patio or ground-level deck: skip ahead to the Alternative Post Installation.

On the ground: follow the procedure on pages 220 to bury the posts in concrete. **NOTE: This requires longer posts to compensate for the buried portion.**

Step A: Cut the Post Holes

1. Lay out the post locations on your deck, following the POST LAYOUT PLAN, on page 139.

NOTE: If a series of posts falls over a deck joist, move the layout just enough so that the posts will be flush against the side of the joist. You can either move the entire structure or move only the affected posts. If you choose the latter, you can cut-to-fit the affected pieces to complete the project—just be aware that the plan measurements might not always apply.

2. Mark a cutout hole for the posts onto the decking boards. Measure each post to find its exact dimensions (they often slightly vary), then mark the cutout onto the decking boards.

3. Drill a starter hole inside each cutout marking, then use a jigsaw with a down-cutting blade to make the cutouts.

Step B: Install the Post Blocking

1. Underneath the deck, measure between the neighboring joists at each post location. Cut two pieces of blocking to fit in between the joists at each location. Use pressure-treated lumber that is the same size as the joists (e.g. 2×10, 2×12, etc.).

2. Get someone to help with this step, so one person is on top of the deck and one is below. Have the top person insert a short length of post (such as the seat support post) into a post cutout, extending it down so it's even with the bottoms of the joists. The person below sandwiches the post with blocking. While the top person uses a level to hold the post perfectly plumb, the bottom person marks the outsides of the blocking onto the neighboring joists.

3. Remove the post, then fasten the blocking to the joists with 16d common nails. Drive three nails or drill three screws through the joists and into the ends of the blocking, making sure the blocking stays on the marks made in step 2.

Drill a starter hole inside the post marks, then make the cutout with a jig saw.

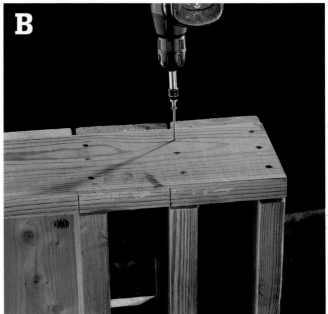

Hold the blocks on their layout marks, and fasten them to the joists at both ends.

Step C: Cut & Install the Posts

1. For the full-height posts: Measure from the bottom of the blocking to the top of the deck surface. Add that dimension to 91¼" to find the total post length. For the seat support post: Add 16½" to the deck-depth measurement above to find the total length. Cut the posts to length (see page 34).

2. If desired, bevel the top ends of the full-height posts at 45°, as shown in the ELEVATION (page 139).

3. Measure from the top end of each full-height post and make a reference mark at 91¼". On the seat support post, make a reference line 16½" from the top end.

4. With one person on top of the deck and one below, set each post into its hole so the reference line is aligned with the deck surface. Use a level to hold the post perfectly plumb, then have the person below clamp the post to the blocking.

5. Drill pilot holes and anchor each post to the blocking with two ⅜" × 7" carriage bolts.

Alternative Post Installation: Setting Posts on a Concrete Patio or a Ground-level Deck

1. Lay out the post locations on your patio or deck; follow the POST LAYOUT PLAN.

2. For concrete patios: Use a hammer drill to drill a hole for each post base anchor. Refer to the base manufacturer for the size and type of anchor to use. Secure the anchor to the concrete, then bolt the post base to the anchor, using the recommended hardware.

For decks: Fasten a post base to the deck at each post location, using the fasteners recommended by the base manufacturer.

3. Cut the full-height posts to length so that they will stand 91¼" above the patio or deck surface when they're installed on the post bases. Cut the seat support post so it will stand 16½" above the surface when installed on its base.

4. If desired, bevel the top ends of the full-height posts at 45°, as shown in the ELEVATION.

5. Set each post on its base and support it with temporary braces so that it stands perfectly plumb. Fasten the post to the base using the fasteners recommended by the base manufacturer.

Use a clamp to help hold the post at the proper height. Anchor the post with carriage bolts.

Alternative Post Installation: Use post bases with metal standoff plates to protect the posts from surface moisture.

Step D: Cut & Shape the Roof Beams

1. Cut the eight 2 × 8 beams to length at 133½".

2. To shape the beam ends, make a mark 2½" down from the top corner at each end. Make another mark 15" in from the bottom corner. Draw a line connecting the two marks. Cut along this diagonal line.

3. At the corner, the four sets of beam pairs intersect with half-lap joints. To mark the notches for the half-lap joints, measure the depth (width) and thickness of the beams. The width of the notches must match the thickness of the beams; the length of the notches must equal half the depth of the beams. Mark the layout of the notches, following the ROOF FRAMING PLAN (page 141).

4. Cut the notches.

TIP: You can save time by clamping two or more beams together and cutting them at once. Using a circular saw or handsaw, cut the outside edges of the notches first. Then, make a series of interior cuts at ⅛" intervals. Use a chisel to remove the waste and smooth the seats of the notches.

5. Test-fit the notches on the ground and make any necessary adjustments for a good fit.

Step E: Install the Roof Beams

1. Mark the sides of the posts that will receive the beams 11¼" down from the top ends.

2. Starting with the beams with the top-down notches, sandwich one set of posts so the notches clear the posts on both sides and the bottom edges of the beams are on the reference marks made in the last step. Clamp the beams in place.

3. Drill two pilot holes for ¼" × 6½" carriage bolts through both beams and the post. On the less-visible beam sides, countersink the holes just enough to completely recess the washer and nut. Fasten the beams to the posts with the carriage bolts.

4. Repeat Steps 2 and 3 to install the other set of parallel beams.

5. Install the perpendicular beams, fitting the notches together so all the beams are flush at the top and bottom edges. Clamp the beams as before, then drill pilot holes and attach the beams with carriage bolts.

TIP: Drill the pilot holes from the outsides of the beam intersections, so you have enough room for the drill bit.

Test-fit the beam joints and make adjustments before installing the beams.

Step F: Install the Roof Slats

1. Cut the 20 roof slats to length at 43".

2. Mark the slat layout on the tops of the roof beams; follow the ROOF SLAT PLAN on page 140.

3. Position each slat on its layout mark so it overhangs the outer roof beams by 6" on both sides. Fasten the slat to each intersecting beam with 2½" deck screws driven through pilot holes.

Step G: Build the Seat Frames

1. Look at the SEAT FRAMING PLAN (page 141) to understand the seat frame layout. There are three, 4-sided seat frames. You can build them on a workbench, then install them—just make sure they fit snugly between the sets of posts.

2. Measure between the posts for each seat frame. Cut the side seat supports to length so they extend from post to post. Cut the end seat supports to length so they fit between the side supports.

3. Lay out the arched cutout on one side support; follow the ELEVATION. Make the cut with a jigsaw or bandsaw, then sand the arch smooth.

Counterbores help hide the bolt hardware. Locate them in the least conspicuous areas.

Drill pilot holes for the roof slats, and fasten them to the roof beams with 2½" deck screws.

Use the support as a pattern to mark the three remaining long seat supports, then make the cuts.

4. Assemble the seat frames with 3½" deck screws drilled through the side supports and into the end supports. Make sure the pieces are flush along their top edges.

5. Measure up from the deck surface, and mark the inside faces of the posts at 16½". Install the seat frames as shown in the SEAT FRAMING PLAN, so their top edges are on the reference marks; fasten through the end seat supports and into the posts with two 3½" lag screws at each location. Using a metal angle and screws, fasten the frame at the outside corner of the lounge.

Step H: Add the Seat Slats

1. Measure between the outside faces of the seat frames to find the lengths of the seat slats. You can either make the slats flush to the frames or overhang the frames by ¼" on either side.

2. Notch the first slat to fit around the posts where the left side frame meets the corner frame; see SEAT SLAT LAYOUT (page 141). Drill pilot holes, and then fasten the slat to the seat frames with pairs of 2½" deck screws.

3. Cut and install the remaining slats, gapping them at 3⁄16". Rip the last slat in each section to fit the remaining space.

Step I: Build the Lattice Screens

How you use the lattice screening is your choice. You may want screens only on the ends of the seats, as shown in the plan drawings, or you might cover the entire backside of the project. To avoid blocking your view behind your deck, you can build short screens that match the deck rail height. The basic procedure for building screens is shown here.

1. Construct a jig for assembling the lattice screens: On a sheet of plywood, fasten two straight 2 × 4s in an "L" pattern, using a framing square to set the pieces at an exact 90° angle.

2. Cut several 2 × 6 spacers from ¾" plywood.

3. Cut the lattice pieces to length from ¾" × ¾" (actual dimensions) lumber; follow the SCREEN LAYOUT on page 140.

4. Using the jig and spacers, assemble the screens according to the drawing, or create your own pattern. Fasten the pieces with waterproof wood glue and 4d finish nails.

5. To install the screens, fasten a lattice backer strip to each post, as shown in the plan detail of the SCREEN LAYOUT, using 6d finish nails. Finally, install the screens against the backer strips.

A flexible wood strip helps you make a perfect curve for the long side seat supports.

H

Notch the slats as needed to fit snugly around the posts. Gap the slats by 3⁄16".

I1

Construct a right-angle jig for assembling the lattice screens.

I2

A right-angle jig and plywood spacers help you keep the lattice screens square as you work.

With its similar structure to our Classic gazebo (page 152), this example shows how simple embellishments, like decorative brackets and post trim, can add a sense of grandeur.

Classic 8-Sided Gazebo

The traditional octagonal gazebo has timeless elegance. Viewed from any angle, its eight symmetrical sides give it an eye-catching, sculptural quality—a perfect centerpiece for the landscape. Inside the gazebo, an elevated floor adds a sense of loftiness, while open-air sides make it a great spot for escaping the sun and catching summer breezes.

The gazebo on page 152 measures nine feet across and has cedar decking laid in an octagonal pat-tern. Look up from the inside and you see an attrac-tive panel ceiling of 1 × 6 cedar boards. The lattice panels help enclose the interior while giving the entire structure a light, airy feel. If you prefer more ornamentation, you can easily omit the upper lattice panels and add decorative brackets or scrollwork.

Not surprisingly, this project involves lots of angled cuts. If you've been looking for a reason to buy a compound miter saw, this is your ticket. It makes the project much, much easier.

Modest in scale, this charming gazebo demonstrates the appeal of a simpler design, enhanced by leafy vines rather than architectural ornament.

Material List

Description (No. finished pieces)	Quantity/Size	Material
Foundation		
Concrete	field measure	3,000 PSI concrete
Concrete tube forms	1 @ 16"-dia., 8 @ 12"-dia.	
Compactible gravel	2.5 cu. ft.	
Framing		
Posts (8)	8 @ 10'	6 × 6 cedar
Perimeter beams (16)	8 @ 8'	2 × 6 pressure-treated
Double joists (8)	8 @ 10'	2 × 6 pressure-treated
Angled joists (16)	8 @ 8'	2 × 6 pressure-treated
Roof beams (8)	4 @ 10'	6 × 8 cedar
Hip rafters (8)	8 @ 8'	2 × 8 cedar
Intermediate rafters (16)	8 @ 10'	2 × 6 cedar
Purlins (8)	2 @ 8'	2 × 8 cedar
Collar ties (4)	4 @ 10'	2 × 6 cedar
Rafter hub (1)	1 @ 2'	8 × 8 cedar
Wood sphere	1 @ 10"-dia., with dowel screw	
Pad (center pier) (2)	Cut from stringers	2 × 12 pressure-treated
Framing anchors		
Joists to posts	8, with nails	Simpson U26-2
Angled joists to perim. beams	16, with nails	Simpson U26
Angled joists to double joists	16, with nails	Simpson LSU26
Anchor bolts	9 @ ⅝" × 12"	Galvanized J-bolt
Posts to piers	8, with fasteners	Simpson ABU66
Perimeter beams to posts	32	½" × 6" lag screws & washers
Metal anchors—rafters to beams	24	Simpson H1
Metal hangers—rafters to hub	8, with nails	Simpson FB26
Posts to roof beams	8, with fasteners	Simpson 1212T
Beams to roof beams	8, with nails	3" × 12" × 14-gauge galv. plate
Stair stringers to perimeter beam	6, with nails	Simpson L50
Stairs		
Compactible gravel	4.5 cu. ft.	
Concrete form	2 @ 8'-0"	2 × 4
Stair pad	7 @ 60-lb. bags	Concrete mix
Stringers (3)	2 @ 8'-0"	2 × 12 pressure-treated
Stair treads (6)	2 @ 10'-0"	2 × 6 cedar
Stair risers (3)	1 @ 10'-0"	1 × 8 cedar

Description
(No. finished pieces)

Description (No. finished pieces)	Quantity/Size	Material
Finishing Lumber		
Decking	15 @ 8'-0", 6 @ 10'-0"	2 × 6 cedar
Deck starter	1 @ 1'-0"	2 × 8 cedar
Fascia	4 @ 10'-0"	2 × 4 cedar
Lattice	4 panels @ 4 × 8'	Cedar lattice
Stops	15 @ 8'-0" (horizontal)	⁵⁄₄ × ⁵⁄₄ cedar
	10 @ 10'-0" (vertical)	
Rails (37)	19 @ 8'-0"	2 × 4 cedar
Roofing		
Roof sheathing	26 @ 8'-0", 14 @ 10'-0"	1 × 6 T&G V-joint cedar
Asphalt shingles	256 sq. ft.	
15# building paper	300 sq. ft.	
Metal drip edge	36 linear ft.	
Galvanized flashing	3 linear ft.	
Roofing cement	1 tube	
Fasteners		
16d common nails		
16d galvanized common nails		
16d galvanized box nails		
16d galvanized casing nails		
10d galvanized common nails		
8d galvanized box nails		
8d galvanized finish nails		
3d galvanized finish nails		
Roofing nails, to fit roofing material		
1½" galvanized joist hanger nails		
Masonry screws or nails		
3" deck screws		
Construction adhesive		

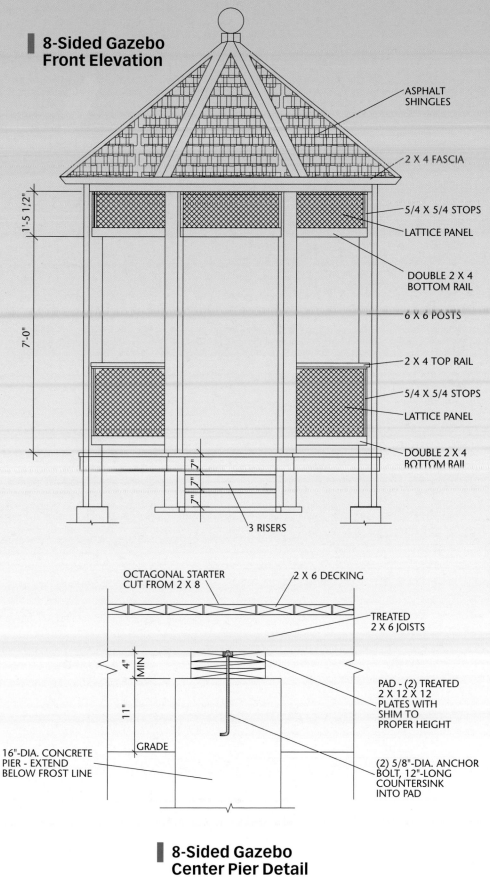

8-Sided Gazebo
Front Elevation

ASPHALT
SHINGLES

2 X 4 FASCIA

5/4 X 5/4 STOPS

LATTICE PANEL

DOUBLE 2 X 4
BOTTOM RAIL

6 X 6 POSTS

2 X 4 TOP RAIL

5/4 X 5/4 STOPS

LATTICE PANEL

DOUBLE 2 X 4
BOTTOM RAIL

1'-5 1/2"

7'-0"

7" 7"

7" 7"

3 RISERS

OCTAGONAL STARTER
CUT FROM 2 X 8

2 X 6 DECKING

TREATED
2 X 6 JOISTS

4" MIN

11"

GRADE

16"-DIA. CONCRETE
PIER - EXTEND
BELOW FROST LINE

PAD - (2) TREATED
2 X 12 X 12
PLATES WITH
SHIM TO
PROPER HEIGHT

(2) 5/8"-DIA. ANCHOR
BOLT, 12"-LONG
COUNTERSINK
INTO PAD

8-Sided Gazebo
Center Pier Detail

8-Sided Gazebo
Floor Framing Plan

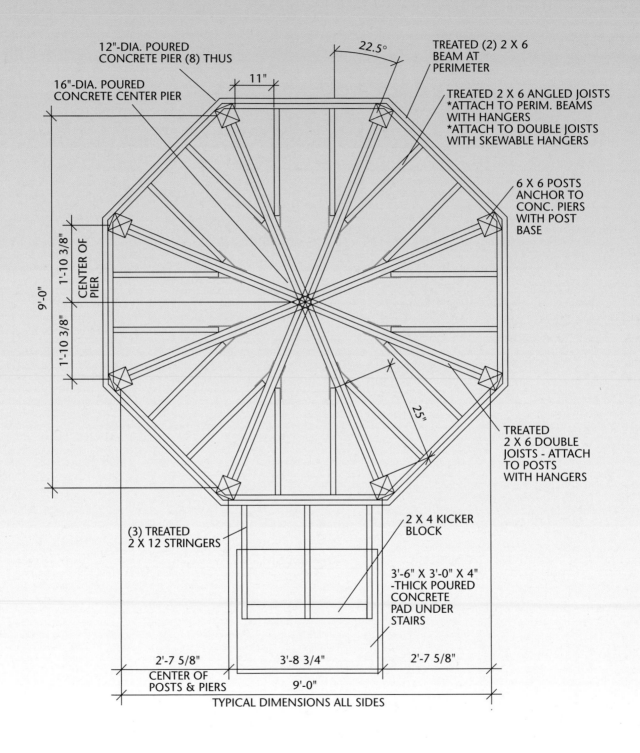

12"-DIA. POURED
CONCRETE PIER (8) THUS

16"-DIA. POURED
CONCRETE CENTER PIER

11"

22.5°

TREATED (2) 2 X 6
BEAM AT
PERIMETER

TREATED 2 X 6 ANGLED JOISTS
*ATTACH TO PERIM. BEAMS
WITH HANGERS
*ATTACH TO DOUBLE JOISTS
WITH SKEWABLE HANGERS

6 X 6 POSTS
ANCHOR TO
CONC. PIERS
WITH POST
BASE

9'-0"

1'-10 3/8"

CENTER OF PIER

1'-10 3/8"

25"

TREATED
2 X 6 DOUBLE
JOISTS - ATTACH
TO POSTS
WITH HANGERS

(3) TREATED
2 X 12 STRINGERS

2 X 4 KICKER
BLOCK

3'-6" X 3'-0" X 4"
-THICK POURED
CONCRETE
PAD UNDER
STAIRS

2'-7 5/8"

CENTER OF
POSTS & PIERS

3'-8 3/4"

2'-7 5/8"

9'-0"

TYPICAL DIMENSIONS ALL SIDES

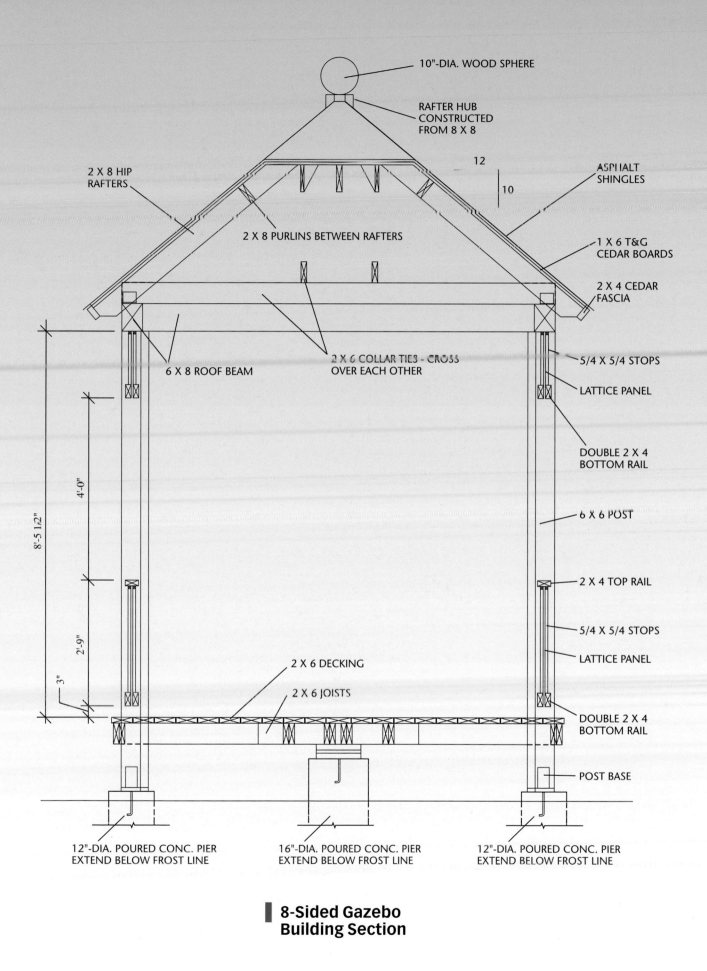

10"-DIA. WOOD SPHERE

RAFTER HUB CONSTRUCTED FROM 8 X 8

2 X 8 HIP RAFTERS

2 X 8 PURLINS BETWEEN RAFTERS

12

10

ASPHALT SHINGLES

1 X 6 T&G CEDAR BOARDS

2 X 4 CEDAR FASCIA

6 X 8 ROOF BEAM

2 X 6 COLLAR TIES - CROSS OVER EACH OTHER

5/4 X 5/4 STOPS

LATTICE PANEL

DOUBLE 2 X 4 BOTTOM RAIL

6 X 6 POST

2 X 4 TOP RAIL

5/4 X 5/4 STOPS

LATTICE PANEL

8'-5 1/2"

4'-0"

2'-9"

3"

2 X 6 DECKING

2 X 6 JOISTS

DOUBLE 2 X 4 BOTTOM RAIL

POST BASE

12"-DIA. POURED CONC. PIER EXTEND BELOW FROST LINE

16"-DIA. POURED CONC. PIER EXTEND BELOW FROST LINE

12"-DIA. POURED CONC. PIER EXTEND BELOW FROST LINE

8-Sided Gazebo Building Section

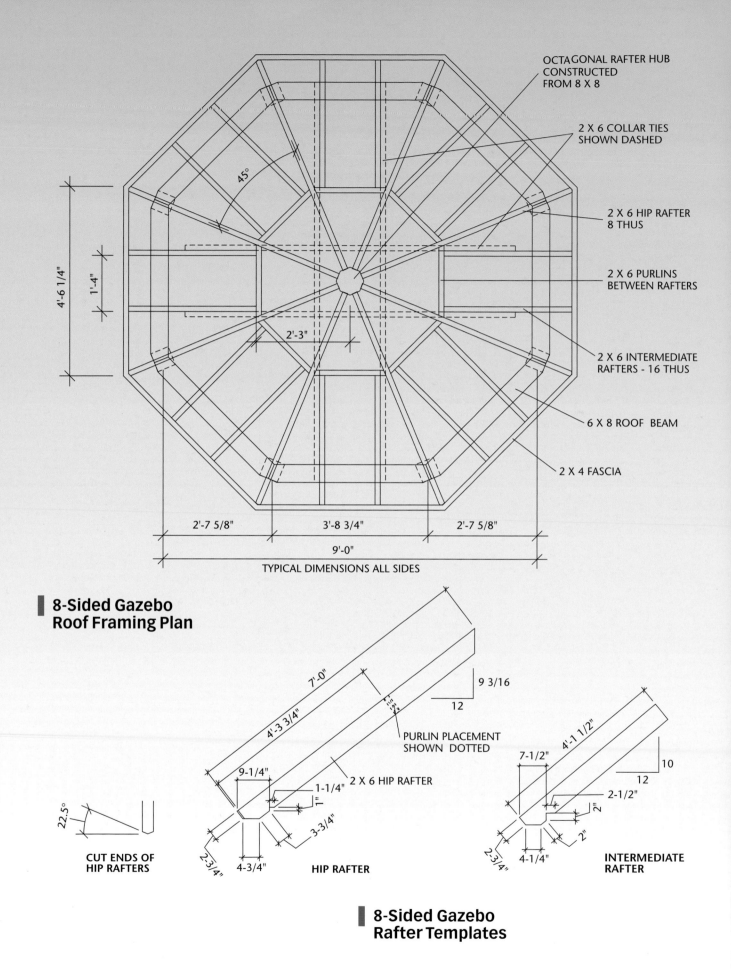

OCTAGONAL RAFTER HUB CONSTRUCTED FROM 8 X 8

2 X 6 COLLAR TIES SHOWN DASHED

2 X 6 HIP RAFTER 8 THUS

2 X 6 PURLINS BETWEEN RAFTERS

2 X 6 INTERMEDIATE RAFTERS - 16 THUS

6 X 8 ROOF BEAM

2 X 4 FASCIA

45°

4'-6 1/4"

1'-4"

2'-3"

2'-7 5/8"   3'-8 3/4"   2'-7 5/8"

9'-0"

TYPICAL DIMENSIONS ALL SIDES

8-Sided Gazebo Roof Framing Plan

7'-0"

9 3/16 / 12

4'-3 3/4"

PURLIN PLACEMENT SHOWN DOTTED

9-1/4"

1-1/4"
1"
3-3/4"

2 X 6 HIP RAFTER

2-3/4"   4-3/4"

HIP RAFTER

22.5°

CUT ENDS OF HIP RAFTERS

4'-1 1/2"

10 / 12

7-1/2"

2-1/2"
2"
2"

2-3/4"   4-1/4"

INTERMEDIATE RAFTER

8-Sided Gazebo Rafter Templates

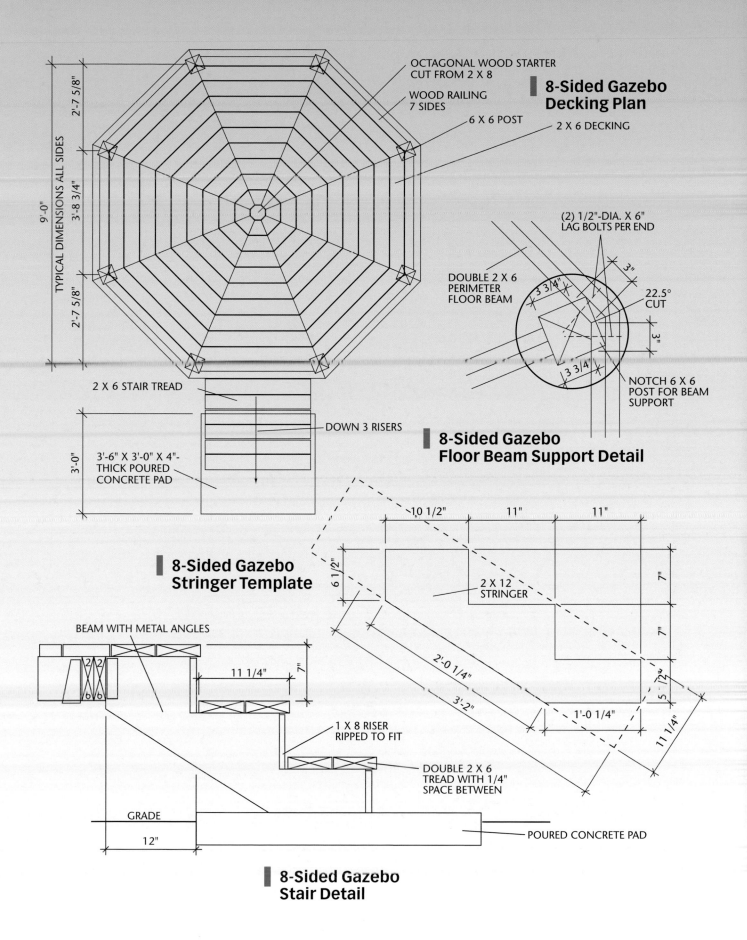

8-Sided Gazebo Decking Plan

OCTAGONAL WOOD STARTER CUT FROM 2 X 8

WOOD RAILING 7 SIDES

6 X 6 POST

2 X 6 DECKING

TYPICAL DIMENSIONS ALL SIDES

9'-0"

2'-7 5/8"

3'-8 3/4"

2'-7 5/8"

2 X 6 STAIR TREAD

3'-0"

3'-6" X 3'-0" X 4"-THICK POURED CONCRETE PAD

DOWN 3 RISERS

8-Sided Gazebo Floor Beam Support Detail

(2) 1/2"-DIA. X 6" LAG BOLTS PER END

DOUBLE 2 X 6 PERIMETER FLOOR BEAM

3 3/4"

3"

22.5° CUT

3"

3 3/4"

NOTCH 6 X 6 POST FOR BEAM SUPPORT

8-Sided Gazebo Stringer Template

10 1/2"

11"

11"

6 1/2"

2 X 12 STRINGER

7"

7"

2'-0 1/4"

3'-2"

1'-0 1/4"

5 1/2"

11 1/4"

8-Sided Gazebo Stair Detail

BEAM WITH METAL ANGLES

2/2

6/6

11 1/4"

7"

1 X 8 RISER RIPPED TO FIT

DOUBLE 2 X 6 TREAD WITH 1/4" SPACE BETWEEN

GRADE

12"

POURED CONCRETE PAD

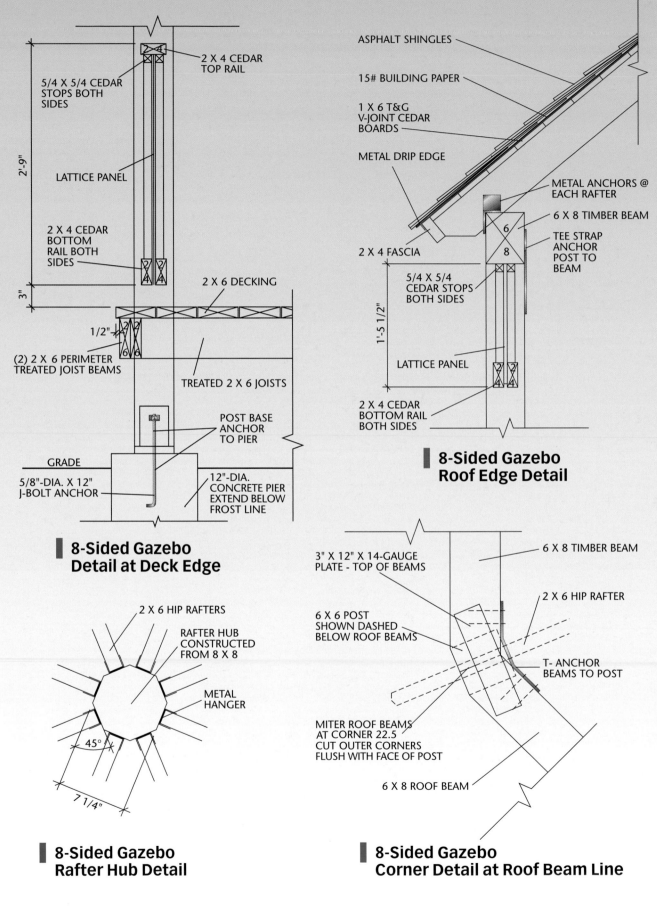

8-Sided Gazebo Detail at Deck Edge

2 X 4 CEDAR TOP RAIL

5/4 X 5/4 CEDAR STOPS BOTH SIDES

2'-9"

LATTICE PANEL

2 X 4 CEDAR BOTTOM RAIL BOTH SIDES

3"

2 X 6 DECKING

1/2"

(2) 2 X 6 PERIMETER TREATED JOIST BEAMS

TREATED 2 X 6 JOISTS

POST BASE ANCHOR TO PIER

GRADE

5/8"-DIA. X 12" J-BOLT ANCHOR

12"-DIA. CONCRETE PIER EXTEND BELOW FROST LINE

8-Sided Gazebo Roof Edge Detail

ASPHALT SHINGLES

15# BUILDING PAPER

1 X 6 T&G V-JOINT CEDAR BOARDS

METAL DRIP EDGE

METAL ANCHORS @ EACH RAFTER

6 X 8 TIMBER BEAM

TEE STRAP ANCHOR POST TO BEAM

2 X 4 FASCIA

5/4 X 5/4 CEDAR STOPS BOTH SIDES

1'-5 1/2"

LATTICE PANEL

2 X 4 CEDAR BOTTOM RAIL BOTH SIDES

8-Sided Gazebo Rafter Hub Detail

2 X 6 HIP RAFTERS

RAFTER HUB CONSTRUCTED FROM 8 X 8

METAL HANGER

45°

7 1/4"

8-Sided Gazebo Corner Detail at Roof Beam Line

3" X 12" X 14-GAUGE PLATE - TOP OF BEAMS

6 X 8 TIMBER BEAM

2 X 6 HIP RAFTER

6 X 6 POST SHOWN DASHED BELOW ROOF BEAMS

T- ANCHOR BEAMS TO POST

MITER ROOF BEAMS AT CORNER 22.5 CUT OUTER CORNERS FLUSH WITH FACE OF POST

6 X 8 ROOF BEAM

How to Build the Classic 8-Sided Gazebo

Step A: Pour the Concrete Pier Footings

NOTE: See page 212 for instructions on laying out and pouring concrete pier footings. Use 12"-dia. cardboard tube forms for the eight outer piers and a 16"-dia. form for the center pier.

1. Set up batter boards in a square pattern, and attach tight mason's lines to form a 9 × 9-ft. square. Take diagonal measurements to make sure the lines are square to one another. Attach two more lines that run diagonally from the corners and cross in the center of the square—this intersection represents the center of the center footing.

2. Measure 31⅝" in both directions from each corner and make a mark on a piece of tape attached to the line.

3. At each of the nine points, use a plumb bob to transfer the point to the ground, and mark the point with a stake. Remove the mason's lines.

4. Dig holes for the forms and add a 4" layer of gravel to each hole. Set the forms so the tops of the outer forms are 2" above grade and the center form is 11" above grade. Level the forms and secure them with packed soil. Restring the mason's lines and confirm that the forms are centered under the nine points.

5. Fill each form with concrete, and then screed the tops. Insert a ⅝" × 12" J-bolt in the center of the form. Use a plumb bob to align the J-bolt with the point on the line layout. On the outer footings, set the bolts so they protrude ¾" to 1" from the concrete. On the center footing, set the bolt to protrude 5". Let the concrete cure completely.

Step B: Set the Posts

1. Use a straight board to mark reference lines for squaring the post anchors. Set the board on top of one of the outer footings and on the center footing. Holding the board against the same side of the J-bolts, draw a pencil line along the board across the tops of the footings. Do the same for the remaining footings.

2. Place a metal post anchor on each perimeter footing and center it over the J-bolt. Use a framing square to position the anchor so it's square to the reference line (see photo F, on page 215). Secure the anchor with washers and a nut.

3. Set each post in an anchor, tack it in place with a nail, then brace it with temporary cross braces so that it's perfectly plumb. Secure the post to the anchor, using the fasteners recommended by the manufacturer. **Note: You will cut the posts to length during the construction of the roof frame.**

Step C: Install the Perimeter Floor Beams

1. Starting at one of the posts that will be nearest to the stairs, measure from the ground and mark the post at 20½". Draw a level line at this mark around all four sides of the post. Transfer this height mark to the other posts, using a mason's line and a line level. These marks represent the tops of the 2 × 6 perimeter beams and the double joists of the floor frame.

2. Measure down 5½" from the post marks and make a second mark on all sides of each post. Notch the outer posts to accept the inner member of the

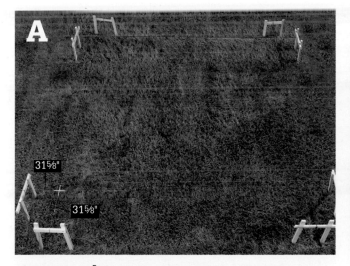

Measure in 31⅝" from the corners of the string layout to mark the centers of the outside piers.

Set a board across the center and each outer footing and mark a line across the top of the outer footing.

perimeter floor beams, as shown in the FLOOR BEAM SUPPORT DETAIL, on page 157, using a handsaw or circular saw and a chisel.

3. Cut the inner members of the perimeter floor beams to extend between the centers of the notches of adjacent posts, angling the ends at 22½°. Set the members into the notches and tack them to the posts with two 16d galv. common nails. See photo C.

4. Cut the outer members of the perimeter beams to fit around the inner members, angling the ends at 22½° so they fit together at tight miter joints (you may have to adjust the angles a little). Anchor the perimeter beams to the posts with two ½" × 6" lag screws at each end, as shown in the FLOOR BEAM SUPPORT DETAIL. Fasten the inner and outer beams together with pairs of 10d galvanized common nails driven every 12".

Step D: Install the Double Joists

1. Fasten metal hangers to the inside centers of the posts so the tops of the joists will be flush with the upper line drawn in Step C (also, see the FLOOR FRAMING PLAN, on page 156).

2. Cut two 2 × 6 joists to span between two opposing posts, as shown in the FLOOR FRAM-ING PLAN (check the boards for crowning, and make sure to install them crown-up). Nail the joists together with pairs of 10d galvanized common nails spaced every 12".

3. Set the double joist into the hangers and leave it in place while you build and fit the wood

pad that supports the joists at the center pier (see the CENTER PIER DETAIL, on page 153).

4. Cut two 2 × 12 plates—one from two of the boards you'll use for the stair stringers—and cut a shim at 11¼". Use treated plywood or treated lumber for the shim (if necessary, sand a lumber shim to the correct thickness with a belt sander.) Test-fit the pad; then remove the joist.

5. Fasten together the plates and shim with 16d galvanized nails. Drill a counterbored hole for the anchor nut and washer into the top plate, then drill a ⅝" hole through the center of the plates and shim. Secure the pad to the pier with construction adhesive, anchor nut, and washer.

6. Install the double joist, fastening it to the hangers with the recommended nails and toenailing it to the center pad with 10d galvanized nails.

7. Cut and assemble two double joists that run perpendicular to the full-length double joist. Install the joists at the midpoint of the full-length joist, toe-nailing them to the joist and pad.

8. Cut the remaining four double joists so their inside ends taper together at 45°. Install the joists following the FLOOR FRAMING PLAN.

Step E: Install the Angled Floor Joists

1. Mark the perimeter beam 11" from the post sides to represent the outside faces of the sixteen floor joists (see the FLOOR FRAMING PLAN). Then, measure from the inside face of each post toward the center and mark both sides

Cut the post notches by making horizontal cuts with a handsaw or circular saw, and then remove the remaining material with a chisel.

Miter the ends of four of the double joists so they meet flush with the full-length joist and those perpendicular to it.

of the double joists at 25"—this mark represents the end of the angled joist.

2. Install metal joist hangers on the perimeter beams and skewable (adjustable) hangers on the double joists, using the recommended fasteners.

3. Cut and install the 2 × 6 angled floor joists, following the hanger manufacturer's instructions.

Step F: Pour the Stair Pad

1. Using stakes or mason's line, mark a rectangular area that is 39 × 49", positioning its long side 10½" from the perimeter beam. Center the rectangle between the two nearest posts.

2. Excavate within the area to a depth of 7". Add 4" of compactible gravel and tamp it thoroughly.

3. Build a form from 2 × 4 lumber that is 36 × 42" (inner dimensions). Set the form with stakes so that the inside face of its long side is 12" from the perimeter beam and the form is centered between the nearest posts. Make sure the top of the form is level and is 19½" from the top of the perimeter beam.

4. Fill the form with concrete and screed the top flat with a 2 × 4. Float the concrete, if desired (see page 219), and add a broomed or other textured finish for a slip-resistant surface. Round over the edges of the pad with a concrete edger. Let the concrete cure, and then remove the form and backfill around the pad with soil or gravel.

Step G: Build the Stairs

NOTE: The STRINGER TEMPLATE, on page 157, is designed for a gazebo that measures 21" from the stair pad to the top of the floor deck. If your gazebo is at a different height, adjust the riser dimension of the steps to match your project: divide the floor height (including the decking) by three to find the riser height for each step.

1. Use a framing square to lay out the first 2 × 12 stair stringer, following the STRINGER TEMPLATE: Starting at one end of the board, position the framing square along the top edge of the board. Align the 11" mark on the square's blade (long part) and the 7" mark on the tongue (short part) with the edge of the board. Trace along the outer edges of the blade and tongue, then use the square to extend the blade marking to the other edge of the board. The tongue mark represents the first riser.

2. Measure 1½" from the bottom mark and draw another line that is parallel to it—this is the cutting line for the bottom of the stringer (the 1½" is an allowance for the thickness of the treads of the first step).

3. Continue the step layout, starting at the point where the first riser mark intersects the top edge of the board. Draw lines for the tread of the first step and the riser of the second step. Repeat this process to draw one more step and a top cutting line.

4. Measure 10½" from the top riser and make a mark on the top cutting line. Draw a perpendicular line from the cutting line to the opposite edge of the board—this line represents the top end cut.

5. Cut the stringer and test-fit it against the stair pad and perimeter beam. Make any necessary adjustments. Using the stringer as a pattern, trace the layout onto the two remaining stringer boards, and then cut the stringers.

Fasten the angled floor joists to the sides of the double joists with skewable metal anchors.

Fill the 2 × 4 form for the stair pad with concrete, then screed the top with a straight piece of 2 × 4.

6. Attach the stringers to the perimeter floor beam with metal angles, following the layout shown in the FLOOR FRAMING PLAN.

7. From scrap pressure-treated 2 × 4 lumber, cut kicker blocks to fit between the bottom ends of the stair stringers. Fasten the blocks to the concrete pad with construction adhesive and masonry screws or nails, then nail through the sides of the stringers into the kickers with 16d galv. common nails.

Step H: Install the Decking

1. Cut an octagonal starter piece from a cedar 2 × 8: Draw two lines across the board to make a 7¼ × 7¼" square. Make a mark 2⅛" in from each corner, and then connect the marks to form an octagon. Cut the starter piece and position it in the center of the floor frame, with each point centered on a double joist. Drill pilot holes and attach the piece with 3" deck screws.

2. Cut the 2 × 6 deck boards for each row one at a time. The end cuts for each boards should be 22½°, but you may have to adjust the angles occasionally to make tight joints. Gap the boards, if desired, but make sure the gaps are consistent—use scrap wood or nails as spacers. Drill pilot holes and drive two screws wherever a board meets a framing member. Periodically measure to make sure the boards are parallel to the perimeter beams. Overhang the perimeter beams by ½" with the outer row of decking.

3. Install the 2 × 6 treads and 1 × 8 riser boards on the stairs following the STAIR DETAIL, on page 157.

Step I: Set the Roof Beams

1. Measure up from the floor deck and mark one of the posts at 101½". Transfer that mark to the remaining posts, using a mason's line and a line level. Mark a level cutting line around all sides of each post, then cut the posts with a reciprocating saw or handsaw.

2. On the top of each post, draw a line down the middle that points toward the center of the structure. Cut each of the four 6 × 8 roof beams in half so you have eight 5-ft.-long beams.

3. Set each roof beam on top of two neighboring posts so its outside face is flush with the outside corners of the posts. Mark the inside face of the roof beam where it meets the post centerlines—these marks represent cuts at each end (see the CORNER DETAIL AT ROOF BEAM LINE, on page158). Also mark the underside of the beam by tracing along the outside faces of the posts—these lines show you where to trim off the beams so they will be flush with the outside post faces. Use a square to extend the marks down around the post sides to help keep your cuts straight.

4. Starting from the end-cut marks, cut the beam ends at 22½°. Trim off the corners at the underside marks. Mark and cut the remaining beams, test-fitting the angles as you go.

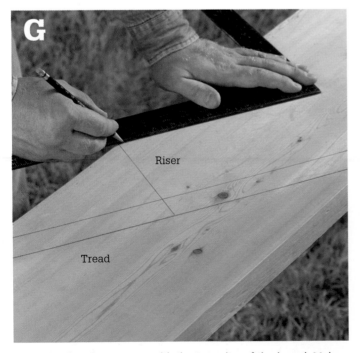

Align the framing square with the top edge of the board. Make the 11" tread mark by tracing along the square's tongue, the riser mark along the blade.

Install the decking by completing one row at a time.

5. Install the beams, securing them to the posts with metal T-anchors. Bend the side flanges of the anchors, as shown in the CORNER DETAIL AT ROOF BEAM LINE, and fasten the anchors with the recommended fasteners. Tie the beams together with galvanized metal plates fastened with 16d galvanized box nails.

Step J: Install the Hip Rafters

1. Cut the roof hub from an 8 × 8 post, following the RAFTER HUB DETAIL on page 158. You can have the hub cut for you at a lumberyard or cut it yourself using a table saw or circular saw (see photo A, page 106). Cut the post at 16", then mark an octagon on each end: make a mark 2⅛" in from each corner, and then join the marks. The cuts are at 45°. If you use a circular saw, extend the cutting lines down the sides of the post to ensure straight cuts.

2. Draw a line around the perimeter of the hub, 3½" from the bottom end. Center a metal anchor on each hub side, with its bottom flush to the line, and fasten it to the hub using the recommended nails.

3. Cut two pattern 2 × 6 hip rafters, following the RAFTER TEMPLATES on page 156. Tack the rafters to opposing sides of the hub and test-fit the rafters on the roof beams. The bottom rafter ends should fall over the post centers. Make any necessary adjustments to the rafter cuts.

4. Use a pattern rafter to mark and cut the six remaining hip rafters. Install the rafters, toenailing the bottom ends to the roof beams with one 16d common nail on each side. Fasten the top ends to the hangers with 1½" galvanized joist hanger nails, then install metal hangers at the bottom rafter ends.

Step K: Install Purlins & Intermediate Rafters

1. On each side of each hip rafter, measure up from the cut edge at the lower rafter end and make a mark at 51¾"—these marks represent the lower faces of the purlins (see the ROOF FRAMING PLAN, on page 156; the BUILDING SECTION, on page 153; and the RAFTER TEMPLATES).

2. Cut the 2 × 6 purlins, beveling the ends at 22½°. Position them between the rafters so their top edges are flush with the top edges of the rafters. Endnail or toenail each purlin to a rafter with 16d common nails.

3. Mark the layout for the intermediate rafters onto the tops of the roof beams, following the ROOF FRAMING PLAN.

4. Cut a pattern intermediate rafter, following the RAFTER TEMPLATES. Test-fit the rafter and make any necessary adjustments. Use the pattern rafter to mark and cut the fifteen remaining rafters.

5. Install the rafters, endnailing their top ends to the purlins and toenailing their bottom ends to the

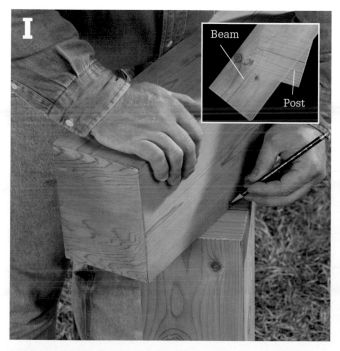

Mark the inside faces of the beams at the post centerlines. Mark the beam undersides along the outside post faces.

Attach the rafters to the hangers on the roof hub, driving the nails at a slight angle, if necessary.

roof beams with 16d nails. Install metal anchors to secure the bottom rafter ends to the roof beams.

Step L: Install the Collar Ties

1. Cut two 2 × 6 collar ties to span between the outsides of the roof beams, as shown in the ROOF FRAMING PLAN. Clip the top corners of the collar ties so they don't project above the top edges of the intermediate rafters.

2. Install the ties to the outside faces of neighboring intermediate rafters, as shown in the ROOF FRAMING PLAN—it doesn't matter which rafters you use, as long as the basic configuration matches the plan. Fasten the collar ties with 10d nails.

3. Set two uncut 2 × 6 collar ties on top of—and perpendicular to—the installed collar ties so both ends extend beyond the intermediate rafters on opposing sides of the roof (see the ROOF FRAMING PLAN). Mark the ends of the ties by tracing along the top rafter edges.

4. Cut the marked collar ties, and then clip the top corners. Fasten the collar ties to the outside faces of the intermediate rafters with 10d nails.

Step M: Add the Fascia & Roof Sheathing

1. Cut the 2 × 4 fascia, mitering the ends at 22½°. Install the fascia with its top edges ¾" above the rafters so it will be flush with the roof sheathing—use 16d galvanized casing nails.

2. Install the 1 × 6 tongue-and-groove roof sheathing, starting at the lower edge of the roof. Angle-cut the ends of the boards at 22½°, cutting them to length so their ends break on the centers of the hip rafters. Fit the tongue-and-groove joints together, and facenail the sheathing to the hip and intermediate rafters with 8d galvanized box nails.

Step N: Install the Roofing

1. Install metal drip edge along the bottom edges of the roof, angle-cutting the ends.

2. Lay 15# building paper over the sheathing and drip edge. Overlap the paper at each hip by 6".

3. Install the asphalt shingles on one section of the roof at a time. Trim the shingles flush with the hip ridges.

4. Cover the hip ridges with manufactured cap shingles or caps you cut from standard shingles.

5. Piece in metal flashing around the roof hub, and seal all flashing seams and cover all exposed nail heads with roofing cement.

6. Install the wood sphere on the center of the roof hub, using a large dowel screw.

Step O: Build the Overhead Lattice Screens

1. On the side faces of each post, mark the center of the post width. Then measure over, toward the gazebo center, one-half the thickness of the lattice

Bevel-cut the ends of the purlins so they meet flush with the rafter faces, and install them between the hip rafters.

Install the collar ties so that the upper pair rest on top of, and are perpendicular to, the lower pair.

Miter the ends of the sheathing boards and make sure the tongue-and-groove joints are tight before nailing.

panels and make a second mark. Use a level to draw a plumb line, starting from the second mark and extending down 17½" from the roof beam (see the ROOF EDGE DETAIL, on page 158). Draw a level line across the post face at the end of the vertical line (at the 17½" mark). Also, snap a chalk line between the vertical lines on the underside of the beams— these will guide the placement of the top inner stops.

2. Cut a cedar 2 × 4 rail to span between each set of posts, so the bottom rail edge is on the level line and the side face is on the plumb line—bevel the ends at 22½°. Fasten the rails to the posts with 3" deck screws.

3. Cut ⁵⁄₄ × ⁵⁄₄ (about 1⅛ × 1⅛" actual dimension) cedar inner stops to span between posts underneath the roof beams. Bevel the ends at 22½° and fasten the stops to the beams with 8d galvanized finish nails so their side faces are flush to the chalk lines.

4. The vertical stops of the overhead screens and the screens below the railings (Step P) are ⁵⁄₄ × ⁵⁄₄s that have one edge beveled at 22½°. It will save time to rip all of them at once, using a table saw, if available—you'll need about 110 linear feet.

5. Cut and install the inner vertical stops with their sides flush to the plumb lines drawn on the posts.

6. Cut eight lattice panels at 16 × 39⅝". Set the panels against the inner stops and rails and fasten them with 3d galvanized finish nails.

7. Cut and install the outer rails and stops to complete the screens. Fasten the rails with 3" deck screws driven through the inner rails, and fasten the stops with 8d galvanized finish nails driven into the posts and beams.

Step P: Build the Railings & Lower Lattice

1. Measure up from the deck and mark the side faces of each post at 3" and 36". Draw level lines across the faces at these marks. Draw a plumb line between the level marks by finding the post center and moving inward one half the thickness of the lattice, as you did in Step O.

2. Cut the 2 × 4 cedar top rails to fit between seven pairs of posts (skipping the two posts flanking the stairs), as shown in the DETAIL AT DECK EDGE, on page 158. Miter the rail ends at 22½° and install them with 3" deck screws so they are centered on the posts and their top faces are on the upper level lines.

3. Cut and install the 2 × 4 inner bottom rails and ⁵⁄₄ × ⁵⁄₄ stops, following the procedure in Step O.

4. Cut the lattice panels at 31 × 39⅝". Fasten the panels against the stops and lower rails with 3d galvanized finish nails.

5. Cut and install the outer bottom rails, securing them with screws, then cut and install the outer horizontal and vertical stops.

Shingle the roof sides individually, then cover the hip ridges with caps, overlapping the shingles equally on both sides.

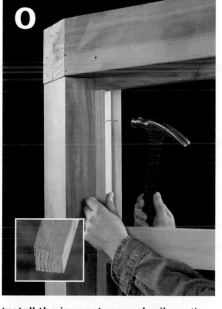

Install the inner stops and rails on the layout lines. The vertical stops are beveled at 22½° (INSET).

Set the lattice panels against the inner stops and rails, and fasten them with 3d galvanized finish nails.

Adding a wood deck below, as shown in this four-post structure, can turn a party shelter into a comfortable remote patio.

Party Shelter

A simple outdoor shelter is all about versatility. Rain or shine, it's always ready for picnics, outdoor projects, playing with the kids, or just lounging in the shade. And you never have to stop the party because of the weather.

The large shelter on page 169 covers a 12 × 16-foot area—plenty of room for a deck with a picnic table, or a sandbox and play structure. The sturdy post-and-beam design is ideal for custom add-ons, such as bamboo shades or hanging plants and vines. It's also easy to dress up with decorative details that match your house.

To simplify construction, the shelter's roof is framed with pre-built wood trusses. They are a standard type (6-in-12 slope and 10-foot. span) that should be available in stock at a local lumberyard or home center. You may also decide to order custom trusses built to your specifications. Be sure to specify the roof slope, roof span, and amount of overhang beyond the side beams (to create an eave). You may have to give several weeks' lead-time for custom trusses.

This multi-functional backyard landscape features a custom party shelter with arbor-style roof to define and shade the main patio space.

Dramatic embellishments, including a pagoda-style roof and traditional architrave, make this custom shelter as eye-catching as it is practical.

Material List

Description (No. finished pieces)	Quantity/Size	Material
Foundation		
Batterboards/braces	10 @ 8'-0"	2 × 4
Drainage material	1⅔ cu. ft.	Compactible gravel
Concrete tube forms	6 @ 14"-dia.	
Concrete	field measure	3,000 PSI concrete
Beam framing		
Posts (6)	6 @ 12'	6 × 6 rough-sawn cedar
Side beams (4)	4 @ 16'	2 × 8 pressure-treated
End beams (2)	2 @ 12'	2 × 8 pressure-treated
Lateral beams (4)	4 @ 10'	2 × 8 pressure-treated
Diagonal supports (8)	4 @ 8'	4 × 4 cedar
Roof Framing		
Gable braces (8)	4 @ 10', 2 @ 8'	2 × 4
Trusses, 2 end and 11 common (13)	13 @ 10' span	2 × 4 with 6-in-12 pitch
Purlins (10)	20 @ 8'	2 × 4
Metal hurricane ties	22, with nails	Simpson H-1
Metal hurricane ties	4, with nails	Simpson H-2.5
Roofing		
Metal roofing panels	8 @ 4' × 8'	with ridge cap and sealer strip
Gable Finishes		
Gable-end purlin blocking (16)	3 @ 8'	2 × 2
Blocking (8)	5 @10'	1 × 6
Gable sheathing (4)	2 @ 4 × 8'	¾" CDX plywood
Gable end fascia (4)	4 @ 8'	1 × 6 cedar
Side fascia (2)	4 @ 10'	1 × 8 cedar
Siding (14)	14 @ 8'	cedar siding with 6" reveal
Fasteners		
1½" deck screws		
2½" deck screws		
6d galvanized common nails		
8d galvanized common nails		
8d joist hanger nails		
10d galvanized common nails		
⅜" × 4" galvanized lag screws	48, with washers	
⅜" × 5" galvanized lag screws	12, with washers	
10d ringshank nails		
6d galvanized casing nails		
6d siding nails		
1" self-tapping metal roofing screws with rubber washers (as specified by metal roofing manufacturer)		
2½" self-tapping metal roofing screws with rubber washers (as specified by metal roofing manufacturer)		

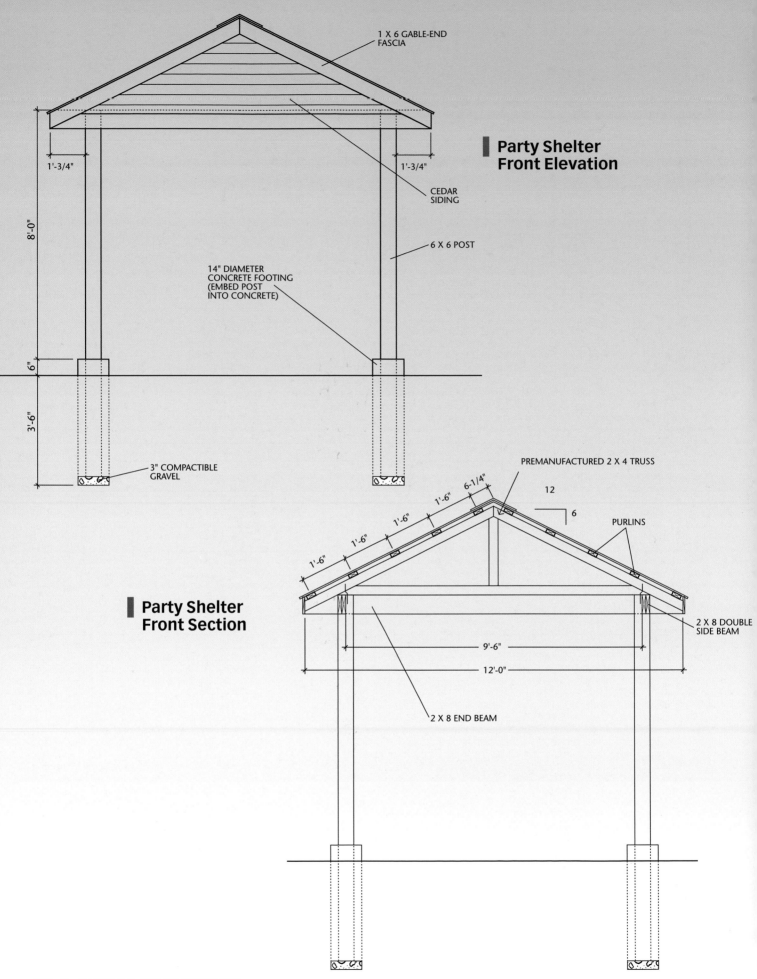

1 X 6 GABLE-END FASCIA

Party Shelter Front Elevation

CEDAR SIDING

6 X 6 POST

1'-3/4"

1'-3/4"

8'-0"

6"

3'-6"

14" DIAMETER CONCRETE FOOTING (EMBED POST INTO CONCRETE)

3" COMPACTIBLE GRAVEL

PREMANUFACTURED 2 X 4 TRUSS

6-1/4"

1'-6"

1'-6"

1'-6"

1'-6"

12

6

PURLINS

Party Shelter Front Section

2 X 8 DOUBLE SIDE BEAM

9'-6"

12'-0"

2 X 8 END BEAM

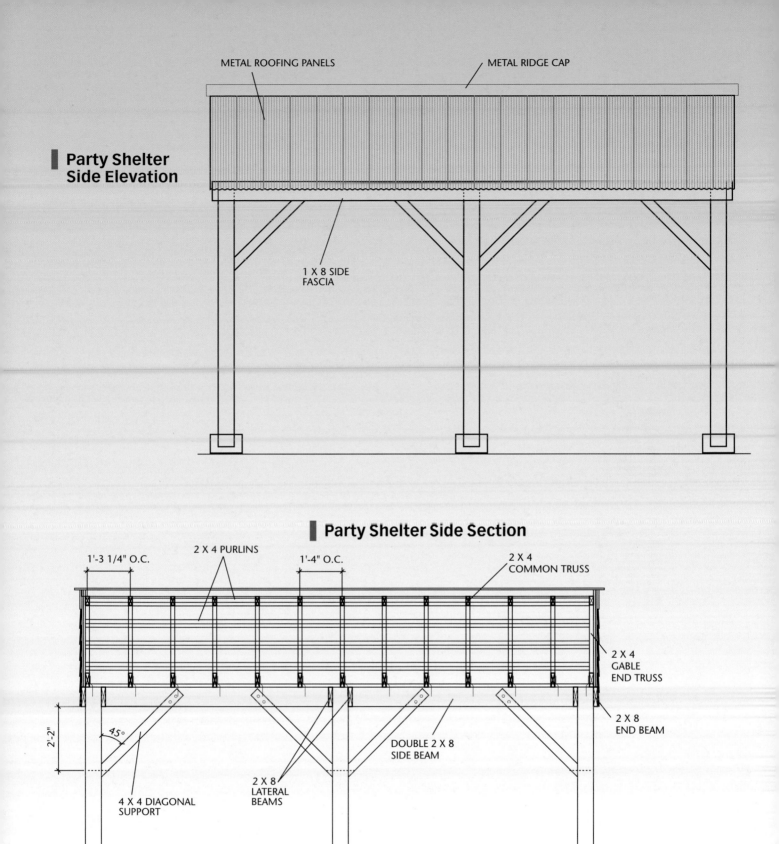

Party Shelter Side Elevation

METAL ROOFING PANELS

METAL RIDGE CAP

1 X 8 SIDE FASCIA

Party Shelter Side Section

1'-3 1/4" O.C.

2 X 4 PURLINS

1'-4" O.C.

2 X 4 COMMON TRUSS

2 X 4 GABLE END TRUSS

2 X 8 END BEAM

DOUBLE 2 X 8 SIDE BEAM

2'-2"

45°

4 X 4 DIAGONAL SUPPORT

2 X 8 LATERAL BEAMS

Party Shelter Beam Framing Plan

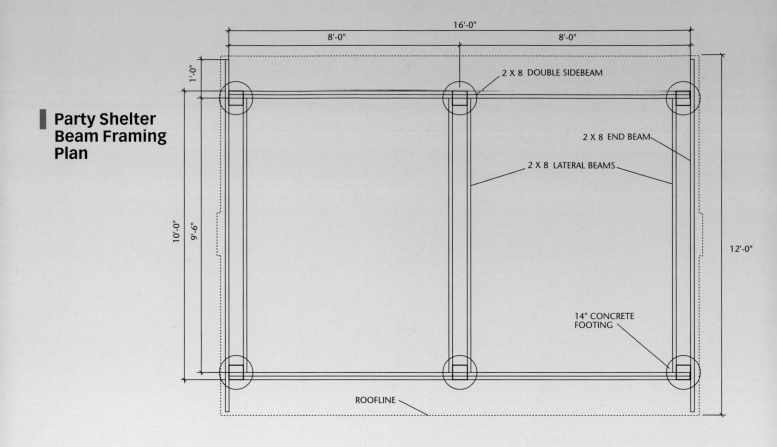

16'-0"

8'-0"   8'-0"

1'-0"

2 X 8 DOUBLE SIDEBEAM

2 X 8 END BEAM

2 X 8 LATERAL BEAMS

10'-0"

9'-6"

12'-0"

14" CONCRETE FOOTING

ROOFLINE

Party Shelter Diagonal Support Detail

Party Shelter Gable-End Detail

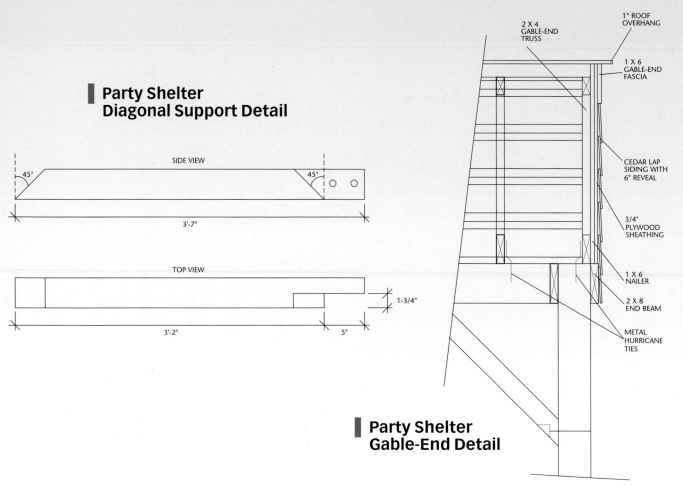

SIDE VIEW

45°   45°

3'-7"

TOP VIEW

1-3/4"

3'-2"   5"

2 X 4 GABLE-END TRUSS

1" ROOF OVERHANG

1 X 6 GABLE-END FASCIA

CEDAR LAP SIDING WITH 6" REVEAL

3/4" PLYWOOD SHEATHING

1 X 6 NAILER

2 X 8 END BEAM

METAL HURRICANE TIES

How to Build the Party Shelter

Step A: Locate the Footings

1. Lay out the rough location of the party shelter with stakes and string, in an area 10 ft. wide and 16 ft. long. Make sure the surface is relatively flat and even.

2. Build ten 2 × 4 batterboards (page 213). Fasten the cross pieces about 2" below the tops of the stakes, using 2½" deck screws.

3. Following the rough layout, establish the exact location of the front walls by positioning a pair of batterboards 12" outside the front rough layout string. Run a level mason's string roughly 3" inside the layout string, then remove all the rough layout stakes and string.

4. Measure along the front mason's string, and mark the centerpoint of the first post at 12", using masking tape. Measure and mark the second post at 114" from the first mark.

5. Set up additional batterboards and stretch two mason's strings perpendicular to the front wall string, so the strings intersect the centerpoints of the front posts. Use the 3-4-5 triangle method to establish right angles for both side wall strings (refer to page 213).

6. Measure along both side wall strings and mark the centerpoint of the end posts with masking tape at 186". Set up batterboards and run a mason's string that intersects the centerpoints for the back wall.

7. Check the mason's strings for square by measuring diagonally from corner to corner, adjusting the strings until the measurements are equal.

8. From the centerpoint of the front posts, measure along the side walls 93" and mark the centerpoints of the center posts, using masking tape. Set up batterboards and run a mason's string across the centerpoints.

9. Transfer the six post centerpoints to the ground using a plumb bob, then drive wooden stakes to mark their locations.

Step B: Install the Posts & Pour the Footings

1. Remove the mason's strings, leaving the batterboards in place. Dig 16"-diameter holes at least 42" deep, using a power auger or clamshell digger. Make sure the holes are centered on the stakes.

NOTE: Check with the local building department for size and depth requirements for footings in your area. Also see page 212.

Run mason's strings to determine the exact locations of the centerpoints of the posts.

Place a 12-ft. post in the footing hole and align with the mason's strings. Plumb the post and brace it on adjacent sides with 2 × 4s staked to the ground.

2. Pour 3" of compactible gravel into each footing hole. Cut 14"- diameter concrete tube forms to length, so the footings will be 6" above the ground. Insert the forms into the holes, then pack soil around each for support.

3. On each batterboard, measure 3" out from the original location and tack a new nail, then retie the mason's strings to establish the outside face of each wall.

4. Place a 12-ft. 6 × 6, rough-cut cedar post into the front corner concrete form tube. Align the post with the mason's strings in both directions.

5. Attach two 2 × 4 braces to the post on adjacent sides, using 2½" deck screws. Drive a pointed 2 × 4 stake into the ground next to the end of each brace. Check the post on adjacent sides for plumb, using a carpenter's level, making adjustments as necessary. Attach the braces to the stakes with two 2½" deck screws.

6. Install and brace the five remaining posts, then mix concrete and fill the form tubes to anchor the posts. Tamp the concrete with a long stick or rod to eliminate any air pockets. Recheck the posts for plumb, making necessary adjustments to the braces. Let the concrete cure for 1 week.

Step C: Notch the Posts

1. Measure up from the ground 102" and mark one of the front posts. Transfer the mark onto each side of the post, using a combination square.

2. From the height reference line, run a level mason's line across the faces of each of the five remaining posts and mark. Transfer the line to all sides of the posts with a combination square, then cut off the tops of all the posts at the line, using a reciprocating saw or handsaw.

3. Mark a 3" deep × 7¼" long notch on the outside face of each post. Cut out the notches with a reciprocating saw.

Step D: Install the Side Beams

NOTE: Refer to the BEAM FRAMING PLAN on page 172.

1. Cut four 2 × 8s at 192", using a circular saw, then clamp the boards together in pairs to make the side beams. Make sure the crowned edges are up and the ends are flush. Nail together using 10d common nails in rows of three, spaced every 16".

2. From the front end of each side beam, measure across the top edge and mark the truss locations at 1½" and 15¼". Then, measuring from the 15¼"

Mark 3" × 7¼" notches on the outside face of each beam and cut out with a reciprocating saw.

mark, make a mark every 16"—at 32", 48", 64" and so on, to the end of the side beam. Make a mark 1½" in from the remaining end. Following the plans, draw an "X" next to each mark, designating to which side of the line the trusses go. The first two trusses on each beam are closer together than the remaining trusses.

3. Lift the beams into the notches with the crown up. Clamp into position so the ends of the beams are flush with the edges of the posts.

4. Counterbore two ½"-deep holes using a 1" spade bit, then drill ¼" pilot holes into each beam at the post center locations. Drive ⅜" × 5" galvanized lag screws with washers into each hole.

Step E: Install the End Beams

NOTE: Refer to the BEAM FRAMING PLAN.

1. Cut two 2 × 8 end beams at 144", using a circular saw, then measure in from each end and mark a reference line at 12".

2. Position each end beam against the posts, with the top edge flush with the post tops. Match the reference lines to the outside faces of the side beams, and clamp the end beam in place.

3. Drill a pair of ½"-deep counterbored holes using a 1" spade bit, then drill 3½"-deep, ¼" pilot holes at each location. Position the holes side by-side, so one bores into the 3" post top created by notching, and the other into the end of the side beams.

4. Fasten the end beams to the posts, using ⅜" × 4" lag screws with washers.

Step F: Install the Lateral Beams

NOTE: Refer to the BEAM FRAMING PLAN.

1. At each pair of posts, measure the span between the interior faces of the side beams. Cut four 2 × 8 lateral beams to size, approximately 114", using a circular saw.

2. Lift each beam into position between the side beams and against the side of the remaining 3" section of the post tops. Make sure the top edge of the beams are flush with the tops of the posts and clamp in place.

Build the double side beams and lift into the notches. Drill counterbored pilot holes at each post, and secure with lag screws.

Cut the end beams to length, clamp in position, and drill counterbored pilot holes into the post and side beams. Fasten with lag screws.

3. Drill a pair of ½"-deep counterbored holes using a 1" spade bit, then drill 3½"-deep, ¼" pilot holes at each location.

4. Fasten the lateral beams with ⅜" × 4" lag screws with washers.

Step G: Install the Diagonal Supports

1. Cut eight 4 × 4 diagonal supports to size, following the DIAGONAL SUPPORT DETAIL on page 172.

2. At each post, measure down from the side beam and mark at 26". Position the mitered end of the support against the post, aligned with the mark, and the notched-out end against the bottom edge of the inner member of the side beam. Make sure the support is centered on the post, then clamp the support to the side beam.

3. At the notched end, drill a pair of ½"-deep counterbored holes, using a 1" spade bit, then drill ¼" pilot holes into the side beams. Attach the support with ⅜" × 4" lag screws with washers (two at each lateral beam end).

4. Measure up from where the support meets the post and mark 3" on-center. Drill a ½"-deep counterbored hole straight into the support at the mark, using a 1" spade bit, then drill a ¼" pilot hole into the post. Drive a ⅜" × 4" lag screw with washer into each hole and fasten tightly.

Step H: Install the Gable-end Trusses

1. To make the gable-end truss braces, cut 2 × 4s at 36" and 120", using a circular saw. Cut four pieces of each dimension to build four braces. Fasten the 36" pieces at one end of the 120" pieces, using 2½" deck screws.

2. Use two braces at each gable end. Place the 36" end of the brace at the top of the end beam, roughly 36" in from the post. Position the opposite end of the brace at the post, place a scrap piece of 2 × 4 between the brace and post, then clamp the brace at both the post and end beam.

3. Place the gable trusses on the ends of the side beams, flush against the braces. Align each truss with the reference marks on the side beams, then measure the overhang of each rafter tail to ensure proper placement.

4. Check to make sure the truss is plumb using a level, and clamp the truss to the braces. Use wood shims at the braces to keep the truss plumb, if necessary. Toenail the truss to the side beams, using 10d galvanized common nails.

5. Drive a 10d nail into the rafter tail of each gable truss and stretch a mason's string between the two ends. Make sure the string is flush across the tails; this string will serve as a guide for installing the common trusses.

Measure and cut the lateral beams to size, and clamp in position. Drill counterbored pilot holes and secure the beams with lag screws.

G

Notch out one end
of the diagonal supports
and cut the other end
at a 45° angle. Fasten
the supports in position
with ⅜" × 4" lag screws.

H

Gable-end
truss brace

Align gable trusses
with the reference lines
on the side beams.
Check for plumb, then
clamp trusses to 2 × 4
braces. Toenail in place
with 10d common nails.
INSET: Gable-end
hurricane tie.

Step I: Install the Common Trusses

1. Install three common trusses, following the truss layout on the top of the side beams. Align the tails of each truss with the mason's string. Toenail into place with 10d galvanized common nails.

2. Measure from one end of the 2 × 4 starter purlin at 96" and mark the 16" on-center truss spacing, following the measurements used for the side beams: mark at 1½" and 15¼", then every 16" for the remaining trusses. Following your plans, mark an "X" on one side, indicating the truss placement.

3. Measure and mark 8" down from the peak on the installed trusses. Position the purlin with its lower edge on the 8" mark, and the truss layout marks aligned with the trusses. Make sure the gable-end truss is plumb, then fasten the purlin in place with 10d galvanized ringshank nails. Align the remaining trusses with the reference marks on the purlin, and fasten in place.

4. Continue installing trusses, working along the purlin and aligning each truss with the layout marks on the side beams and the starter purlin. Check each truss for plumb, then toenail it to the side beams with 10d galvanized common nails and fasten to the purlin using 10d galvanized ringshank nails.

5. At the end of the first starter purlin, measure and mark a second 96" 2 × 4 with the same truss spacing, continuing the span to the rear gable-end truss. Align the new purlin with the reference mark on the rear gable-end truss and common trusses, make sure the rear gable-end truss is plumb, and attach the purlin with 10d galvanized ringshank nails.

6. Install the remaining trusses. Align each with the marks on the side beams and starter purlin. Check each for plumb, then toenail in place with 10d galvanized common nails, and fasten to the starter purlin with 10d galvanized ringshank nails.

7. With the trusses installed, secure each using metal hurricane ties. Fasten the hurricane ties to the side beams with 8d galvanized common nails and to the rafter tails with 8d joist hanger nails.

Step J: Install the Purlins

1. At each gable end, measure from the lower edge of the starter purlin and mark every 18" along the rafter chords to the tails, following the FRONT SECTION on page 170. Snap a chalk line across the rafter chords between each pair of marks.

2. Align 2 × 4 purlins across the trusses, flush with the ends of the gable-end trusses and aligned

Align the common trusses with the reference lines on the side beams and the starter purlins. Toenail trusses in place using 10d common nails. INSET: Hurricane tie for common trusses.

with their chalk lines, then fasten with 10d galvanized ringshank nails. (The last purlin should fall 2¼" from the ends of the rafter tails.) Repeat for the other side of the roof, and then remove the gable-end truss braces.

3. Fasten 2 × 2 blocking to the top of each gable-end rafter chord between the purlins, using 10d galvanized common nails.

Step K: Install the Blocking & Gable-end Sheathing

NOTE: Refer to the GABLE-END DETAIL on page 172.

1. Add 1 × 6 blocking to the chords and struts of the gable-end trusses. Measure and cut pieces to length as needed, using a rafter square to mark the angles for the 6-in-12 roof pitch. (Refer to page 222 for rafter square techniques.) Install the blocking over the rafter chords so the top edge is flush with the top of the purlins and blocking. Fasten the 1 × 6 blocking to the truss members with 6d common nails.

2. Measure the triangular shape of the gable-end wall, from the top edge of the end beam to the top edge of the blocking. Divide the area into two equal-sized triangular areas, and cut ¾" CDX plywood to fit. Attach the sheathing with 1½" deck screws.

Step L: Install the Fascia

1. Measure, mark, and cut 1 × 6 gable-end fascia boards—two for each gable end—long enough to extend from the peak to several inches past the end of the rafter tails following the FRONT ELEVATION on page 172. Use a rafter square to mark the peak-ends of the boards for a 6-in-12 roof pitch, then cut the angles.

2. Fasten the gable-end fascia boards to the gable sheathing, so the top edge of the boards are flush with the top of the sheathing. Use 6d galvanized casing nails.

3. Measure the span between the gable-end fascia boards at each end of the party shelter, then cut 1 × 8s to size for side fascia boards. Cut smaller board lengths to fit, if necessary, making sure seams fall on the ends of rafter tails. Fasten with 6d galvanized casing nails driven into the ends of the rafter tails. Make sure the top edge of the side fascia boards do not protrude above the top of the last row of purlins.

4. Trim the ends of the gable-end fascia flush with the side fascia, using a handsaw. Drive three 6d galvanized casing nails through the gable-end fascia, into the ends of the side fascia.

Install 2 × 4 purlins across the rafter chords of the trusses, spaced every 18" on-center. Fasten with 10d ringshank nails.

Attach 1 × 6 blocking to the chords and struts of the gable-end trusses. Make sure the blocking covers the ends of the purlins. Cut triangular pieces of plywood sheathing and fasten them with 1½" deck screws.

Cut side fascia boards to span between the gable-end fascia boards. Fasten to the ends of the rafter tails with 6d galvanized casing nails.

Gable-end fascia

Rafter tail

Side fascia

Install metal roofing so each panel overlaps the preceding panel. Fasten to the purlins, using self-tapping screws with rubber washers.

Step M: Install the Metal Roofing

NOTE: Follow the instruction provided by the manufacturer when installing metal roofing.

1. Lay the first roof panel across the purlins and position it so the finished edge of the panel extends approximately 2" beyond the gable-end fascia, and 2" past the side fascia.

2. Drive 1" roofing screws with rubber washers through the roof panel into the purlins. Space the fasteners according to the manufacturer's directions.

NOTE: Do not drive screws into the portion of the panel that will be overlapped by the next panel.

3. Install the subsequent panels, overlapping each preceding panel according to the manufacturer's directions. Work from one gable end to the other. Install the final panel so the finished edge overhangs the gable-end fascia by 2".

Step N: Install the Ridge Cap

1. Measure 6¼" down from the roof peak. Mark the location for the pre-formed rubber sealer strip. It should fall over the center of the starter purlin. Mark a reference line along both sides of the entire roof length.

2. Run a bead of exterior-grade silicone caulk along the reference line, then install the sealer strip. Install sealer strips to both sides of the peak.

3. Apply a caulk bead to the top of the sealer strip, then center the pre-formed metal ridge cap over the

peak so it overhangs the finished edges of the gable-end roof panels by 2". At each rib of the roof panels, drive 2½" roofing screws with rubber washers through the ridge cap, sealer strip, and roof panel and into the starter purlins.

Step O: Install the Gable Siding

NOTE: Refer to the FRONT ELEVATION and the GABLE-END DETAIL.

1. At each gable end, measure along the end beam—from fascia board to fascia board—and cut a 2"-wide starter strip (ripped from a piece of siding) to length. Use a framing square or rafter square to mark cutting lines on the ends to match the 6-in-12 roof pitch, then trim with a circular saw. Nail the strip to the end beam, flush with the bottom edge, using 6d siding nails.

2. Measure and mark a cutting line that matches the 6-in-12 roof pitch onto the end of a scrap piece of siding, using a framing square or a rafter square. Cut the siding at the roof pitch line, and use it as a template to mark siding for cutting.

3. Measure, mark, and cut the first piece of siding to length. Place the siding over the starter strip, overlapping the bottom ¼". Fasten with pairs of 6d siding nails, spaced every 12". With 8' material, you may need two pieces (and you'll center the joint).

4. Cut the next siding board so it overlaps the one below, creating a consistent reveal (amount of exposed siding). Be sure to keep the siding level. Continue to cut and install siding pieces until reaching the peak of the gable.

5. Seal all exposed lag screw heads and counterbored holes with silicone caulk. Finish as desired.

Roof cap

Sealer strip

Roof panel

Attach sealer strips (INSET) near the roof peak with a bead of caulk, then drive screws at each rib in the roof panels to secure the ridge cap.

O

Cut siding so each piece overlaps the previous to create a consistent reveal. Install siding up to the gable peak.

Connecting arbors with a traditional arch design creates an elegant border that frames the view beyond.

Wall of Arbors

With a wall of arbors, each arbor is self-supporting yet easily links to additional arbors to create anything from a pairing to a boundary wall. Planted with roses or flowering vines, it becomes a luxurious ornamental accent that can serve as a barrier or a welcoming entryway.

The arbor project beginning on page 183 is made entirely of copper. If you're new to soldering, this is a good project to start with—the size is manageable, and the joints don't have to be watertight. If you mess up a joint, you can always reheat the solder, pop off the fittings, and start over. Where precision counts is in the alignment of the connecting Ts, so the arbors fit together properly. See page 234 for step-by-step instructions on cutting and soldering copper pipe.

Cutting List

Description (No. finished pieces)	Quantity/Size	Material
Top of Arbor (8)	2"	½" copper pipe
Arch (8)	14¾"	½" copper pipe
Arch (8)	15"	½" copper pipe
First and last side panel (8)	8 @ 20"	½" copper pipe
First and last side panel (4)	4 @ 9¾"	½" copper pipe
Middle side panel (20)	20 @ 9¾"	½" copper pipe
Arch horizontal (16)	19½"	½" copper pipe
Arch horizontal brace (4)	19½"	½" copper pipe
Pipe (5)	10 @ 10'	½" copper pipe
Dowel (4)	6–8"	⅜" dowel
Jig cleats (2)	at least 46"	1 × 2
1" deck screws	8	
Scraps (2)	1 @ 8'	10 × 40" × ½" or thicker Plywood
½" elbows (8)	45°	copper
½" elbows (4)	90°	copper
#3 rebar (4)	36" sections	
½" tees (20), tee (12)		copper

Note: The measurements above are for two connected arbors.

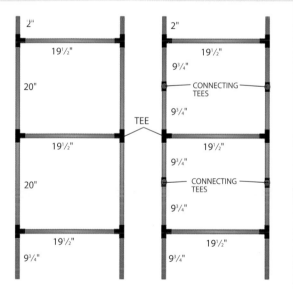

Wall of Arbors First & Last Side Panels

Wall of Arbors Middle Side Panel

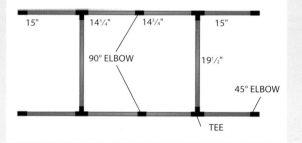

Wall of Arbors Plan

How to Build the Wall of Arbors

Step A: Cut the Pipe & Build a Support Jig

1. Measure, mark, and cut the copper pipe. Clean and flux the pipes.

2. To build a support jig, start with two scraps of plywood at least 10" wide and 35 to 40" long. Draw a line down the center of each piece of plywood; then drill two ⅜" holes, 20" apart along the line. Glue a 6 to 8" piece of dowel into each hole.

3. On each of two 1 × 2s, draw a pair of marks 42½" apart. Lay the 1 × 2s across the pieces of plywood, aligning the marks on the 1 × 2s with the lines on the plywood to set the exact spacing for the sides of the arch. Secure the 1 × 2s to the plywood, using 1" screws. See photo D on page 184.

Step B: Construct the Leg Assemblies

1. To construct a first and last side panel, slide a 9¾" length of pipe over each dowel, then alternate tees and pipe as indicated (see photo B).

2. Fit 19½" lengths of pipe between pairs of tees to form horizontal supports.

3. Construct a middle side panel following the MIDDLE SIDE PANEL on page 183.

Step C: Solder the Leg Assemblies

Disassemble the pieces and solder the joints in each leg assembly, working from the ground up. When the joints are cool, set the assemblies aside.

NOTE: In order to connect the arbors, it's very important that you solder the connecting tees so they're exactly perpendicular to the plane of the leg assemblies.

Step D: Construct the Arch

1. Working on a flat surface, connect two 14¾" lengths of pipe, using a 90° elbow. Add a tee, then a 15" length of pipe to each side. Repeat to form a second, identical arch.

2. Slide a 45° elbow onto each dowel of the support jig, and then slide the legs of the arches onto those elbows.

3. Add 19½" lengths of pipes between sets of tees, forming horizontal supports as shown in the PLAN on page 183.

4. Disassemble the pieces and build the arch assembly, soldering as you go (see page 235). When the joints are cool, set the assembly aside.

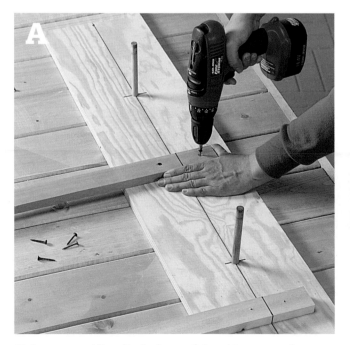

Make a support jig: attach pieces of dowel to scraps of plywood, then use 1 × 2s as spacers to set the distance between the sides of the jig.

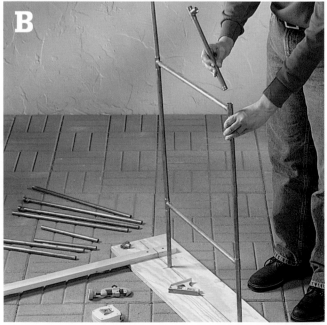

Dry fit the leg assemblies: alternate pipe and tees to form the legs, and then add horizontal supports.

5. Put the leg assemblies back onto the support jig and fit the arch assembly into place; solder the joints.

6. Repeat Steps B, C, and D to build as many arbors as necessary.

Step E: Install the First Arbor

1. If you're building a wall of arbors, use stakes and string to create a straight line for positioning of the arbors. Set the arbors in place, 19½" apart and aligned with the string.

2. Push down on the sides of the first arbor to mark the position of the legs on the ground; remove the arbor. At two opposite corners, drive a 3-ft. piece of rebar about 18" into the ground.

CAUTION: Buried utility lines are dangerous. Have your provider mark the utilities before digging any holes or driving anything deep into the soil (see page 21).

3. Fit two legs of the arbor over the buried rebar, firmly anchoring it in place.

Step F: Connect the Remaining Arbors

1. Flux the ends of a 19½" piece of pipe as well as the connecting tees on the inside faces of the first two arbors. Set the second arbor into place, aligned with the strings and 19½" from the inside face of the first arbor. Add the horizontal braces that connect the arbors.

2. Mark the leg positions and anchor two legs on the second arbor with rebar.

3. Solder the joints on the horizontal braces.

4. Repeat this process to install the remaining arbors.

Disassemble the pieces and solder each joint, working from the ground up.

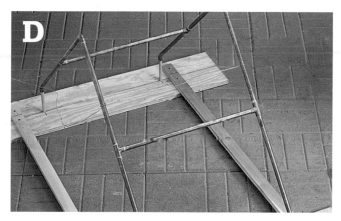

Using 90° elbows, pipe, and tees, build the arch assemblies. Connect the arches with horizontal braces.

Position the first arbor, and press its legs into the ground to mark their positions. At two opposite corners, drive 36" pieces of rebar 18" into the ground. Slide the arbor over the rebar.

Position and anchor the second arbor. Add horizontal braces, then solder them into position.

Freestanding Arbor

A freestanding arbor is a great project for the workshop. When you're done with construction, you can move the arbor anywhere you like. Perch it at the edge of your garden as an entryway, or anchor it to your deck and add some boards for built-in bench seating.

The arbor on page 188 is built entirely of cedar, giving it a distinctive Asian styling and making it a nice complement to a natural wood deck or a Craftsman-style house (of course out in the garden anything goes, stylewise). If you plan to paint the arbor, you can save money by using pressure-treated lumber instead of cedar. For safety, it's a good idea to anchor the arbor with stakes to prevent strong winds, or your kids, from tipping it over.

A portal-shaped arbor is a classic garden ornament, as shown in these three structures that were inspiration for our project (page 188). Adding your own details to the overhead beams and side frames is an easy way to personalize your creation.

Material List

Description (No. finished pieces)	Quantity/Size	Material
Posts		
Leg fronts (4)	4 @ 8'	2 × 4" Cedar
Leg sides (4)	4 @ 8'	2 × 4" Cedar
Cross beams (2)	1 @ 8'	2 × 4" Cedar
Top beams (2)	2 @ 8'	2 × 6" Cedar
Side Panels	2 @ 8'	2 × 6" Cedar
Side rails (2)	1 @ 8'	2 × 4" Cedar
Side spreaders (2)	1 @ 8'	2 × 6" Cedar
Roof		
Trellis strips (9)	5 @ 8'	1 × 2" Cedar
Cross strips (15)	5 @ 10"	1 × 2" Cedar
	10 @ 7"	
Braces (4)	1 @ 8'	2 × 6" Cedar
Hardware & Fasteners		
#10 × 2½" galvanized wood screws		
⅜"-dia. × 2½" galvanized lag screws	8	
6" galvanized lag screws	4	
2½" deck screws		
3" deck screws		

Freestanding Arbor Trellis Insert

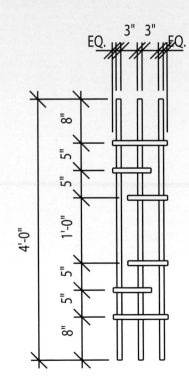

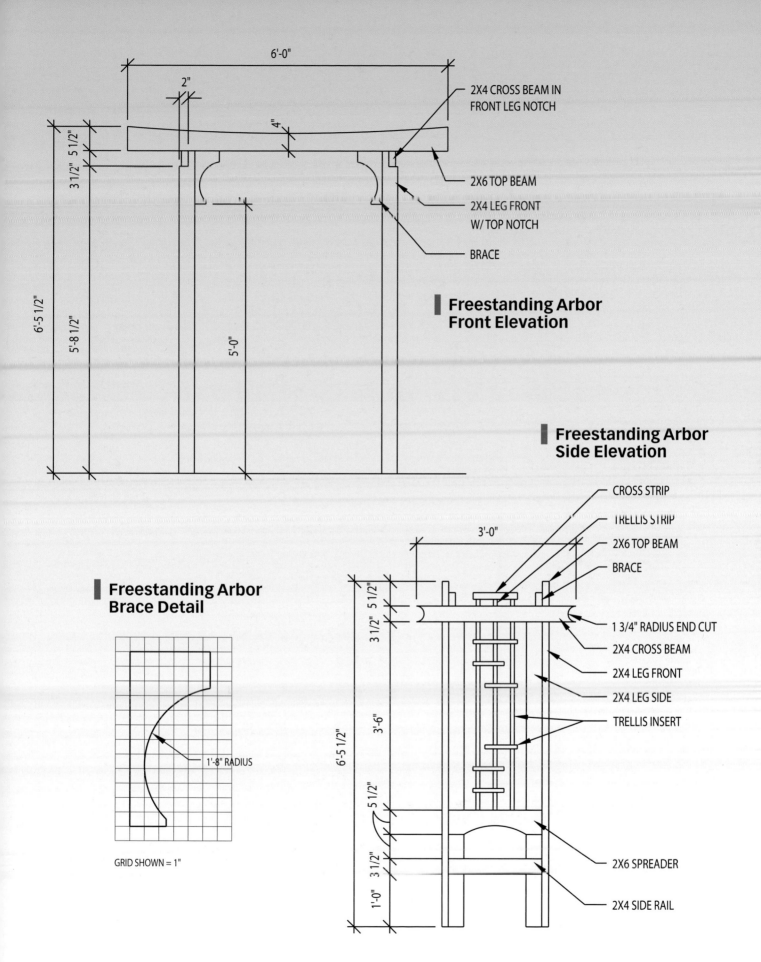

6'-0"

2"

4"

2X4 CROSS BEAM IN
FRONT LEG NOTCH

3 1/2" 5 1/2"

2X6 TOP BEAM

2X4 LEG FRONT
W/ TOP NOTCH

BRACE

6'-5 1/2"

5'-8 1/2"

5'-0"

Freestanding Arbor
Front Elevation

Freestanding Arbor
Side Elevation

Freestanding Arbor
Brace Detail

1'-8" RADIUS

GRID SHOWN = 1"

CROSS STRIP

TRELLIS STRIP

3'-0"

2X6 TOP BEAM

BRACE

3 1/2" 5 1/2"

1 3/4" RADIUS END CUT

2X4 CROSS BEAM

2X4 LEG FRONT

2X4 LEG SIDE

3'-6"

TRELLIS INSERT

6'-5 1/2"

5 1/2"

3 1/2"

1'-0"

2X6 SPREADER

2X4 SIDE RAIL

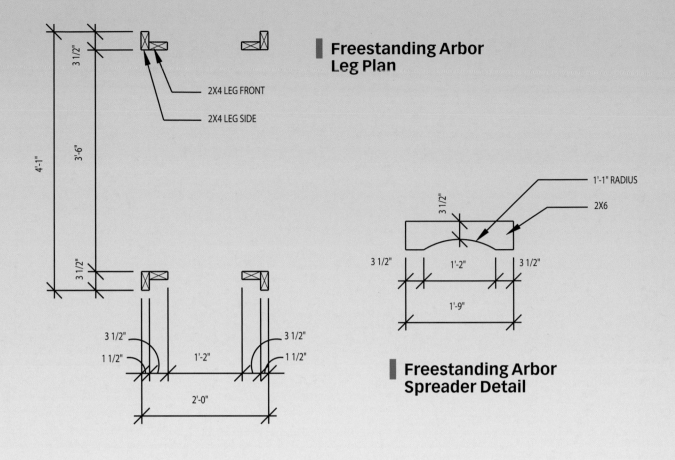

Freestanding Arbor Leg Plan

2X4 LEG FRONT

2X4 LEG SIDE

3 1/2"

4'-1"

3'-6"

3 1/2"

3 1/2"

1 1/2"

1'-2"

3 1/2"

1 1/2"

2'-0"

Freestanding Arbor Spreader Detail

1'-1" RADIUS

2X6

3 1/2"

3 1/2"

1'-2"

3 1/2"

1'-9"

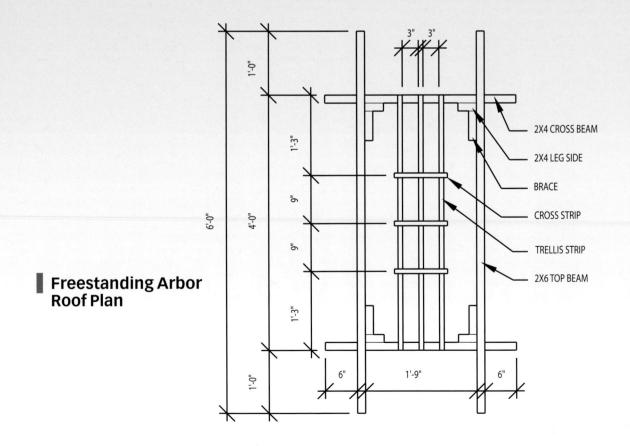

Freestanding Arbor Roof Plan

3" 3"

1'-0"

1'-3"

9"

9"

1'-3"

1'-0"

6'-0"

4'-0"

6"

1'-9"

6"

2X4 CROSS BEAM

2X4 LEG SIDE

BRACE

CROSS STRIP

TRELLIS STRIP

2X6 TOP BEAM

How to Build the Freestanding Arbor

Step A: Make the Legs

1. Cut the leg fronts and leg sides to length at 72" each. Position the leg sides at right angles to the leg fronts, with their top and bottom edges flush. Apply moisture-resistant glue to the joint. Attach the leg fronts to the leg sides by driving evenly spaced 2½" screws through the faces of the leg fronts and into the edges of the leg sides.

2. Use a jigsaw to cut a 3½"-long × 2"-wide notch at the top outside corner of each leg front. These notches cradle the cross beams when the arbor is assembled.

Step B: Cross beams, Rails, & Spreaders

1. Cut cross beams to length. Cut a small arc at both ends of each cross beam. Start by using a compass to draw a 3½"-diameter semicircle at the edge of a strip of cardboard. Cut out the semicircle, and use the strip as a template for marking the arcs. Cut out the arcs with a jigsaw. Sand the cuts smooth.

2. Cut two side spreaders to length at 21". The spreaders fit just above the side rails on each side. Mark a curved cutting line on the bottom of each spreader (see SPREADER DETAIL, page 190). To mark the cutting lines, draw starting points 3½" in from each end of a spreader. Make a reference line 2" up from the bottom of the spreader board. Tack a casing nail on the reference line, centered between the ends of the side spreader. With the spreader clamped to the work surface, also tack nails into the work surface next to the start/end points lines on the side spreader. Slip a thin strip of metal or plastic between the casing nails so the strip bows out to create a smooth arc. Trace the arc onto the side spreader, then cut along the line with a jigsaw. Sand smooth. Use the first spreader as a template for marking the second spreader. Cut and sand the second spreader.

3. Cut the side rails to length at 21".

Step C: Assemble the Side Frames

1. Lay two leg assemblies parallel on a work surface, with the notched board in each leg facing up. Space the legs so the inside faces of the notched boards are 21" apart. Set a 36" long cross beam into the notches, overhanging each leg by 6". Also set a side spreader and a side rail between the legs for spacing.

Create four legs by fastening leg sides to leg fronts at right angles.

2. Drill ⅜" pilot holes in the cross beam. Attach the cross beam to each leg with glue. Drive two ⅜"-dia. × 2½" lag screws through the cross beam and into each leg.

3. Position the side spreader between the legs so the top is 29½" up from the bottoms of the legs. Position the side rail so the top is 18" up from the leg bottoms. Drill counterbored pilot holes in the spreader and rail. Keeping the legs parallel, attach the pieces with glue and drive 3" deck screws through the outside faces of the legs and into the ends of the side rail and side spreader.

Step D: Attach the Side Trellis Pieces

1. Cut three vertical trellis strips to length for each side frame. Space them so they are 2⅜" apart, with the ends flush with the top of the cross beam.

2. Drill counterbored pilot holes to attach trellis strips to the cross beam and side spreader with 2½" deck screws. Repeat the procedure for the other side frame.

Step E: Shape Top Beams & Shape the Sides

1. Cut two top beams to length at 72" each. Following the same technique used to create the

arcs on the spreaders, draw 1½"-deep arcs at the top edges of the top beams, starting at the ends of each of the boards.

2. Cut the arcs with a jigsaw, and sand the edges smooth with a drum sander.

Step F: Assemble Top & Sides

1. Mark a centerpoint for a lag screw 12¾" from each end of each top beam. Drill a ¼" pilot hole through the top edge at the centerpoint. Set the top beams on top of the cross beams of the side frames. Mark the pilot hole locations onto the cross beams. Remove the top beams and drill pilot holes into the cross beams. Secure the top beams to the cross beams with 6" lag screws.

2. Cut four braces to length, and transfer the brace cutout pattern to each board. Cut the patterns with a jigsaw. Attach the braces at the joints where the inside faces of the legs meet the top beams, using 2½" deck screws.

3. Because the side frames are fairly heavy and bulky, you will need to brace them in an upright position to fasten the top beams between them. Using a pair of 1 × 4 braces, connect the tops and bottoms of the side frames.

4. Cut and attach three trellis strips (each at 48") between the top beams.

A piece of cardboard acts as a template when you trace the outline for the arc on the cross beams.

Lag-screw the cross beams to the legs, and fasten the spreaders and rails with deck screws to assemble the side frames.

Attach trellis strips to the cross brace and spreader with deck screws.

Step G: Add Trellis Cross Strips

1. Cut the cross strips to 7" and 10" lengths. For each side, add one 10" strip to the side trellis pieces, a few inches down from the cross beams, using 2½" wood screws driven through pilot holes.

2. Attach the first 7" strips below the 10" strips at 3" intervals, staggering the pattern as desired (photo G). You can adjust the sizes and placements of the cross strips, but for best appearance, retain some symmetry of placement.

3. Fasten 10" cross strips to the top trellis strips. Center the cross strips on the trellis strips, and space the cross strips at 3" intervals to match the side details.

4. Finish the project as desired.

OPTION: Create an outdoor seat by installing two 2 × 10 cedar boards on top the side rails of the frame. Overhang the rails by 6" or so, and attach the seat boards to the rails with 3" deck screws.

Use long pieces of 1 × 4 to brace the side frames in an upright, level position while you attach the top beams.

Lock the legs in a square position after assembling the arbor by tacking strips of wood between the front and back legs.

Attach the trellis cross strips to spice up the design and assist climbing plants.

Trellis Gate

A vine-filled trellis forms a charming garden entryway. With a built-in gate, a trellis is perfect for enclosing a space while adding tasteful decoration. The human scale and simple ornamentation of the project on page 197 make it a welcoming entry without taking over your yard. If you want your trellis gate to span an existing opening, you can easily adjust the width of the gate and length of the trellis tie beams to fit your space.

The trellis gate is best suited to a location where it receives plenty of sunlight to ensure abundant foliage growth. For plantings, choose perennials rather than annuals, since they will produce more luxurious growth over time.

Traditional wrought iron gate hardware adds a nice complement to a painted gate. Ornamental Victorian brackets like those used here are available at home centers or through architectural supply houses (see page 236). You might also hunt for some unique hardware and decorative pieces at architectural salvage dealers.

Three variations on our trellis gate design offer inspiration for custom styling: classical profiles cut into the beam ends of this trellis (left) lend a stately, traditional quality; an arched overhead section (right) changes the look dramatically, adding a fanciful touch; stout, unfinished posts and a simplified construction (below) give this garden entrance a rustic feel.

Cutting List

Description (No. finished pieces)	Quantity/Size	Material
Foundation		
Gate posts (2)	2 @ 8'	pressure-treated 4 × 4
Concrete	field measure	
Concrete tube forms (2)	field measure	12" dia.
Gravel	field measure	compactable gravel
Frames		
Horizontal braces (2)	12"	2 × 2
(8)	15¾"	2 × 2
(6)	33"	2 × 2
Vertical braces (4)	17"	2 × 2
(2)	54½"	2 × 2
Trellis posts (4)	87½"	2 × 4
Victorian millwork brackets (2)		
Stop (1)	46½"	1 × 2
Top		
Tie beams (2)	72¾"	2 × 4
Rafters (4)	33"	2 × 2
Stakes (2)	24"	pressure-treated or composite
Gate		
Frame top/bottom (2)	40½"	2 × 4
Frame vertical (2)	32¾"	2 × 4
Diagonal brace (1)	49½"	2 × 4
Pickets (7)	45¼"	1 × 4
(2)	45¼"	1 × 6
Fasteners		
3" corrosion-resistant lag screws		
1½" corrosion-resistant deck screws		
2½" corrosion-resistant deck screws		
6d corrosion-resistant finish nails		
1¼" corrosion-resistant deck screws		
Hinge hardware		
Gate handle		
Flexible PVC pipe	52½"	

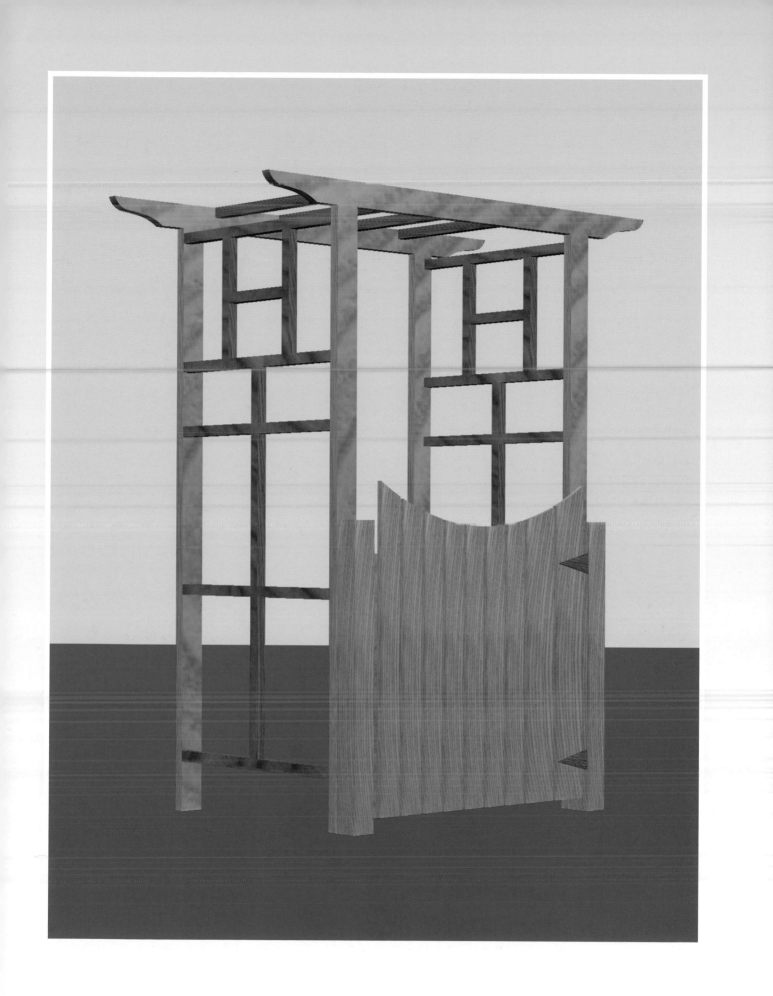

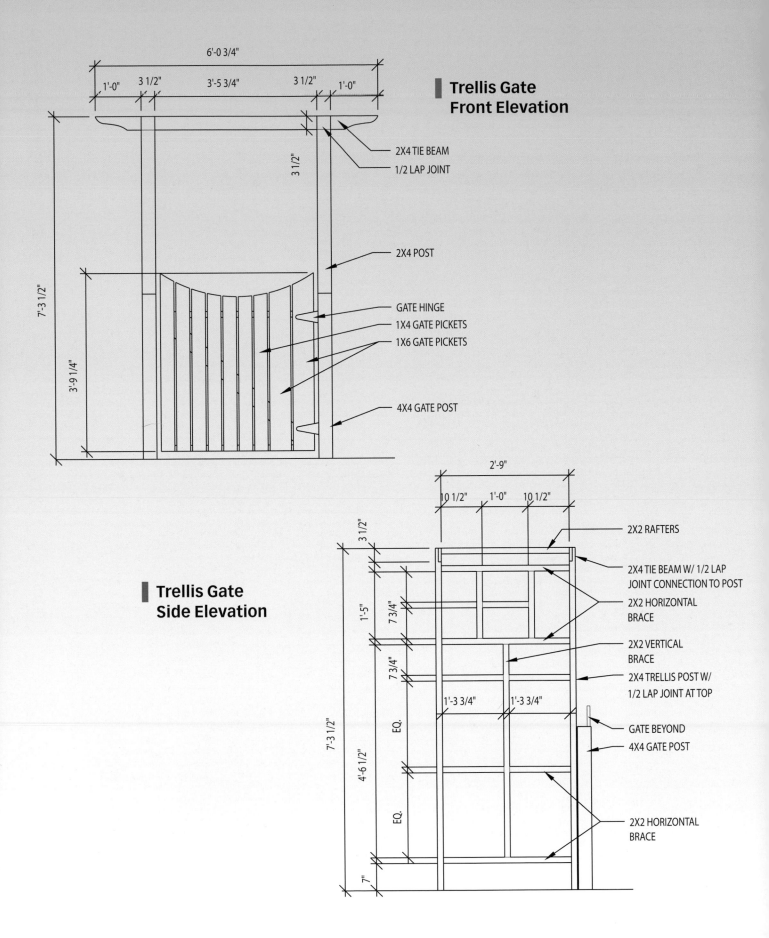

**Trellis Gate
Front Elevation**

6'-0 3/4"

1'-0" 3 1/2" 3'-5 3/4" 3 1/2" 1'-0"

3 1/2"

2X4 TIE BEAM

1/2 LAP JOINT

7'-3 1/2"

3'-9 1/4"

2X4 POST

GATE HINGE

1X4 GATE PICKETS

1X6 GATE PICKETS

4X4 GATE POST

**Trellis Gate
Side Elevation**

2'-9"

10 1/2" 1'-0" 10 1/2"

3 1/2"

1'-5"

7 3/4"

7 3/4"

1'-3 3/4" 1'-3 3/4"

EQ.

EQ.

7'-3 1/2"

4'-6 1/2"

7"

2X2 RAFTERS

2X4 TIE BEAM W/ 1/2 LAP
JOINT CONNECTION TO POST

2X2 HORIZONTAL
BRACE

2X2 VERTICAL
BRACE

2X4 TRELLIS POST W/
1/2 LAP JOINT AT TOP

GATE BEYOND

4X4 GATE POST

2X2 HORIZONTAL
BRACE

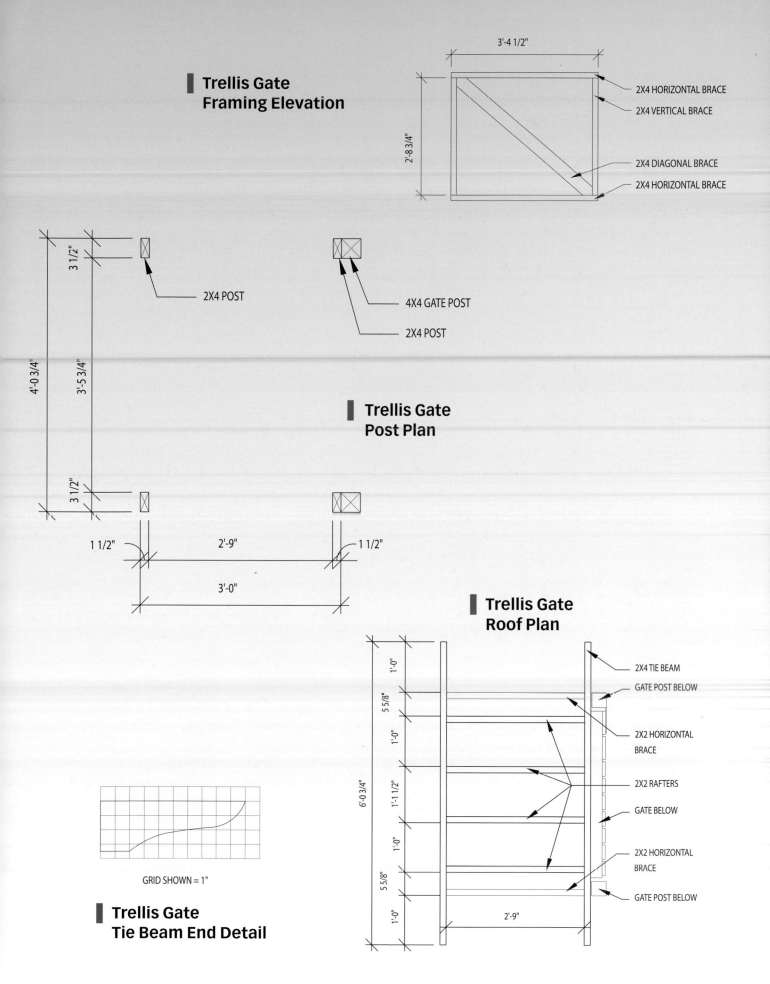

**Trellis Gate
Framing Elevation**

3'-4 1/2"

2'-8 3/4"

2X4 HORIZONTAL BRACE
2X4 VERTICAL BRACE
2X4 DIAGONAL BRACE
2X4 HORIZONTAL BRACE

3 1/2"

2X4 POST

4X4 GATE POST
2X4 POST

**Trellis Gate
Post Plan**

4'-0 3/4"

3'-5 3/4"

3 1/2"

1 1/2"

2'-9"

1 1/2"

3'-0"

**Trellis Gate
Roof Plan**

1'-0"

5 5/8"

1'-0"

1'-1 1/2"

6'-0 3/4"

1'-0"

5 5/8"

1'-0"

2'-9"

2X4 TIE BEAM
GATE POST BELOW
2X2 HORIZONTAL BRACE
2X2 RAFTERS
GATE BELOW
2X2 HORIZONTAL BRACE
GATE POST BELOW

GRID SHOWN = 1"

**Trellis Gate
Tie Beam End Detail**

How to Build the Trellis Gate

Step A: Install the Gate Posts & Assemble the Trellis Frames

1. Set 4 × 4 gate posts in concrete; follow the procedure shown on page 220 (check with the local building department for recommendations on gate-post depth). Position the posts so their inside faces are 41¾" apart, and make sure they are perfectly plumb. If you desire a broader or narrower gate, determine the gate width, then add 1¼" to that dimension to find the inside post spacing (this leaves a ⅝" gap at either side of the gate).

2. Cut all of the pieces for the trellis gate. For those building a custom width, make the tie beams for the trellis about 32" longer than the width of the gate.

3. Mark the cuts for the half-lap joints on the tie beams and trellis posts; follow the FRONT ELEVATION on page 198. Set a circular saw to a depth of ¾". Cut first on your layout marks, then make a cut about every ⅛" in between. Remove the waste wood and smooth the lap surface with a sharp chisel.

Step B: Anchor the Frame to the Gate Posts

1. Referring to the POST PLAN on page 199 and to your own gate measurements, mark the positions of the trellis frame on the ground, using stakes and string. Make sure the layout is square by measuring from corner to corner and adjusting the stakes until these diagonal measurements are equal.

2. On a flat surface, lay out all of the pieces for both sides of the trellis (to make sure everything fits and the assemblies are square). Refer to ELEVATION DETAILS, pages 198 to 199. Drill pilot holes, and fasten the pieces together with 2½" galvanized deck screws at each joint. Do not attach the tie beams in this step.

3. Set one trellis frame into position, with the inside face of the frame flush with the inside face of the gate post. Drive a 24" pressure-treated stake behind the opposite side of the frame to hold the trellis in position. Drill three evenly spaced pilot holes through the frame and into the gate post. Attach the frame to the post, using 3" lag screws.

Cut and lay out the pieces for each side of the trellis frame, then secure each joint with 2½" corrosion-resistant deck screws. INSET: Set the blade depth on a circular saw to ¾". Make the joint, then make a cut every ⅛" to ¼" in the joint area. Remove the waste material, using a chisel.

Position the trellis frames, clamping them against the gate posts. Attach the frames to the gate posts with 3" lag screws.

4. Repeat #1 and #2 to attach the other trellis frame to the opposite post.

5. Make a cardboard template for the shaped ends of the tie beams; follow the TIE BEAM DETAIL on page 199. Transfer the shape onto the ends of the tie beams. Cut out the shapes using a jigsaw or bandsaw, and sand the contours smooth.

6. Paint, stain, and/or seal the pieces as desired. Coat all sides and edges, and allow the finish to thoroughly dry.

Step C: Secure the Free Trellis Posts

1. Measure between the frame sides to make sure they are parallel and square to the plane of the posts.

2. Drive a 24"-long stake behind each unattached trellis post, measure again for square, then anchor the stakes to the posts with lag screws driven through pilot holes.

Step D: Install the Tie Beams

1. Position a tie beam flush with the top of the posts. Clamp the beam into place and drill pilot holes

Square the trellis frames, then secure the free end of each frame to a stake, using a lag screw.

Clamp the tie beams to the trellis posts, then attach with five 1¼" corrosion-resistant deck screws at each joint.

Attach four evenly spaced rafters between the tie beams, using 2½" corrosion-resistant deck screws.

through it and into each post. Drive five 1¼" corrosion-resistant deck screws into each joint to attach the tie beam to the posts.

2. Repeat #1 to install the remaining tie beam.

Step E: Attach the Rafters

Hold a 2 × 2 rafter in position between the tie beams, flush with the tops of the beams. Drill pilot holes through the tie beams, one into each end of the rafter; secure the rafter with 2½" corrosion-resistant deck screws. Repeat, placing a total of four evenly spaced rafters across the span of the tie beams.

Step F: Add the Trim

Set a millwork bracket into place at each of the corners between the tie beams and the trellis posts. Drill pilot holes and secure the brackets, using finish nails.

Step G: Build the Gate Frame

1. Lay out the parts of the gate frame and measure from one corner to the diagonally opposite corner. Repeat at the opposite corners. Adjust the pieces until these measurements are equal, meaning the frame is square. Secure each joint, using 2½" corrosion-resistant deck screws.

2. Measure again for squareness, then position the 2 × 4 diagonal brace so it runs from corner to

corner, resting against the gate frame. Mark the angle of the cutting lines, then cut the brace to fit, using a circular saw. Use 2½" corrosion-resistant deck screws to secure the diagonal brace into position.

Step H: Add the Pickets

1. Clamp a 2 × 4 across the bottom of the frame to act as a reference for the length of the pickets (see photo H). Position the pickets flush with the lower edge of the clamped 2 × 4.

2. Align the right edge of a 1 × 6 picket flush with the right edge of the frame. Drill pilot holes and attach the siding to the frame, using 1½" corrosion-resistant deck screws.

3. Set scraps of ⅝" plywood in place as spacers, then add a second 1 × 6 picket. Continuing to use the ⅝" plywood as spacers, cover the remainder of the frame with 1 × 4 pickets.

Step I: Hang the Gate

1. Measure and mark the hinge positions on the gate. Drill pilot holes and drive screws to secure the hinges to the gate.

2. Shim the gate into position, centered within the opening. Use a carpenter's level to make sure the gate is level and plumb. Mark the hinge-side post to

Add millwork brackets at each corner where the tie beams and the trellis frame posts meet. Secure with finish nails.

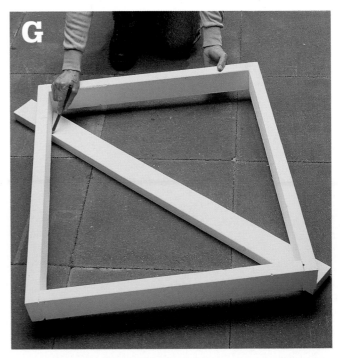

Lay out the gate frame pieces, check for square, and secure the joints with 2½" corrosion-resistant deck screws. Mark and cut the diagonal brace, then screw it in place, using 2½" corrosion-resistant deck screws.

gate is level and plumb. Mark the hinge-side post to indicate the hinge screw locations, then drill pilot holes. Fasten the hinges to the post, using the screws provided with the hinge hardware.

3. Mark the position of the stop. Drill pilot holes and secure the stop to the post, using 1½" corrosion-resistant deck screws.

Step J: Shape the Pickets & Add the Gate Handle

1. Cut a piece of flexible PVC pipe 52½" long (or 12" longer than the width of your gate). Clamp the PVC at the top of the outside edges of the last picket on each side of the gate.

2. Tack a nail just above the top of the frame at the center of the gate. If this happens to be between two pickets, set a wood scrap behind the picket to hold the nail. Adjust the PVC until it fits just below the nail and creates a pleasing curve.

3. Trace the curve of the PVC onto the pickets. Remove the pipe and cut along the marked line, using a jigsaw. Sand the tops of the pickets and finish as necessary.

4. Mark the handle location on the gate. Drill pilot holes and secure the handle, using the screws provided by the manufacturer.

Clamp a 2 × 4 across the bottom of the gate frame as a guide, then attach the pickets. Begin with two 1 × 6s on the hinge side, then finish with 1 × 4s. Use scraps of ⅝" plywood as spacers.

Clamp a 1 × 2 stop to the latch-side gate post and secure with 1½" corrosion-resistant deck screws.

Clamp the ends of a length of PVC pipe at each end of the gate top. Bend the pipe down to create the curve, and trace. Cut the pickets to shape, using a jigsaw.

The Nuts & Bolts

Picked a project? This chapter will help you get started on the practical matters of shopping for materials and learning some basic construction skills. When you begin the building process, look here for detailed steps on certain procedures, like building foundations and installing roofs.

In This Section

- Buying Lumber
- Finishes for Outdoor Projects
- Other Building Materials
- Hardware & Fasteners
- Tools
- Building Foundations
- Cutting Roof Rafters
- Roofing
- Working with Copper Pipe

Cedar

Redwood

Pressure-treated Pine

Buying Lumber

There are a few choices of lumber for outdoor building projects. Availability varies by location, but generally the options are redwood, cedar, and pressure-treated pine. All of these share one vital characteristic: they are resistant to rot and insects. Standard lumber, such as untreated pine, is too vulnerable to decay and infestation for use on outdoor structures.

Redwood

The best all-around lumber for outdoor applications, redwood is beautiful, strong, and easy to work with. It's also expensive. Redwood is naturally resistant to rot and insects. However, only all-heart (heartwood) redwood is suitable for ground contact.

Redwood comes in two basic classifications: heartwood, from the inner portion of the tree; and sapwood, from the tree's outer layers. Heartwood is harder, darker, and generally more attractive than sapwood. Of course, it also costs more. Because redwood is available in several grades, you can use less expensive cuts on inconspicuous areas of your project and spend more for the critical parts.

Redwood has a high tannin content and will turn black if it contacts hardware containing iron. To prevent black stains and streaks, use only stainless steel; aluminum; or high quality, galvanized steel hardware. Stainless steel offers the best protection, but it is the most expensive.

Cedar

Cedar, specifically western red cedar, has many of the same properties as redwood. It's attractive, lightweight, easy to work with, and naturally rot-resistant. It's also available in heartwood and sapwood, the former being the higher quality. As with

redwood, anything but stainless steel, aluminum, and galvanized hardware will stain the wood, and even galvanized hardware may produce some discoloration.

Both cedar and redwood are available with rough or smooth surfaces. For example, S4S cedar is milled smooth on all four sides; S2S is smooth on two sides and rough on two sides. A rough surface can add to the lumber's actual dimensions, so you might have to adjust your measurements accordingly.

Pressure-treated lumber

Typically, treated pine or fir lumber is chemically treated to stand up to outdoor exposure. It's the least expensive option but is a perfectly suitable material, if not the most attractive.

Most treated lumber has a greenish color resulting from the chemical treatment, but you might prefer the brownish version, if available. Both types weather to a silvery gray. For parts that will be on or within 12" of the ground, use only lumber rated for "Ground Contact."

Because of its strength and affordability, treated lumber is a good option for the concealed structural parts of a project. You can still use redwood or cedar—or even a higher quality treated lumber—for the more visible parts, and no one's the wiser.

Arsenic and old lumber

Prior to 2004, most pressure-treated lumber was treated with CCA (chromated copper arsenate), which contains arsenic. The lumber industry is now using non-arsenic treatments for all residential-use lumber. However, as in the old days, it's recommended that you wear a dust mask when cutting treated lumber. Never burn the scraps.

Finishes for Outdoor Projects

Redwood, cedar, and pressure-treated lumber all change to a weathered gray over time. But finishing the wood helps it to look better, longer; it also helps inhibit mildew and fungal growth and makes it more resistant to water damage. Unfortunately, no single finish does it all. In fact, the only finish that truly protects wood from discoloration is a well-maintained paint job.

Thus, the paradox of outdoor finishes: clear finishes expose the wood's natural beauty but leave it more vulnerable to the damaging effects of the sun. Heavier and less transparent finishes provide more UV protection but obscure the wood's natural coloring.

Here is an overview of the basic types of finishes. For more information about your specific application, contact the finish manufacturer. The lumber resources on page 236 also have helpful tips on protecting redwood, cedar, and southern yellow pine.

Clear Finishes

Water repellants (or water sealers) are clear, wax-based liquids that seal the wood's pores to inhibit water damage. Some include a mildewcide and/or a fungicide for added protection in damp areas (check the manufacturer's recommendations about using these formulas on seats, tables, and other direct-contact surfaces).

Clear finishes with a UV-blocking formula will slow discoloration and sun bleaching somewhat but won't do much in the long run. The wax wears off, and water-repellant finishes must be reapplied every 1 to 2 years.

Clear varnish, such as polyurethane, spar varnish, and marine varnish, form a sealed layer on top of the wood. As the wood expands and contracts, an inflexible varnish may crack and peel. For this reason, many experts recommend against varnish for outdoor projects.

Stain

There are three classes of stain: transparent, semi-transparent, and solid-body. "Exterior" formulas typically offer some UV protection, but for the most part, transparent stain does little more than color the wood.

Semi-transparent stain is a thicker version, offering a little more protection from the sun. It penetrates the wood, like transparent stain, leaving the wood's texture intact but producing a more consistent pigmented color.

Solid-body (or solid-color) stains are a cross between stain and paint. Like paint, they form an opaque film over the surface, yet they allow more of the wood's texture to show. Solid-body stains come in latex and oil-based versions. The California Redwood Association recommends oil-based stain for redwood.

Paint

Paint is the most durable outdoor finish and the best at hiding unsightly wood. You'd be nuts to spend the extra money on redwood or cedar just to cover it with paint, but pressure-treated lumber is another story. However, because treated lumber often contains a lot of water when you buy it, make sure it's dry before painting.

Redwood with clear finish

Cedar with transparent stain

Treated pine with semi-transparent stain

Rough cedar with solid-body stain

Treated pine with paint

Lattice panels (above) are bought in sheets but can be cut to size using a circular saw with a carbide-tipped blade. For decorative curved cuts use a jigsaw or a reciprocating saw with a fine-toothed blade.

There are many ways to incorporate materials into a finished project. Here, bamboo screens are hung by simple hooks to add texture and shade (right).

Other Building Materials

Gardens and outdoor rooms have always inspired creative uses of materials. While plywood is great for storage sheds, gazebos and garden spaces call for something more charming or unexpected. Here are just a few ideas for expanding your materials list.

Lattice

Prefabricated lattice panels provide instant structure without totally enclosing a space. They're commonly available in cedar and redwood, in diagonal and square patterns. Lattice is also available in low-maintenance plastic or vinyl that can be painted or left bare. Most wood lattice comes in 4 × 8-ft. panels, in ½", ¾", and 1" total panel thicknesses.

Wood lattice panels are made up of individual slats stapled and sometimes glued together and are actually fairly strong as a flat barrier. They should never be used for structural support, however. Look for lattice with well-concealed staples and uniform slats.

When working with lattice, mark your cuts with a chalk line, and use a circular saw with a carbide-tipped blade to make the cuts. You can cut right through the staples, but make sure to wear safety glasses. For curved cuts, you can use a jigsaw or a reciprocating saw with a fine-toothed blade to minimize splintering. Fasten lattice panels with nails or screws driven through pilot holes to prevent splitting the wood.

Copper Pipe

Copper is great for outdoor projects. It never rusts or corrodes, it develops a beautiful patina over time, and it assembles like a toy construction set. Your local hardware store or home center carries copper pipe in rigid and flexible forms, ranging upward from ¼" in diameter.

To build with copper, simply join lengths of pipe with copper fittings and solder the pieces together (see pages 234 to 235). Copper works well by itself, as in the Wall of Arbors (page 182), or integrated with a wood structure, as in the Wood & Copper Arbor (page 64).

Bamboo

One of nature's most versatile building materials, bamboo is a woody grass with a tough outer layer that needs no protective finish. It's also naturally rot-resistant. A bamboo mat or series of spaced poles is great for adding extra shade to an overhead or to create a privacy screen. Light filtering through bamboo creates a warm, sun-dappled interior.

Bamboo is available from importers and domestic growers in a huge variety of species, colors, textures, and sizes (Resources, page 236). You can order anything from pre-cut and assembled grass mats to split slats to individual poles up to 6" in diameter. Bamboo is usually assembled and secured with rust-proof wire, but suppliers also carry rope, raffia, and other tie materials for creating various traditional and custom effects.

Like tree lumber, bamboo weathers to a silvery gray. You can slow this process somewhat by applying a wax or liquid floor polish. Check with the supplier about working with and maintaining your specific type of bamboo.

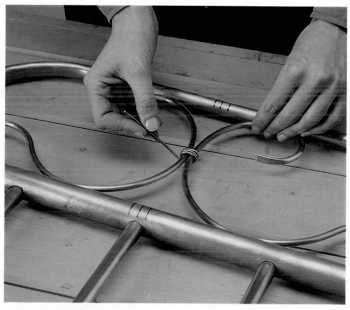

You can build simple frames with rigid copper pipe, then use thin flexible pipe and copper wire to create decorative accents.

Hardware & Fasteners

All hardware for outdoor projects must be rust resistant. This includes nails, screws, hinges, nuts, and bolts—essentially any metal used for holding things together. The most common type is galvanized steel, which has a zinc coating or other treatment to prevent corrosion. Aluminum and stainless steel hardware are naturally rust-proof.

For nails, use hot-dipped galvanized steel rather than the smoother, electroplated type. Hot-dipped fasteners are recognizable by their rough, silver-colored coating, which provides better rust protection than electroplating and is less likely to stain redwood and cedar. Stainless steel fasteners are really the only guaranteed protection against staining, but the cost usually makes them impractical for all but the most critical applications.

Framing connectors

Some of the projects in this book call for framing connectors—galvanized metal plates and fittings used to reinforce framing connections. All of the connectors called for in the plans are Simpson Strong-Tie® brand and are identified by a specific part number. These connectors are commonly available at lumberyards and home centers. If you can't find what you need at the store, try the manufacturer's online catalog (www.strongtie.com). You can also order custom-made connectors.

IMPORTANT: Framing connectors and anchors are effective only when they are installed correctly, using the specified type and number of fasteners. If your nails are too thin, for example, the connector might shear them off, setting your framing free. Always follow the manufacturer's instructions.

Commonly used framing connectors and anchors include: Joist hanger (A), angled joist hanger (B), rafter tie (C), post-beam caps (D), stair cleat (E), hurricane tie (F), post base assembly (G), joist tie (H), and angle bracket (I).

Tools

H ere's a look at many of the hand and power tools mentioned in this book.

Power Tools (right): Some power tools are essential, including the circular saw (A) and drill with keyless chuck (B). Others just make jobs a lot easier: the power miter saw (C) makes quick, accurate cuts at any angle; the reciprocating saw (D), the ultimate multipurpose saw, is easily portable and makes straight or curved cuts in almost any material, including heavy timbers; a jigsaw (E) is best for clean, detailed curved cuts in various materials, especially thin sheets and fragile products; a ½" hammer drill (F) is a heavy-duty drill with a hammering motion for effective drilling into masonry, stone, and concrete.

Hand Tools (below): These include standard carpentry tools—plus a few landscaping tools for digging holes, chipping stone or concrete, and leveling the ground.

Rental & Landscape Tools (above): When you need the big guns, it usually makes more sense to rent than to buy. You might need any of these tools for clearing your project site or building the foundation: power auger (A), power tamper (B), power sod cutter (C), pick (D), weed trimmer (E), come-along (F), and garden rake (G).

Building Foundations

The two types of foundations used in the projects in this book are the concrete pier and the concrete slab. Many of the projects also involve setting structural posts in the ground with concrete, so that procedure is shown here as well.

Regardless of what the plans in this book call for, your foundation must comply with the local building codes. The main reasons for this are climate and weather. In Arizona, for example, foundation piers don't need to be as deep as in Minnesota, where the ground might freeze to a depth of four feet each year. High winds and poor soil are other factors that must be accounted for on a case-by-case basis.

REMEMBER: Have all your utility lines marked before you start digging into your yard (see page 21).

Concrete Pier Foundation

A concrete pier foundation consists of poured-concrete cylinders that support wood posts. The piers, or footings, are the same as those used for deck construction. They are easy to make using cardboard forms that you cut to size.

To anchor the posts to the footings, it's best to use galvanized metal post bases. There are several easy-to-use adjustable types available, which are secured to the footing by means of a J-bolt set into the concrete. After the concrete is dry, you bolt down the base, set and plumb the post, and fasten the post to the base.

Pier foundations work well for gazebos because they allow you to build an elevated floor while keeping the structure securely planted in the earth. Some projects call for pads made from pressure-treated 2× lumber instead of posts. The pads are anchored to the piers using J-bolts (inset photo, below).

Constructing a pier foundation is not difficult work, but it's important that the pier layout is accurate and the concrete forms are set properly. Use batter boards and mason's lines to lay out the pier positions and check your work by taking measurements and applying some simple geometry.

Before starting your project, ask the local building department about the required diameter and depth of your piers and what type of post anchors to use. In most areas, concrete piers must extend into the ground below the frost line and stand at least 2" above the ground to protect the posts from moisture. Cardboard forms for piers are commonly available in 8", 10", 12", and 16" diameters.

Tools & Materials

Circular saw ▪ Drill ▪ Mason's line ▪ Sledgehammer ▪ Line level ▪ Framing square ▪ Plumb bob ▪ Shovel ▪ Post hole digger ▪ Reciprocating saw or handsaw ▪ Utility knife ▪ Ratchet wrench ▪ 2 × 4 lumber ▪ 2½" screws ▪ Stakes ▪ Nails ▪ Masking tape ▪ Cardboard concrete forms ▪ Paper ▪ Concrete mix ▪ J-bolts ▪ Post bases ▪ Straight board ▪ Wood sealer-preservative ▪ Scrap lumber for braces ▪ Lag screws

Step A: Construct the Batter Boards

1. Cut two 24"- long 2 × 4 legs for each batter board (for most projects you'll need eight batter boards total). Cut one end square and cut the other end to a sharp point, using a circular saw. Cut one 2 × 4 crosspiece for each batter board at about 18".

2. Assemble each batter board using 2½" screws. Fasten the crosspiece about 2" from the square ends of the legs. Make sure the legs are parallel and the crosspiece is perpendicular to the legs.

Step B: Set the Batter Boards & Establish Perpendicular Mason's Lines

1. Measure and mark the locations of the piers with stakes, following your project plan.

2. Set two batter boards to form a corner about 18" behind each stake, as shown in the illustration. Drive the batter boards into the ground until they are secure, keeping the crosspieces roughly level with one another.

3. Stretch a mason's line between two batter boards at opposing corners (not diagonally) and tie the ends to nails driven into the top edge of the crosspieces; align the nails and line with the stakes. Attach a line level to the line, and pull the line very taut, making sure it's level before tying it.

4. Run a second level line perpendicular to the first: Tie off the end that's closest to the first string, then stretch the line to the opposing batter board while a helper holds a framing square at the intersection of the lines. When the lines are perpendicular, drive a nail and tie off the far end.

5. Confirm that the lines are exactly perpendicular, using the 3-4-5 method. Starting at the intersection, measure 3 ft. along one string and make a mark onto a piece of masking tape. Mark the other string 4 ft. from the intersection. Measure diagonally between the two marks; the distance should equal 5 ft. Reposition the second string, if necessary, until the diagonal measurement is 5 ft.

Step C: Mark the Footing Locations

1. Following your plan, measure from the existing lines and use the 3-4-5 method to add two more perpendicular lines to form a layout with four 90° corners. Use the line level to make sure the mason's

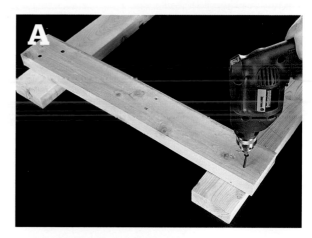

Cut the batter board pieces from 2 × 4 lumber and assemble them with screws.

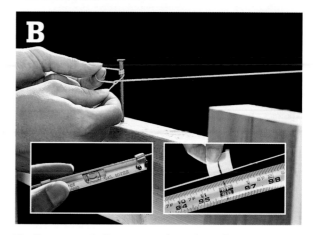

Tie the mason's lines securely to the nails, and level the lines with a line level (INSET LEFT). Use tape to mark points on the lines (INSET RIGHT).

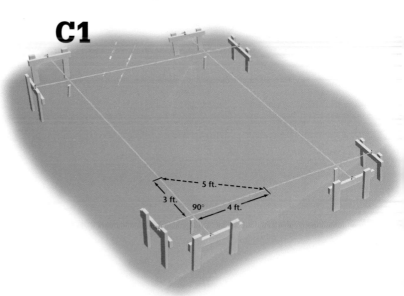

Use the 3-4-5 method to add two more perpendicular lines to form a layout with four 90° corners.

C2

Use a plumb bob to mark the pier locations. Drive a stake into the ground directly below the plumb bob pointer.

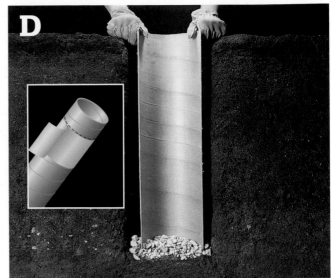

D

Wrap paper around the form to mark a straight cutting line (INSET). Set the forms in the holes on top of the 4" gravel layer.

lines are level. The intersections of the lines should mark the centers of the piers.

2. Check the squareness of your line layout by measuring diagonally from corner to corner: when the measurements are equal, the frame is square. Make any necessary adjustments.

3. Plumb down with a plumb bob and place a stake directly under each line intersection. If your plan calls for additional piers, measure and mark those points on the lines, then plumb down and plant the stakes.

4. Untie each line at one end only, then coil the line and place it out of the way. Leaving one end tied will make it easier to restring the lines later.

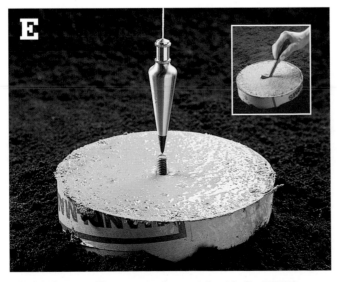

E

Fill the forms with concrete, then set the J-bolts (INSET). Check with a plumb bob to make sure the bolts are centered.

Step D: Set the Forms

1. Dig holes for the forms, centering them around the stakes. Make the holes a few inches larger in diameter than the cardboard forms. The hole depth must meet the local building code requirements—add 4" to the depth to allow for a layer of gravel. For deep holes, use a post hole digger or a rented power auger. Add 4" of gravel to the bottom of each hole.

2. Cut each cardboard form so it will extend 2" above the ground level. The top ends of the forms must be straight, so place the factory-cut end up, whenever possible. Otherwise, mark a straight cutting line using a large piece of paper with at least one straight edge: Wrap the paper completely around the form so that it overlaps itself a few inches. Position the straight edge of the paper on the cutting mark, and align the overlapping edges of the paper with each other. Mark around the tube along the edge of the paper. Cut the tube with a reciprocating saw or handsaw.

3. Set the tubes in the holes and fill in around them with dirt. Set a level across the top of each tube to make sure the top is level as you secure the tube with dirt. Pack the dirt firmly, using a shovel handle or a stick.

Step E: Pour the Concrete

1. Restring the mason's lines and confirm that the forms are positioned accurately.

2. Mix the concrete following the manufacturer's directions; prepare only as much as you can easily work with before the concrete sets. Fill each form

with concrete, using a long stick to tamp it down and eliminate air pockets in the concrete. Overfill the form slightly.

3. Level the concrete by pulling a 2 × 4 on edge across the top of the form, using a side-to-side sawing motion. Fill low spots with concrete so that the top is perfectly flat.

4. Set a J-bolt into the wet concrete in the center of the form. Lower the bolt slowly, wiggling it slightly to eliminate air pockets. Use a plumb bob to make sure the bolt is aligned exactly with the mark on the mason's line. Make sure the bolt is plumb and extends 3/4" to 1" above the concrete. Smooth the concrete around the bolt and let the concrete cure.

Step F: Install the Post Bases

1. Mark a reference line on the top of each pier to help with aligning the post bases. Place a long, straight board across two piers, setting it on the same side of each J-bolt. Hold the board against the bolts and trace along the edge (bolt-side) of the board onto the tops of the piers.

NOTE: If your footing layout is square or rectangular, make reference marks that follow the perimeter of the building. If you're building a gazebo, set the board across the center pier and each of the outside piers.

2. Place a post base on each pier so it's centered over the J-bolt. Add the washers and loosely screw the anchor nut onto the J-bolt. Use a framing square to position the base square with the reference line, then tighten the nut with a ratchet wrench.

3. Place the metal pedestals into the post bases.

Step G: Set the Posts

1. Make sure the bottom post ends are square; cut them, if necessary. Seal the bottom ends with a wood sealer-preservative, to prevent rot.

2. Place each post in its base, hold it plumb, and tack in one 16d galvanized common nail. Have a helper set up two perpendicular cross braces. Use a level to plumb the post, and secure the braces to the post and to stakes in the ground, using screws. Hold the level on two adjacent post faces to make sure the post is perfectly plumb. Nail the post to the base with 16d nails.

3. Drill pilot holes for the lag screws that anchor the posts to the bases (check with the manufacturer for the recommended size of lag screw). Install the lag screws with a ratchet wrench. Leave the braces in place until the top post ends are securely framed into the structure. Cut away the exposed portions of the forms with a utility knife.

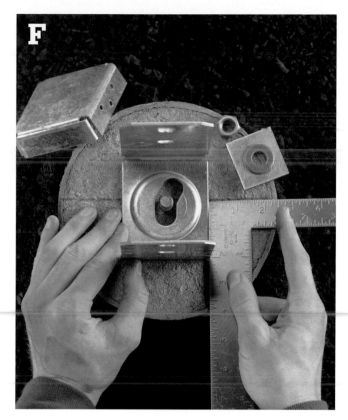

Set the post base over the J-bolt and use a framing square and reference line to position the base before securing it.

Plumb and brace the posts, then secure the posts to the bases with galvanized nails and lag screws.

Concrete Slab Foundation

The slab foundation commonly used for outbuildings is called a slab-on-grade foundation. This combines a 3½"- to 4"-thick floor slab with a 8"- to 12"-thick perimeter footing that provides extra support for the walls of the building. The whole foundation can be poured at one time using a simple wood form.

Because they sit above ground, slab-on-grade foundations are susceptible to frost heave and in cold-weather climates are suitable only for detached buildings. Specific design requirements also vary by locality, so check with the local building department regarding the depth of the slab, the metal reinforcement required, the type and amount of gravel required for the subbase, and whether plastic or an other type of moisture barrier is needed under the slab.

The slab shown in this project has a 3½"-thick interior with a 8"-wide × 8"-deep footing along the perimeter. The top of the slab sits 4" above ground level, or grade. There is a 4"-thick layer of compacted gravel underneath the slab and the concrete is reinforced internally with a layer of 6" × 6" 10/10 welded wire mesh (WWM). (In some areas, you may be required to add rebar in the

foundation perimeter—check the local code.) After the concrete is poured and finished, 8"-long J-bolts are set into the slab along the edges. These are used later to anchor the wall framing to the slab.

A slab foundation typically requires a lot of concrete: An 8 × 10-ft. slab designed like the one in this project calls for about 1.3 cubic yards of concrete; a 12 × 12-ft. slab, about 2.3 cubic yards. Considering the amount involved, you'll probably want to order ready-mix concrete delivered by truck to the site (most companies have a one-yard minimum). Order air-entrained concrete, which will hold up best, and tell the mixing company that you're using it for an exterior slab.

An alternative for smaller slabs is to rent a concrete trailer from a rental center or landscaping company; they fill the trailer with one yard of mixed concrete and you tow it home with your own vehicle.

If you're having your concrete delivered, be sure to have a few helpers on-hand when the truck arrives; neither the concrete nor the driver will wait for you to get organized. Also, concrete trucks must be unloaded completely, so designate a dumping spot for any excess. Once the form is filled, load a couple of wheelbarrows with concrete (in case you need it) then have the driver dump the rest. Be sure to spread out and hose down the excess concrete so you aren't left with an immovable boulder in your yard.

If you've never worked with concrete, finishing a large slab can be a challenging introduction; you might want some experienced help with the pour.

4" compacted gravel

8"-thick perimeter

Welded wire mesh

Plywood form

Trench slope 45°

3½"-thick slab

Tools & Materials
Circular saw ▪ Drill ▪ Mason's line ▪ Sledgehammer ▪ Line level ▪ Framing square ▪ Shovel ▪ Wheelbarrow ▪ Rented plate compactor ▪ Bolt cutters ▪ Bull float ▪ Hand-held concrete float ▪ Concrete edger ▪ Compactible gravel ▪ 2 × 3 & 2 × 4 lumber ▪ 1¼" & 2½" deck screws ▪ ¾" A-C plywood ▪ 8d nails ▪ 6" × 6" 10/10 welded wire mesh ▪ 1½" brick pavers ▪ J-bolts ▪ 2"-thick rigid foam insulation

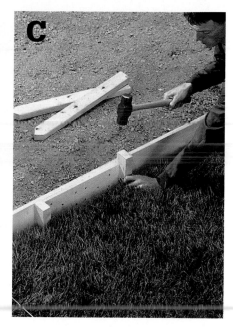

Measure down from the layout lines and temporary cross strings to check the depth of the excavation.

Assemble the form pieces with 2½" deck screws, then check the inner dimensions of the form. For long runs, join pieces with plywood mending plates.

Drive stakes every 12" to support the form, using the mason's lines to make sure the form remains straight.

Step A: Excavate the Site

1. Set up batter boards and run level mason's lines to represent the outer dimensions of the slab (see page 213). Use the 3-4-5 method to make sure your lines are perpendicular, and check your final layout for squareness by measuring the diagonals.

2. Excavate the area 4" wider and longer than the string layout—this provides some room to work. For the footing portion along the perimeter, dig a trench that is 8" wide × 8" deep.

3. Remove 3½" of soil over the interior portion of the slab, then slope the inner sides of the trench at 45°. Set up temporary cross strings to check the depth as you work.

4. Add a 4" layer of compactible gravel over the entire excavation and rake it level. Compact the gravel thoroughly, using a rented plate compactor.

Step B: Build the Form

1. Cut sheets of ¾" A-C plywood into six strips of equal width—about 7⅞", allowing for the saw cuts. To make sure the cuts are straight, use a table saw or a circular saw and straightedge.

2. Cut the plywood strips to length to create the sides of the form. Cut two sides 1½" longer so they can overlap the remaining two sides. For sides that

are longer than 8 ft., join two strips with a mending plate made of scrap plywood; fasten the plate to the back sides of the strips with 1¼" screws.

3. Assemble the form by fastening the corners together with screws. The form's inner dimensions must equal the outer dimensions of the slab.

Step C: Set the Form

1. Cut 18"-long stakes from 2 × 3 lumber—you'll need one stake for every linear foot of form, plus one extra stake for each corner. Taper one end of each stake to a point.

2. Place the form in the trench and align it with the mason's lines. Drive a stake near the end of each side of the form, setting the stake edge against the form and driving down to 3" above grade.

3. Measuring down from the mason's lines, position the form 4" above grade. Tack the form to the stakes with partially driven 8d nails (driven through the form into the stakes). Measure the diagonals to make sure the form is square and check that the top of the form is level. Drive the nails completely.

4. Add a stake every 12" and drive them down below the top edge of the form. Secure the form with two 8d nails driven into each stake. As you work, check with a string line to make sure the form sides are straight and measure the diagonals to check for square.

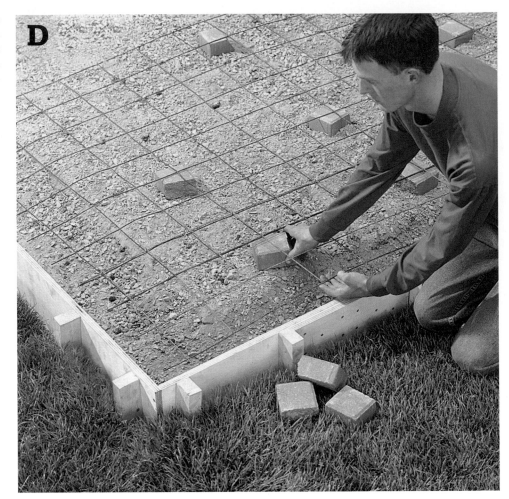

Lay out rows of wire mesh, tie the rows together, then prop up the mesh with brick pavers or metal bolsters.

Step D: Add the Metal Reinforcement

1. Lay out rows of 6" × 6" 10/10 welded wire mesh so their ends are 1" to 2" from the insides of the forms. Cut the mesh with bolt cutters or heavy pliers, and stand on the unrolled mesh as you cut, to prevent it from springing back. Overlap the rows of mesh by 6" and tie them together with tie wire.

2. Prop up the mesh with pieces of 1½"-thick brick pavers or metal bolsters.

3. Mark the layout of the J-bolts onto the top edges of the form, following your plan. (J-bolts typically are placed 4" to 6" from each corner and every 4 ft. in between.)

Step E: Pour the Slab

1. Starting at one end, fill in the form with concrete, using a shovel to distribute it. Use the shovel blade or a 2 × 4 to stab into the concrete to eliminate air pockets and settle it around the wire mesh and along the forms. Fill with concrete to the top of the form.

2. As the form fills, have two helpers screed the concrete, using a straight 2 × 4 or 2 × 6 that spans the form: Drag the screed board along the top of the form, working it back and forth in a sawing motion. Throw shovelfuls of concrete ahead of the screed board to fill low spots. The goal of screeding is to make the surface of the concrete perfectly flat and level, if not smooth.

3. Rap the outsides of the form with a hammer to settle the concrete along the inside faces of the form. This helps smooth the sides of the slab.

Step F: Finish the Concrete & Set the J-bolts

1. Immediately after screeding the concrete, make one pass with a bull float to smooth the surface. Add small amounts of concrete to fill low spots created by the floating, then smooth those areas with the float. Floating forces the aggregate down and draws the water and sand to the surface.

2. Set the J-bolts into the concrete 1¾" from the outside edges of the slab. Work the bolts into the concrete by wiggling them slightly to eliminate air pockets. The bolts should be plumb and protrude 2½" from the slab surface. After setting each bolt, smooth the concrete around the bolt, using a magnesium or wood concrete float.

3. Watch the concrete carefully as it dries. The bull-floating will cause water (called bleed water) to rise, casting a sheen on the surface. Wait for the bleed water to disappear and the surface to become dull. Pressure-test the concrete for firmness by stepping on it with one foot: if your foot sinks ¼" or less, the concrete is ready to be finished.

NOTE: Air-entrained concrete may have very little bleed water, so it's best to rely on the pressure test.

4. Float the concrete with a hand-held magnesium or wood float, working the float back and forth until the surface is smooth. If you can't reach the entire slab from the sides, lay pieces of 2"-thick rigid foam insulation over the concrete and kneel on the insulation. Work backwards to cover up any impressions.

5. Use a concrete edging tool to round over the slab edge, running the edger between the slab and the form. If you want a very smooth finish, work the concrete with a trowel.

6. Let the concrete cure for 24 hours, then strip the forms. Wait an additional 24 hours before building on the slab.

Screed the concrete after filling the form, using two people to screed, while a third fills low spots with a shovel.

Float the slab with a bull float, then set the J-bolts at the marked locations (INSET).

Setting Posts in Concrete

Burying posts in the ground with concrete provides strength and lateral stability, making it a good foundation system for small- to mid-scale projects. The concrete also helps protect the posts from ground moisture, so they last longer than they would if buried directly in the soil. However, it's a good idea to treat the bottom ends of posts before burying them, as an added measure against rot (see Protecting Buried Posts, below).

When digging postholes, make them 6" deeper than the post footing depth specified by the local building code. This leaves room for a layer of gravel that keeps water from collecting at the base of the post. Also follow the building code specs for posthole diameter; as a minimum, the holes should be several inches larger in diameter than the post size—about 8" for 4 × 4 posts, and 12"–14" for 6 × 6 posts.

FYI ▸ Protecting Buried Posts

The most vulnerable part of a buried post is the bottom end, which soaks up water when untreated, and the point where the post emerges from the ground or surrounding concrete. Here are a couple of popular methods for protecting posts against rot from moisture contact.

Stand posts in a pan of wood preservative and let them soak overnight. This protects the porous end grain from moisture.

Coat the buried portion of posts with roofing tar, covering the ends and all sides up to several inches above the points where they will emerge from the ground.

Tools & Materials Plumb bob ▪ Stakes & string ▪ Hand maul ▪ Power auger or posthole digger ▪ Shovel ▪ Coarse gravel ▪ Carpenter's level ▪ Concrete ▪ Mason's trowel ▪ Pressure-treated, cedar, or redwood 4 × 4 posts ▪ Scrap lengths of 2 × 4

Drop a plumb bob from each post reference mark on the string to pinpoint the post centers on the ground.

Dig postholes 6" deeper than specified by local building code. Pour 4" to 6" of gravel into each hole to improve drainage.

Position each post in its hole. Brace the post with scrap pieces of 2 × 4 on adjacent sides, and adjust it until it is plumb.

Step A: Mark Post Locations

1. Transfer the marks from the string to the ground, using a plumb bob to pinpoint the post locations.

2. Mark each post location with a stake, and remove the string.

Step B: Dig Postholes

1. Dig postholes, using a power auger (available at rental centers) or posthole digger. Make each hole 6" deeper than the post footing depth specified by local building code or 12" past the frost line in cold climates. Keep the holes as narrow as possible, usually about twice the width of the post. Corner and gate posts usually require wider footings for extra stability. Check local regulations.

2. Pour a 6" layer of gravel into each hole for improved drainage.

Step C: Position the Posts

1. Position each post in its hole. Check posts for plumb with a level. Adjust posts to the correct height by adding or removing gravel until each post is at the same height.

2. Brace each post with scrap 2 × 4s secured to adjacent sides.

3. If you're setting more than one post, make sure they're properly aligned with one another, using mason's string. Adjust if necessary.

Step D: Fill the Postholes

1. Mix concrete and fill each posthole, overfilling them slightly.

2. Check to make sure each post is still plumb, then use a mason's trowel to shape the concrete around the bottom of the post to form a rounded crown that will shed water.

3. Let the concrete cure for 2 days before removing the braces.

Fill the postholes with pre-mixed concrete, overfilling each slightly. Recheck the post for plumb and shape the concrete into a crown to shed water.

Cutting Roof Rafters

R afters are the main structural members of a framed roof. On a gazebo, the rafters attach at the walls or wall beams and are joined together at their top ends by the roof hub.

All the framed roofs in the plans have a designated slope, or rafter angle. This is shown in the plans by the roof-slope indicator (see RAFTER TEMPLATE, right).

Roof slope is expressed as the amount of vertical rise for every 12" of horizontal run. This indicator shows a 6-in-12 roof, which rises 6" for every 12" of run. The roof slope is used to lay out the rafter cuts.

The key to roof framing is to cut two pattern rafters, test-fit them, and make cuts as needed until they fit properly. Use one of the pattern rafters to lay out the remaining rafters.

Tools & Materials Circular saw
- Framing square ■ 4-ft. level ■ 2× lumber
- 8d, 10d, and 16d common nails

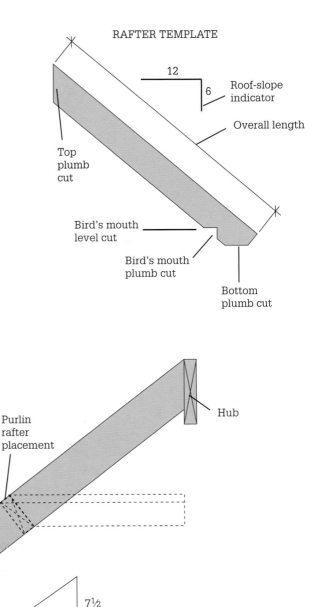

RAFTER TEMPLATE

12

6 Roof-slope indicator

Overall length

Top plumb cut

Bird's mouth level cut

Bird's mouth plumb cut

Bottom plumb cut

Hub

Purlin rafter placement

Hip Rafter

7½

12

NOTE: The following instructions are based on the sample rafter template shown here, which is designed for a 6-in-12 roof slope.

Step A: Mark the Plumb Cuts

1. Select a straight board to use for the pattern rafter. Mark the top plumb cut near one end of the board: Position a framing square with the 6" mark of the tongue (short part) and the 12" mark of the blade (wide part) on the top edge of the board. Draw a pencil line along the outside edge of the tongue.

2. Starting from the top of the plumb-cut mark, measure along the top edge of the board and mark the overall length of the rafter, then use the square to transfer this mark to the bottom edge of the board. Position the square so the tongue points down, and align the 6" mark of the tongue and the 12" mark of the blade with the bottom board edge, while aligning the tongue with the overall length mark. Draw a line along the tongue. If the bottom end cut of the rafter is square (perpendicular to the edges) rather than parallel to the top end, mark a square cut at the overall length mark.

Step B: Mark the Bird's Mouth Cuts

1. Measure from the bottom of the lower plumb cut and mark the plumb cut of the bird's mouth. Position the square as you did for the lower plumb cut and draw a line across the board face at the new mark.

2. Measure along the bird's mouth plumb cut and mark the bird's mouth level cut. Use the square to draw the level cut—it must be perpendicular to the bird's mouth plumb cut.

(above) Position the framing square at the 6" and 12" marks to draw the top and bottom plumb-cut lines.

(left) Mark the bird's mouth level cut by squaring off of the bird's mouth plumb cut.

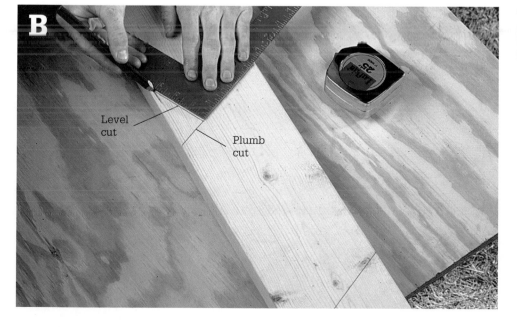

A speed square is a handy tool for marking angled cuts— using the degree of the cut or the roof slope. Set the square flange against the board edge and align the PIVOT point with the top of the cut. Pivot the square until the board edge is aligned with the desired DEGREE marking or the rise of the roof slope, indicated in the row of COMMON numbers. Mark along the right-angle edge of the square.

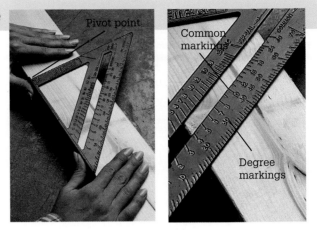

Step C: Make the Cuts

1. Cut the rafter ends at the plumb-cut lines, using a circular saw or power miter saw.

2. Set the base of a circular saw to cut at the maximum depth. Make the bird's mouth cuts, overcutting slightly to complete the cut through the thickness of the board. As an alternative to overcutting (for aesthetic reasons), you can stop the circular saw at the line intersections, then finish the cuts with a handsaw.

3. Select another straight board to use as a second pattern rafter. Use the original pattern rafter to trace the cutting lines onto the duplicate, then make the cuts.

Cut the bird's mouth by overcutting the lines just until the blade cuts entirely through the board.

Step D: Test-fit the Rafters

1. Cut a 12"-long spacer block from material that matches the roof hub or ridge board.

2. With a helper or two, set the two rafters in place on top of the walls, holding the spacer block between the top rafter ends. Make sure the rafters are in line with each other (perpendicular to the walls) and are plumb.

3. Check the cuts for fit: The top-end plumb cuts should meet flush with the spacer block, and the bird's mouths should sit flush against the wall plates. Make sure the top ends are at the same elevation. Recut any angles that don't fit and test-fit the rafters again.

4. Write "PAT" on the pattern rafter, then use it to trace the cutting lines onto the remaining rafters. Before marking, check each rafter for crowning and mark the crowned edge; always install the crowned edge up (see page 60).

5. Cut the remaining rafters.

Test-fit the pattern rafters, using a spacer to represent the ridge board or roof hub.

Roofing

A watertight roof, as opposed to a partial-shade roof, consists of a base layer of sheathing and a top layer of shingles or other roofing material. The sheathing may be exterior-grade plywood, tongue-and-groove decking boards, or 1× or 2× lumber.

The plans in this book call for specific roofing materials. Of course, you might choose a different type for your project. The three basic types of roofing are shown here:

Asphalt shingles are the standard roofing material for outdoor structures, just as they are for houses. For the money, asphalt shingles are the most durable and low-maintenance option, and they come in a wide range of colors and styles.

Cedar shingles are a big step up in price from asphalt, but their visual appeal is undeniable. The type shown here is the factory-sawn shingle with flat, tapered sides. Cedar shingles are less expensive and easier to install than hand-split cedar shakes.

Metal roofing has been used on everything from cathedrals to chicken coops and has seen new popularity in residential construction. Today's metal roofing is extremely durable and easy to install. And it sounds great when it rains.

The type of sheathing you use depends on the roofing material. CDX plywood is the simplest option for asphalt and cedar shingles. Both shingle types must be installed over 15# building paper (also called tar paper or roofing felt), which goes over the sheathing.

Another sheathing option is decking boards. Typically sold in ⁵⁄4 dimension (about 1" thick), board sheathing creates an attractive underside to the roof, and the nails won't show through, as they can with plywood sheathing.

For metal roofing, you must install purlins—evenly spaced rows of 1× or 2× boards nailed perpendicular to the rafters.

Sheathing & Building Paper

A

Install the plywood sheathing so the vertical joints are staggered between rows.

Step A: Install the Sheathing

1. Lay a full sheet of CDX plywood on top of the rafters at one of the lower corners of the roof. Position the edges of the sheet ⅛" from the fascia (or the outside edges of the rafters) and make sure the inside end of the sheet falls over the center of a rafter; trim the sheet, if necessary.

2. Fasten the sheet to the rafters with 8d box nails spaced every 6" along the edges and every 12" in the field of the sheet.

3. Cut and install the next sheet to complete the first row, leaving a ⅛" gap between the sheet ends.

Tools & Materials Framing square
■ Circular saw ■ Stapler ■ Fascia & trim material
■ 6d and 8d galvanized finish nails ■ CDX plywood roof sheathing ■ 8d box nails ■ 15# building paper ■ Hammer
■ Utility knife

4. Start the second row with a half-length sheet so the vertical joints will be staggered between rows. Measure from the top of the first row to the center of the ridge board, and rip the sheet to that dimension.

5. Install the first sheet of the second row, then cut and install the remaining sheet to complete the row.

6. Sheath the opposite side of the roof following the same process.

Step B: Install the Building Paper

NOTE: If you are installing asphalt shingles, add drip edge along the eaves before laying the building paper.

1. Roll out 15# building paper across the roof along the eave edge. If you've installed drip edge, hold the paper flush with the drip edge; if there's no drip edge, overhang the fascia on the eave by ⅜". Overhang the gable ends by 1" to 2". (On hip roofs, overhang the hip ridges by 6".)

2. Secure the paper with staples driven about every 12".

3. Apply the remaining rows, each overlapping the preceding row by at least 2". Overhang the ridge by 6". Overlap any vertical joints by at least 4".

4. Install the paper on the other roof side(s), again overlapping the ridge by 6".

5. Trim the paper flush with the fascia on the gable ends.

Apply building paper from the bottom up, so the lower paper is overlapped by the paper above it.

Asphalt Shingles

Asphalt shingles come in a variety of styles, but most are based on the standard three-tab system, in which each shingle strip has notches creating three equally sized tabs on the lower half of the strip. When installed, the tabs cover the solid portion of the shingle below it, giving the appearance of individual shingles.

For durability, use fiberglass-based shingles rather than organic-based. Also check the packaging to make sure the shingles comply with the ASTM D 3462 standard for durability. If you choose a specialty style, such as a decorative shingle or a type that is made to appear natural (similar to wood or slate), check with the manufacturer for specific installation instructions.

Prepare the roof for shingles by installing building paper and metal drip edge along the roof perimeter. Drip edge covers the edges of the fascia and supports the shingle edges.

Step A: Install the Drip Edge

NOTE: Install drip edge along the eaves before applying building paper; install drip edge along the gable ends on top of the paper.

Tools & Materials Metal snips ▪ Chalk line ▪ Utility knife ▪ Straightedge ▪ Metal drip edge ▪ Asphalt shingles ▪ 2d roofing nails ▪ Roofing cement ▪ Hammer

1. Cut a 45° miter on the end of a piece of drip edge, using metal snips. Hold the end flush with the corner of the fascia, and fasten the flange of the drip edge to the sheathing with roofing nails driven every 12". To prevent corrosion, use galvanized nails with galvanized drip edge and aluminum nails with aluminum edge. Overlap vertical joints by 2".

2. Apply the building paper over the entire roof (see page 227). Install drip edge along the gable ends, over the paper, cutting 45° miters to meet the ends of the eave drip edge. Overlap horizontal joints by 2", overlapping the higher piece on top of the lower. At the roof peak, trim the front flanges so the opposing edge pieces meet at a vertical joint.

Step B: Install the Starter Course of Shingles

1. Snap a chalk line 11½" up from the front edge of the drip edge (this will result in a ½" overlap for standard 12" shingles).

2. Trim off one-half (6") of the end tab of a shingle, using a utility knife and straightedge.

3. Position the shingle upside-down, so the tabs are on the chalk line and the half-tab overhangs the gable drip edge by ⅜". Fasten the shingle with four 2d roofing nails, about 3½" up from the bottom edge: drive one below each tab, one 2" in from the gable edge, and one 1" from the inside edge. Drive the nails straight and set the heads just flush to avoid tearing the shingle.

Install drip edge along the eaves over the sheathing. Add the building paper, then install edging along the gable ends.

Trim 6" from the end tab to begin the starter row. Position the starter course shingles upside down so the tabs point up.

4. Use full shingles for the remainder of the course, placing them upside down and butting their edges together. Trim the last shingle so it overhangs the gable edge by ⅜".

Step C: Install the Remaining Courses

1. Install the first course of shingles, starting with a full shingle. Position the tabs down and align the shingle edges with those in the starter course. Drive four nails into each shingle: one ⅝" above each tab, and one 1" in from each end, at the same level. Trim the last shingle to match the starter course.

2. Snap a chalk line on the building paper, 17" up from the bottom edge of the first course; this will result in a 5" exposure for each course.

3. Begin the second course with a full shingle, but overhang the end of the first course by ½ of a tab. Begin the third course by overhanging a full tab, then 1½ tabs for the fourth course. Start the fifth course with a full shingle aligned with the first course, to repeat the staggered pattern. Snap a chalk line for each course, maintaining a 5" exposure. After every few courses, measure from the ridge to the shingle edges to make sure the shingles are running parallel to the ridge. If necessary, make slight adjustments with each course until the shingles are parallel to the ridge.

4. Trim the top course of shingles at the ridge. If you are working on a hip roof (gazebo), trim the shingles at each hip ridge.

5. Repeat the procedure to shingle the remaining side(s) of the roof. Overlap the ridge with the top course of shingles and nail them to the other roof side; do not overlap more than 5". On a hip roof, trim the shingles along the hip ridge.

Step D: Install the Ridge Caps

1. Cut ridge caps from standard shingle tabs: taper each tab along the side edges, starting from the top of the slots and cutting up to the top edge. Cut three caps from each shingle—you'll need one cap for every 5" of ridge.

2. Snap a chalk line across the shingles, 6" from the ridge. Starting at the gable ends (for a gable roof) or the bottom edge (for a hip roof), install the caps by bending them over the ridge and aligning one side edge with the chalk line. Fasten each cap with one nail on each roof side, 5½" from the finished (exposed) edge and 1" from the side edge. Maintain a 5" exposure for each shingle. Fasten the last shingle with a nail at each corner, then cover the nail heads with roofing cement.

3. Trim the overhanging shingles along the gable ends: Snap chalk lines along the gable ends, ⅜" from the drip edges (these should line up with the first, fifth, etc., courses). Trim the shingles at the lines. Cover any exposed nails with roofing cement.

Stagger each course of shingles by ½ tab, repeating the pattern after overhanging the edge by 1½ tabs.

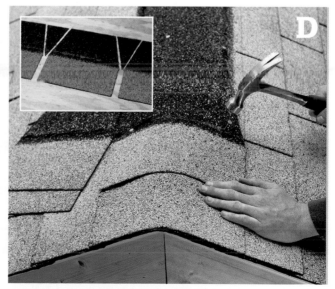

Divide the shingles into thirds, then trim the corners to create the shingle caps (INSET). Install the caps at the ridge.

Cedar Shingles

Cedar shingles come in 16", 18", and 24" lengths and in random widths, generally between 3" and 10" wide. The exposure of the shingles depends on the slope of the roof and the length and quality of the shingles (check with the manufacturer). Because they're sold in a few different grades, make sure the shingles you get are good enough to be used as roofing. Also, be aware that galvanized nails may cause some staining or streaking on the shingles; if you can't accept that, use stainless-steel nails.

The project shown here includes 18" shingles with a 5½" exposure installed on a gable roof. At the ridge, the shingles are covered with a 1× cedar ridge cap, which is easier to install than cap shingles.

Tools & **Materials** Utility knife ▪ Chalk line ▪ Circular saw ▪ Table saw ▪ T-bevel ▪ Cedar shingles ▪ 2 × 4 lumber ▪ 3d & 6d roofing nails ▪ 6d galvanized nails ▪ 1 × 4 and 1 × 6 cedar ▪ Caulk ▪ Hammer

Step A: Install the Starter Course

1. Apply building paper to the entire roof, overhanging the eaves by ⅜" (see page 227).

2. Position the first shingle in the starter course so it overhangs the gable edge by 1" and the eave edge by 1½". Tack or clamp a 2 × 4 spacer to the fascia to help set the overhang. Make sure the butt (thick) end of the shingle is pointing down. Fasten the shingle with two 3d roofing nails, driven 4" up from the butt end and at least 1" from the side edges. Drive the nails just flush with the surface—countersinking creates a cavity that collects water.

3. Install the remaining shingles in the starter course, maintaining a ¼" to ⅜" gap between shingles. If necessary, trim the last shingle to width.

Step B: Install the Remaining Courses

1. Set the first shingle in the first course so its butt and outside edges are flush with the shingles in the starter course and it overlaps the shingle gap below by 1½". Fasten the shingle 1" to 2" above the exposure line and 1" from the side edges.

2. Install the remaining shingles in the first course, maintaining a ¼" to ⅜" gap between shingles.

Install the starter row of shingles, overhanging the gable end by ⅜" and the eave by 1½".

3. Snap a chalk line across the shingles at the exposure line (5½" in this example). Install the second course, aligning the butt ends with the chalk line. Make sure shingle gaps are offset with the gaps in the first course by 1½".

4. Install the remaining courses, using chalk lines to set the exposure. Measure from the ridge periodically to make sure the courses are parallel to the ridge. Offset the shingle gaps by 1½" with the gaps in the preceding three courses—that is, any gaps that are aligned must be four courses apart. Add courses until the top (thin) ends of the shingles are within a few inches of the ridge.

5. Shingle the opposite side of the roof.

Step C: Shingle the Ridge

1. Cut a strip of building paper to 24" wide and as long as the ridge. Fold the paper in half and lay it over the ridge so it overlaps the shingles on both sides of the roof; tack it in place with staples.

2. Install another course of shingles on each side, trimming the top edges so they are flush with the ridge. Cut another strip of building paper 12" wide, fold it, and lay it over these shingles.

3. Install the final course on each side, trimming the ends flush with the ridge. Nail the shingles about 2½" from the ridge.

Step D: Install the Ridge Cap

1. Find the angle of the ridge using a T-bevel and two scraps of 1× board. Position the boards along the ridge with their edges butted together. Set the T-bevel to match the angle.

2. Transfer the angle to a table saw or circular saw and rip test pieces of 1×. Test-fit the pieces on the ridge, and adjust the angles as needed.

3. Cut the 1 × 6 and 1 × 4 cap boards to run the length of the ridge. Join the boards with caulk and 6d galvanized box nails. Attach the cap to the ridge with 6d roofing nails driven every 12".

Install the first course of shingles on top of the starter course, offsetting the shingle gaps 1½" between the courses.

Cover the ridge with 24" of building paper, then a course of trimmed shingles. Repeat with 12" of paper and shingles.

Use a T-bevel and scrap boards to find the ridge angles (above), then cut the 1 × 4 and 1 × 6 for the ridge cap.

Metal Roofing

Metal roofing panels typically are available in 3-ft.-wide panels, with most styles using some form of standing seam design, which adds strength and provides means for joining sheets. You can buy the roofing through metal roofing suppliers and at home centers, but the former typically offer more color options, and they'll custom-cut the panels to fit your project. Most manufacturers supply rubber-washered nails or screws for a watertight seal—use the recommended fasteners to prevent premature rusting due to galvanic action (caused by contact between dissimilar metals).

Install metal roofing over 1 × 4 or 2 × 4 purlins nailed perpendicularly to the rafters at 12" to 24" on center—check with the manufacturer for purlin spacing and load requirements. At gable ends, add blocking between the purlins to provide a nailing surface for the end panels and drip edge.

Step A: Install the Purlins

1. Mark the purlin layout on the top edges of the the rafters, and snap a chalk line for each row. Fasten 2 × 4 purlins to the rafters with 16d common nails; use 8d nails for 1 × 4s. Make sure the upper-most purlins will support the roofing ridge cap.

2. On the gable ends, cut blocking to fit between the purlins, and install it so the outside edges are flush with the outer faces of the outer rafters.

Step B: Install the Roof Panels

1. Set the first roof panel across the purlins so the finished side edge overhangs the gable-end fascia by 2" and the bottom end overhangs the eave by 2". Fasten the panel with self-tapping screws or roofing nails with rubber washers, following the manufacturer's directions for spacing.

2. Install the subsequent panels, overlapping each panel according to the manufacturer's directions.

3. Rotate the final panel 180° from the others, so the finished side edge is at the gable end. Overlap the

Install the purlins across the rafters, then add blocking at the gable ends.

Tools & Materials

Chalk line ▪ Circular saw ▪ Drill ▪ 1 × 4 or 2 × 4 lumber ▪ 16d common nails ▪ Metal roofing panels and pre-formed ridge cap, with fasteners

preceding panel by as much as necessary so the finished edge overhangs the gable edge by 2". Fasten
the final panel.

Step C: Install the Ridge Cap

1. Center the pre-formed ridge cap over the peak
so it overlaps the roofing panels. Make sure the cap
overhangs the gable ends equally on both sides.

**NOTE: some products include ridge-cap
sealing strips.**

2. Fasten the ridge cap to the top purlins.

Install the panels to the purlins
using the manufacturer's
recommended fasteners.

Add the ridge cap at the roof peak,
covering the panels on both roof sides.

Working with Copper Pipe

A soldered pipe joint, also called a sweated joint, is made by heating a copper or brass fitting with a propane torch until the fitting is just hot enough to melt solder. The heat then draws the solder into the gap between the fitting and the copper pipe, forming a strong seal.

Using too much heat is the most common mistake made by beginners. To avoid this error, remember that the tip of the torch's inner flame produces the most heat. Direct the flame carefully—solder will flow in the direction the heat has traveled. Heat the pipe just until the flux sizzles; remove the flame and touch the solder to the pipe. The heated pipe will quickly melt the solder.

Soldering copper pipe and fittings isn't difficult, but it requires some patience and skill. It's a good idea to practice soldering pieces of scrap pipe before taking on a large project.

Step A: Cut the Pipe

1. Measure and mark the pipe. Place a tubing cutter over the pipe with the cutting wheel centered over the marked line. Tighten the handle until the pipe rests on both rollers.

2. Turn the tubing cutter one rotation to score a continuous line around the pipe. Then rotate the cutter in the opposite direction. After every two rotations, tighten the handle. Rotate the cutter until the pipe separates.

Step B: Clean the Pipe & Fittings

To form a good seal with solder, the ends of all pipes and the insides of all fittings must be free of dirt and grease. Remove metal burrs from the inside edge of the cut pipe, using the reaming point on the tubing cutter or a round file. Sand the ends of pipes with emery cloth, and scour the insides of the fittings with a wire brush.

Step C: Flux & Dry-fit the Pipes

1. Apply a thin layer of water-soluble paste flux to the end of each pipe, using a flux brush. The flux should cover about 1" of the end of the pipe.

2. Insert the pipe into the fitting until the pipe is tight against the fitting socket, and twist the fitting slightly to spread the flux. If a series of pipes and fittings (a run) is involved, flux and dry-fit the entire run without soldering any of the joints.

Position the tubing cutter, and score a line around the pipe. Rotate and tighten the cutter until the pipe separates.

Clean inside the fittings with a wire brush, and deburr the pipes with the reaming point on the tubing cutter.

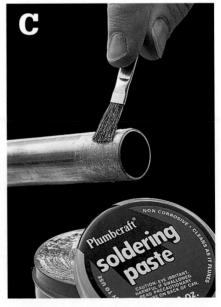

Brush a thin layer of flux onto the end of each pipe. Assemble the joint, twisting the fitting to spread the flux.

When you're sure the run is correctly assembled and everything fits, take it apart and prepare to solder the joints.

Step D: Heat the Fittings

1. Shield flammable work surfaces from the heat of the torch. Although heat-absorbent pads are available for this purpose, you can use a double layer of 26-gauge sheet metal. The reflective quality of the sheet metal helps joints heat evenly.

2. Unwind 8" to 10" of solder from the spool. To make it easier to maneuver the solder all the way around a joint, bend the first 2" of the wire solder to a 90° angle.

3. Open the gas valve and light the propane torch. Adjust the valve until the inner portion of the flame is 1" to 2" long.

4. Hold the tip of the flame against the middle of the fitting for 4 to 5 seconds or until the flux begins to sizzle. Heat the other side of the joint, distributing the heat evenly. Move the flame around the joint in the direction the solder should flow. Touch the solder to the pipe, just below the fitting. If it melts, the joint is hot enough.

Step E: Apply the Solder

Quickly apply solder along both seams of the fitting, allowing capillary action to draw the liquified solder into the fitting. When the joint is filled, solder begins to form droplets on the bottom. A correctly soldered joint shows a thin bead of silver-colored solder around the lip of the fitting. It typically takes about ½" of solder wire to fill a joint in ½" pipe.

If the solder pools around the fitting rather than filling the joint as it cools, reheat the area until the solder liquifies and is drawn in slightly.

NOTE: Always turn off the propane torch immediately after you've finished soldering; make sure the gas valve is completely closed.

Step F: Wipe Away Excess Solder & Check the Joint

1. Let the joint sit undisturbed until the solder loses its shiny color. Don't touch it before then—the copper will be quite hot.

2. When the joint is cool enough to touch, wipe away excess flux and solder, using a clean, dry rag. When the joint is completely cool, check for gaps around the edges. If you find gaps, apply more flux to the rim of the joint and resolder it.

3. If you need to take apart a soldered joint, reverse the process. First, light the torch and heat the fitting until the solder becomes shiny and begins to melt. Then use channel-type pliers to separate the pipe from the fitting. To remove the old solder, heat the ends of the pipe, and use a dry rag to carefully wipe away the melted solder. When the pipe is cool, polish the ends down to bare metal, using emery cloth. Discard the old fittings—they can't be reused.

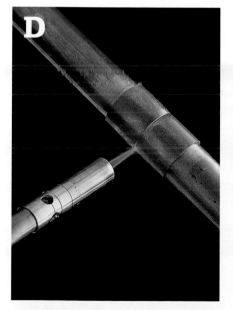

Heat the fitting until the flux begins to sizzle. Concentrate the tip of the torch's flame on the middle of the fitting.

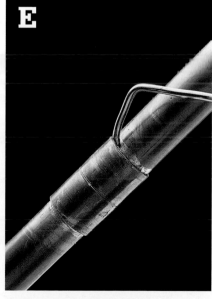

Push ½" to ¾" of solder into each joint, allowing capillary action to draw liquified solder into the joint.

When the joint has cooled, wipe away excess solder with a dry rag. Be careful: The pipes will be hot.

Resources

LUMBER

California Redwood Association
www.calredwood.org

Southern Pine Council
www.southernpine.com
Information on pressure-treated
southern pine lumber

**Western Red Cedar Lumber Association
(WRCLA)**
www.wrcla.org

BAMBOO

Bamboo & Rattan Works, Inc.
www.bambooandrattan.com
Supplier of bamboo and bamboo products

American Bamboo Society
www.americanbamboo.org

STRUCTURAL FIBERGLASS COLUMNS

Architectural Products by Outwater L.L.C.
1-800-835-4400
www.outwater.com
Note: columns used in Classic Pergola are part
#MC-88; column is 8" x 8', plain (not fluted), with
standard Tuscan polyurethane cap and base.

FRAMING CONNECTORS & OTHER ANCHOR SYSTEMS

Simpson Strong-Tie Co.
1-800-999-5099
www.simpsonanchors.com
Supplier of framing connectors, fasteners, and hardware
for connectors, post bases, concrete
and masonry anchors, and anchoring adhesive

Photo Credits

PHOTOGRAPHY CONTRIBUTORS
The following photos are courtesy of:

Amish Country Gazebos
www.amishgazebos.com
800-700-1777
page 19

California Redwood Association
www.calredwood.com
888-CALREDWOOD
pages 15 (right) and 167 (bottom) by Ron Kolb for
Imperial Decks and Enclosures; p. 90 by Charles
Callister, Jr. for Julian Hedges; p. 91 (top) by Marvin
Slobin for Joseph D. Wood; p. 111 (top) by Ernest Braun
for John Tomlinson; page 136 by Ernest Braun for Rex
Higbee; p. 167 (top) by Ernest Braun for Timothy R.
Bitts & Associates.

Cedarshed Gazebos
www.cedarshed.com
800-830-8033
pages 10 (both), 123 (bottom).

Summerwood Products
www.summerwood.com
866-519-4634
pages 74-75 (all).

Walpole Woodworkers
www.walpolewoodworkers.com
800-343-6948
pages 9 (left), 29 (both), 53 (both), 91 (bottom),
186, 187 (bottom), 194, 195 (bottom).

PHOTOGRAPHERS

Alamy
©F1 Online/Alamy: page 23.

John Gregor/ColdSnap Photography
©John Gregor/ColdSnap Photography:
pages 8 (top), 28.

David Livingston
©David Livingston: page 9 (bottom right).

Garden Picture Library/Photolibrary.com
©Brigitte & Phillipe Perdereau/Garden Picture Library,
page 5; ©Jean-Claude Hurni/Garden Picture Library, page
26; ©Steven Wooster/Garden Picture Library, page 110.

Charles Mann
©Charles Mann: pages 11 (left), 14, 111 (bottom),
137, 148.

Jerry Pavia
©Jerry Pavia: pages 6, 8 (bottom), 11 (top right), 41, 123
(top), 166, 182, 187 (top), 195 (top).

Brian Vanden Brink
©Brian Vanden Brink: pages 9 (top right),
11 (bottom right), 12, 13 (both), 52,120.

Jessie Walker
©Jessie Walker: page 40.

Index

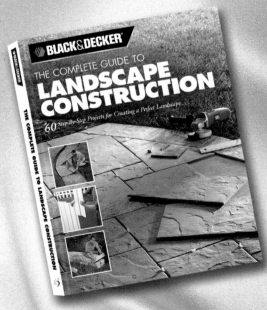

BUILD CUSTOM SHELTER STRUCTURES FOR YOUR OUTDOOR HOME

Turn your landscape into real living space with one or more of these easy-to-build shelters. You'll find complete plans and step-by-step directions for 15 projects, plus exciting chapters for inspiration, planning, and construction basics. Projects include:

- Classic Pergola
- Lattice Gazebo
- Pool Pavilion
- Summer House
- Classic 8-sided Gazebo

CATEGORY: Home Improvement/
Outdoor Landscaping

$24.95 US
£16.99 UK
$29.95 CAN

UPC
0 52944 01574 9

Creative Publishing
international

www.creativepub.com

ISBN – 13: 978-1-58923-285-3
ISBN – 10: 1-58923-285-2

EAN
9 781589 232853

52495